P9-DVD-512

WILD HORSE ANNIE

WILD HORSE ANNIE

VELMA JOHNSTON AND
HER FIGHT TO SAVE THE MUSTANG

ALAN J. KANIA

 UNIVERSITY OF NEVADA PRESS   RENO AND LAS VEGAS

University of Nevada Press, Reno, Nevada 89557 USA
Copyright © 2012 by University of Nevada Press
All rights reserved
Manufactured in the United States of America
Design by Kathleen Szawiola

Library of Congress Cataloging-in-Publication Data

Kania, Alan J.
Wild Horse Annie : Velma Johnston and her fight to save the
mustang / Alan Kania.
    p.   cm.
Includes bibliographical references and index.
ISBN 978-0-87417-873-9 (cloth : alk. paper) —
ISBN 978-0-87417-893-7 (ebook)
1. Johnston, Annie Bronn. 2. Mustang—Conservation—
History—20th century. 3. Wild horses—Conservation—West
(U.S.)—History—20th century. 4. Wild burros—Conservation
—History—West (U.S.)—20th century. 5. Public lands—West
(U.S.)—History—20th century. 6. Horsemen and horsewomen
—West (U.S.)—Biography. 7. Wildlife conservationists—West
(U.S.)—Biography. I. Title.
SF293.M9K36 2013
636.1'3—dc23   2012017295

The paper used in this book is a recycled stock made from
30 percent post-consumer waste materials and meets the require-
ments of American National Standard for Information Sciences—
Permanence of Paper for Printed Library Materials, ANSI/NISO
Z39.48-1992 (R2002). Binding materials were selected for strength
and durability.

22   21   20   19   18   17   16   15   14   13   12
5   4   3   2

CONTENTS

ILLUSTRATIONS

PREFACE

This is the story of an extraordinary woman the world knew as "Wild Horse Annie," whose real name was Velma Ione Bronn Johnston, and her twenty-seven-year national campaign to save, protect, and control the wild horses and burros of the American West. As a photojournalist and equine photographer in New England, I became aware of Wild Horse Annie and her campaign while writing for a newspaper in Massachusetts in 1970. We corresponded and phoned each other to provide information for my articles on her campaign and on what became Public Law (PL) 92-195, the Wild Free-Roaming Horse and Burro Act of 1971.

Her story whetted my interest in her work, and I began making trips to see the situation firsthand and eventually got to meet my correspondent in 1972. "It's a good thing you called first," she advised, "or you would have been greeted with more than just a handshake." Because of the death threats made directly and indirectly against her, Annie greeted unannounced visitors with a smile and an outstretched right hand, but also with a loaded .38 revolver held discretely behind the front door in the other hand.

For the next five years, I worked directly with Annie as I wrote about and photographed the wild horses and burros and researched the issues that Annie confronted during the final years of her campaign. It was during those years that I grew to know and appreciate Annie's unique character, and we became good friends. For many years after Annie's passing, I was pleased to serve on the board of directors of the International Society for the Protection of Mustangs and Burros (ISPMB) on behalf of her successors, Helen Reilly and Karen Sussman, who served as executive directors of the organization. It is my honor to present this homage to my dear friend, whom many know only by her nickname.

I adapted my newspaper and magazine photojournalism background to provide information for her campaign. I also returned to school to earn a graduate degree in nonprofit administration to help my mentor and new best friend. Most of the cases from the 1970s contained in this book were situations that Annie sent me to investigate and photograph on her behalf.

During those seven years that I volunteered my services for Annie, I once investigated an illegal roundup of horses in Nevada. My assignment was to befriend one of the old guard of traditional mustangers who was illegally gathering wild horses and transporting them off the public lands without detection by the Bureau of Land Management (BLM). My curious respect for the heritage of the last of these outlaws brought me to the private ranch of two of the mustanging families participating in the roundup. The beer, fresh steaks, and stories of the prelaw days when mustanging was legal flowed freely. My tape recorder, rolling with their permission, also provided Annie with sufficient information about the current roundup to shut down the operation.

I returned to Annie's home and listened silently on a telephone extension as she made the report to the state director of the Bureau of Land Management. "I'm amazed he got out of there alive!" the director told Annie. While I listened, Annie solemnly looked me squarely in the eyes and slowly nodded her head. At that moment, I realized what my friend was experiencing every day.

In a time when some organizations exploited the animals just to raise funds from naive animal lovers, Annie was determined to maintain the integrity learned from her family. "I will not be a party to any kind of thing that would be misleading to anyone," she explained to me during one phone conversation.

Whereas her family taught her the skills to evaluate complex issues without resorting to knee-jerk reactions, Annie, with nothing more than a high school education, taught herself the fundamentals of range management and its relationship to the welfare of wild horses and burros. She brokered her love for horses with support from a local coalition of fellow horsemen who saw atrocities being committed against the wild horses near Reno and other places throughout the West and worked through the county and state governments to outlaw the practice.

Her focus earned her bipartisan support from state and national politicians. After they listened to Annie's well-researched campaign, even some members of the federal government and those with livestock interests developed respect for Annie. Without the support of professional marketing teams

Velma B. "Wild Horse Annie" Johnston and author Alan Kania spoke during a break of the 1973 National Wild Horse and Burro Advisory Board meeting held in Denver, Colorado. Courtesy of the author.

or fund-raisers, Annie was able to maintain a grassroots campaign that won the admiration of the national and international news media as well.

Annie's campaign was not simply a matter of "save the wild horses," nor was it solely a reaction to the brutality that she documented during round-ups. Instead, it was driven largely by an outrage against a pervasive attitude in America that wild horses were nothing more than commodities, an attitude that she believed ran counter to long-standing national values regarding the horses' contributions to the development of the American West.

During her twenty-seven-year campaign, she never lost sight of her intertwined and complex objectives. The western range was overgrazed, and the livestock industry (and the government agencies originally infused with ranching families) blamed all possible sources of responsibility except their own monopolistic use of the federally owned public lands for private enterprise.

While Annie recognized that wild horses and burros (or any grazing animal on the public land) may reach a population saturation point when they, too, would be responsible for overgrazing the public land, she maintained a three-part objective for her wild horse and burro program. First, the whole-sale slaughter of wild horses and burros had to stop. Thousands of wild horses were gathered in inhumane ways; wild burros were shot and left for predator food on the rangeland. Second, the herds of horses and burros had to be controlled through humane means. Water trapping and other meth-ods could be conducted on an ongoing basis to provide a trickle of horses that would be funneled slowly into a program in which the animals would be adopted by private horse and burro owners instead of shipped to slaughter-houses or warehoused in publicly funded holding pens. Likewise, domestic and wild grazing animals using the public lands would have to be regulated according to range-management principles, not livestock-industry standards. And third, the rangeland itself would have to be managed. The federally con-trolled public land was becoming the personal domain of livestock and hunt-ing (and later mining) private industries with little concern for the general public that also had a vested interest in the *public* lands. Although it was argued that these private industries paid for their use of the public lands through licenses, permits, and local employment, the public land became closed off to public stewardship and long-term conservation of the natural resources.

With this three-part campaign, Annie's advocacy led to Public Law 86-234, the Wild Horse Annie Act of 1959, the national legislation that banned motorized land and air vehicles from hunting and capturing wild horses on federal land. A little more than a decade later, she was able to plug loopholes in that legislation through the passage of Public Law 92-195, the Wild Free-Roaming Horse and Burro Act of 1971, which prohibited capture, injury, or disturbance of wild horses and burros and stipulated that if populations became too large, excess equines would be transferred to suitable areas where wild horses and burros historically roamed. But it was not these legis-lative victories of which she was most proud. Annie often told me her great-est accomplishment was her encouragement of young people to actively par-ticipate in the government process for any cause that they found meaningful.

Annie was a charismatic leader who could unify a nation to stand behind her. Unfortunately, when she died there was no one who had the charisma to bring friend and foe together. Instead, "the wild horse faction" shattered, with pieces scattered among backyard horse lovers and well-financed humane organizations. Without a leader to unify these well-meaning efforts, these groups have been successful in raising money to "save the wild horses" but unsuccessful in making much of a permanent impact. Some organizations, like the Cloud Foundation, have begun to make progress toward becoming productive guardians of Annie's objectives, and I hope they succeed.

ANNIE WANTED HER LIFE'S WORK preserved in the library of a facility where students would have access to all of her personal and professional records. Several attempts were made to create a Wild Horse and Burro Center, but they never got beyond architectural drawings. Some information can be found at the Dickinson Research Center at the National Cowboy and Western Heritage Museum in Oklahoma City, where Wild Horse Annie was inducted into the Hall of Fame. Posthumously, the Cowgirl Hall of Fame in Fort Worth also recognized Annie and maintains a small collection of her letters, photographs, and documents. Fortunately, the Conservation Library (now incorporated into the Western History Collection) of the Denver Public Library was able to offer a permanent repository for most of Wild Horse Annie's files. The library enlisted me to use my seven-year work with Annie to determine the importance of the various case files.

Her administrative backbones were John and Helen Reilly, who helped Annie create the International Society for the Protection of Mustangs and Burros and continued Annie's work after her death in 1977. Annie entrusted a large collection of her personal documents to the Reillys. Several years before their own passing, they helped load the remaining files into my vehicle to be added to the Denver collection. While working on this biography, I also began adding my own personal files to the collection, and the combined material (which has not been publicly shared until now) will eventually be offered to the Wild Horse Annie Collection at the Denver Public Library.

My gratitude goes out to the early supporters of Wild Horse Annie, many of whom risked their professional and personal reputations, careers, and livelihoods to provide her with the support she needed to become self-educated in the realms of range management, wild horse (and burro) heritage, and legislative procedures. Some of their names can be found in the records held in the Denver Public Library Western History Collection; only some individuals and Wild Horse Annie discreetly knew the identities of many others. In writing this book, I was surprised how few of us who personally knew Annie are still alive to share her stories.

I filed a Freedom of Information Act request with the Washington, D.C., office of the Bureau of Land Management, requesting all files, documents, reports, and photographs they had between Mrs. Velma "Wild Horse Annie" Johnston and the BLM officials who communicated with her on a regular basis. Covering an era of twenty-seven years, the BLM could provide only two publicity photographs of quality too poor to use and a public relations video that mentioned her in passing. Fortunately, Annie, a career executive secretary, kept carbon copies of her correspondence to the BLM.

Because I was part of this story, at least for a short time, I found it difficult to write this book with full journalistic objectivity while providing a participatory eye on a little bit of history. Special thanks go to former journalist for the *Christian Science Monitor* and author Ward Morehouse III for keeping me grounded and moving forward to complete this biography.

I want to thank acquisitions editor Matt Becker for accepting this project and being the best writing coach to help transition my 1970s writing style into more contemporary writing—and for tolerating my occasional literary stubbornness. There were times I could sense Annie was rolling her eyes behind us while prodding us to keep going. Writers often covet their prose like each word was divinely mandated. That's why I was most fortunate to have a copy editor, Annette Wenda, to knock me off my pedestal and tweak my words so proficiently. And if you've purchased this book, it was undoubtedly because of the fine marketing work of Barbara Berlin and the design work of Kathleen Szawiola. It's been great fun to work with all of you.

My wife, Terry, never had the opportunity to meet Annie, but she sensed the importance of this biography to me. Very special thanks to Terry for her patience and support for a project that began long before we met.

And personal thanks to my parents, Frank and Genevieve Kania, who stood by me while I went off and pursued that dime-novel fantasy of a wild, free-roaming horse pursuing youthful independence.

WILD HORSE ANNIE

INTRODUCTION

The "wild horse" of the American West has long been a controversial subject. Depending on an individual's perspective of the value of wild horses on the open western ranges, the animals may be interchangeably described as wild horses, feral horses, cayuse, broom-tails, rangs, broncos, mustangs, or, sarcastically, dog-food-on-the-hoof. To Annie, they were simply her "wild ones," and their value was never in question, because she believed they represented the spirit of the American West.

In large part, nineteenth-century writers who created a romantic image of the American West first forged the public image of the wild horse as a principal character in those stories. Foremost among them was German novelist Karl May (1842–1912), who depicted the free-roaming horse as a stoic allegory of independent resolve, an image that would become synonymous with the "West" among his legions of young readers. May effectively drew from his own vivid imagination; he never personally visited the American West about which he so fondly wrote. American novelist Zane Grey (1875–1939) too maintained the image of the wild horse as a metaphor to post–World War I and Depression-era readers for the drive toward a personal quest that always remained just out of reach. Such romantic portrayals existed in tandem with more utilitarian descriptions by early-twentieth-century authors such as Frank Dobie (*The Mustangs*) and Walker Wyman (*The Wild Horse of the West*), who explored the valuable contributions that wild horses made to the Pony Express, early military troops, and the development of the West by eastern settlers.

Yet these more pragmatic literary representations were generally dwarfed by the medium of motion pictures, which also developed in the early 1900s. Like the books of May and Grey, the "western" films of Tom Mix and other silent-film actors continued to equate freedom with the image of the wild horse, a fantasy now made more powerful by the visual images that flickered on motion-picture and later television screens. It was from these origins that the wild horse developed into a romantic symbol of independence, an equation that continues to this day.

Without the glamour of Hollywood or the creative imagination of the writer, the romance of the West was replaced with isolation and difficult conditions as individuals headed west and found harsh winter weather and parching summer drought. Instead of the literature-inspired romance of the wild horse, stark reality created a culture of self-reliance and a less romantic sense of independence among those who chose to stay. Settlers attempted to civilize their homesteads in the West by replacing grasslands with buildings, roads, and towns. The remaining wide-open spaces provided forage to graze their livestock, which then competed with the indigenous animals, including wild horses, for these resources.

For others in the fledgling western livestock industry, the wild horses were increasingly viewed as just another tool of the trade. Captured young wild horses could be incorporated into the riding stock of the ranch—free to any adventuresome cowboy. The horses were more sure-footed than most domestic horses, could survive on sparse vegetation, and could travel long distances between water holes. Moreover, ranchers found the wild horses had an intellect ("a cow savvy") that enabled them to second-guess the moves of other livestock, thus allowing the cowboys to more easily focus on dallying a rope. Even contemporary ranchers still express their appreciation for well-trained wild horses for ranch use.

In the late 1800s, crews of hard-riding cowboys rode long distances to lasso a single wild horse. Since the wild horse was free of a rider and saddle, it usually won the challenge. Later, the cowboys began to adopt a method of gathering wild horses pioneered by the Plains Indians in order to secure larger quantities of the animals. Rather than targeting individual horses, the Plains Indians built U-shaped corral traps with openings that had long wings made of brush, fencing, or anything else that could be used to funnel a band of wild horses toward the center of the corral. Men on horseback would locate a band of five to twelve horses at a time and begin to chase them toward the corral. Another team of men on the ground hid close to the opening of the trap until the horses entered the enclosure. The men then rushed to drag a long canvas tarp to create the illusion that the entrance to the trap was now sealed.

Nineteenth-century mustangers chased wild horses into a corral trap where rodeo skills pitted cowboys against the elusive skills of the range-savvy wild horses. Courtesy of the author; photo taken by an unknown photographer near Maybell, Colorado.

When the easily accessible wild horses on the flats were depleted or escaped to more inaccessible highlands, single-engine aircraft were used to haze the animals out of rugged canyons and barren rimrocks back onto dry lakebeds. The aircraft enabled the pilot to keep up with the evasive maneuvers of the sagacious wild horses. Once a band was flushed from its rugged confines, the pilot could divert to the rest of the herd to quickly pick up another band and send large quantities of horses to the traps.

When the horses were no longer frightened of the droning engine noise, sirens and other noisemakers were added to the plane's fuselage. If that failed to drive the horses, the pilot or passenger peppered the fleeing animals with buckshot from a sawed-off gun. The animals were pursued fifteen to twenty miles from their meager refuges. Fast-moving pickup trucks with ropers riding in the beds easily pulled up next to the exhausted and often injured horses that attempted to break from the rest of the band.

A lasso, anchored with a heavy truck tire or some other weight, was thrown around the horse's neck; the tire bounced off the truck bed as each horse was roped. The frantic horse, with its sides heaving and blood sometimes dripping from its nostrils from a ruptured lung, soon gave up its fight. Another lasso was thrown around the horse's neck and hind legs, preventing it from lashing out at the captors. Handlers pulled or dragged the exhausted horse up a wooden plank onto the bed of the stock truck. Occasionally, the horse's hide caught on the rough planks and was stripped off.

Anecdotal stories of roundups told by mustangers or reported in news-

Wild horses gallop across dry rangeland in Nevada during a 1948 roundup. Photo courtesy of the Gus Bundy family and Special Collections, University of Nevada, Reno Libraries.

papers explained that the animals were loaded into trailers without regard to size, gender, or age and subjected to a long and terrifying haul, often to out-of-state slaughterhouses. The hunters left other horses, too badly hurt to load, to die from the injuries received during the long pursuit by plane and truck. Mares abandoned colts and fillies that were too small to stay with the herd; either the foals starved to death, or predatory animals killed them. More "compassionate" mustangers dispatched a severely injured horse with a bullet to the horse's forehead.

Eventually, the rest of the pursued wild horses found themselves not only contained in the uncomfortably close quarters of the corral trap, but also within fighting distance of the lead stallions of competing bands of horses. The loud grunts and squeals of stallions as they kicked and bit each other were short in duration, but frequently repeated. Other horses attempted to climb the rough-cut wooden corral walls until futility calmed them. They then spent their time wandering the corral trap, kicking up dust and looking in vain for food and water.

Since the horses' destination was the slaughterhouse, transporting food and water to these remote staging areas was an unnecessary burden to these modern-day mustangers. The horses would eventually get water at the stockyard for a temporary weight gain before being driven up the ramp to the scales and on to the slaughterhouse. The modern mustangers no longer respected the horses as living components of the western rangeland and now considered them just another marketable commodity.

Those helping in the roundup were often paid with their choice of a few young horses that could be used for domestic ranching or quickly converted into cash at the slaughterhouse. The very few "professional" mustangers who gathered horses for ranch and rodeo stock (as well as for slaughter) could use their experience to be more careful. The horses that were in better condition got higher prices at auction than the less fortunate horses that were bought in large quantities by the "killer buyers," as the slaughterhouse representatives were known.

With the advent of the airplane roundups, the captured horses were no longer destined primarily for ranches. Instead, an industry developed around these animals. Apart from a select few that were transported to the Northeast to serve as polo ponies or to the South as beasts of burden, most captured wild horses were slated for the slaughterhouses, which in the early twentieth century had been mechanized and vastly increased in number. Once the animals were butchered, the horse meat would be primarily turned into pet food by the approximately two hundred meat-processing plants that opened between 1920 and 1940. So great was the growth in this market that, according to Representative Walter S. Baring of Nevada, who cited an article from the advertising journal *Printer's Ink Monthly,* during the eight years following the end of World War II, one hundred thousand wild horses had been gathered from just his state for the pet-food trade.

ANNIE WAS OUTRAGED that the wild horses were valued more as commodities than living beings, a ranking that contradicted the values of her upbringing. Her father, a horse-drawn freight operator in the pre–motor vehicle era of western America, used wild horses he personally caught from the bands that roamed Nevada. As a result, he could have been described as a mustanger, but with the economic and humane necessity of keeping the welfare of the horse within the interest of both man and beast. It was from her parents that Annie learned to value the horse as a living creature first, a commodity a distant second.

Her advocacy was not based on saving all wild horses and burros. Nor was it in allowing carte blanche control of the "public" lands by the livestock and hunting industries. By 1950 when Annie's campaign began, the western rangeland was already in terrible condition, and there was plenty of blame to be shared on all sides of the issue of range conservation. Rather, her campaign was based on respecting the heritage the wild horse and burro brought to the expansion and development of the West. Few industries, communities, or transportation systems could have developed without having a wild horse or burro involved. The footsteps of man generally followed the hoof prints of a wild equine.

During Annie's early formative years, she saw Reno grow from a ranching and mining-supply town to a respectable community that just happened to have a gambling license. Her family instilled a sense of homesteading ethics found in families that left the comfort of "civilization" and headed west. And she maintained a ranch-life compassion that recognized that both livestock and family were to be treated with respect, and business deals were sealed with a handshake of mutual trust. Bringing an end to exploitation of the wild horses, releasing the monopoly on public-land administration, and reinstating western range conservation were paramount to her. Those were the lines Annie openly chose to draw in adulthood; those were lines you never wanted to cross with Wild Horse Annie.

Standing toe-to-toe with burly representatives of the livestock industry, who grasped their belt buckles as if they were battle shields, was likely not a job that this frail wisp of a woman envisioned as a career objective. Nor did this office secretary ever think she could match wits and intellect with some of the most politically savvy representatives of state and federal government. But while commuting to an office job one morning in 1950 she was mesmerized by dripping blood coming from a horse trailer ahead of her—a sight that would mold the rest of her life in a very public way.

WILD HORSE BLOOD

Blood?

As Velma Johnston drove to work from her small ranch east of Reno, Nevada, she often saw trailers transporting horses between ranches. This particular morning, as she slipped into the flow of traffic, a truck pulling a horse trailer cut in front of her. In the stop-and-go rush-hour traffic, a stream of blood pulsed from the back of the trailer every time the driver used the brake pedal. It was not unusual to see a little urine dripping from the floorboards of a horse trailer, or even the obligatory "road apples." But blood?

Mesmerized by the sight, she diverted from her normal route to her job at the bank and followed the horse trailer toward the slaughterhouses on the Nevada-California border west of Reno. When the tailgate dropped, she saw the source of blood was a young colt that had fallen between two adult stallions wedged into the trailer. The older horses had trampled the yearling to death, and it was his blood that was left along the Nevada road. Outraged, Velma began asking questions: Who was conducting these roundups? Where were they going, and why were these horses being treated this way? She learned the animals had been gathered during a weekend airborne roundup of wild horses. "Although I had heard that airplanes were being used to capture mustangs," Velma once wrote, "like so many of us do when something doesn't touch our lives directly, I pretended it didn't concern me. But one morning in the year 1950, my own apathetic attitude was jarred into acute awareness."[1]

Avid equestrians, Velma Johnston and her husband, Charlie, began asking people why the horses (even wild range horses) ended their lives so tragically. They learned that as the population of wild horses decreased, the horses targeted by the mustangers became less available and had to be hazed from long distances. Smaller bands of horses that grazed on the sparse rangeland now found refuge from the airborne harassment in more rugged territory, where the domestic livestock were less likely to compete for what vegetation was available.

Velma and Charlie followed the paper trail that flowed from federal to state to local authorization of these roundups. Staunch political conservatives, they appreciated laws administered as democratically as possible on a local level. But when small groups of commercially motivated interests unbalanced the conservation of the public lands, the Johnstons began to question the incestuous process for authorizing wild horse roundups. The same individuals gathering the horses or operating the slaughterhouses often supported the county commissioners and law enforcement officers in small ranching communities. How the laws were interpreted on a local level was at the discretion of the local government and livestock operators. As Velma explained to an august assembly of Nevada legislators years later, "Once the big slaughter got underway, the wild horse was doomed, for there were no protective laws whatsoever."[2]

She grasped the challenge to advocate for such laws. Raised on a ranch with a pragmatic understanding of ranch animals, she knew the wild horses needed to be managed efficiently with respect to the conservation of the land. She also had a high level of compassion and ethics that made her consider the horses as living creatures first and livestock second. She could be as headstrong and assertive as any mustanger, but she always enjoyed (and insisted on) being treated and fussed over "like a dame." She lived both geographically and conservatively above the downtown lights of Reno.

When she was enlisted to serve on federal advisory boards, Velma became aware of military-style instruction manuals that set the rudeness for interacting with the public. As Velma described in later years, "I'm used to the velvet glove, soft voice, 'would it be convenient for you to do so-and-so' routine." Once during World War II, Velma took a short-lived job that put her at the beck and call of her employer. She sat obstinately at her desk while her employer repeatedly hollered her last name from his adjoining office. After the third bellow, he came out to see if he had hired a deaf employee. "I informed him I was not," Velma continued, "only used to being treated as a lady."[3]

Privately, she could blush her closest friends with an out-of-character and off-color joke or story. Most important, it was the combination of her dual roles as a mild-mannered Reno secretary and an unyielding champion of the wild horses that made her so effective in her fight to reform the laws favoring wanton mustanging. She would use both of those aspects of her personality to appeal to the public.

ON THE MATERNAL SIDE, Velma claimed George Franklin "Frank" Clay, a Nevada County, California, hydraulic miner whose grandfather was a cousin to Henry Clay. It was Henry Clay (1777–1852) who led the "war hawks" who pushed the United States into the War of 1812. He then spent the next four decades working for international peace and to reconcile the embattled factions within his own country. President John Quincy Adams admirably described Clay as a "half educated" man who was self-taught through life's experience and who had "all the virtues indispensable to a popular man." Velma's own journey into American politics would lead an army of children in a letter-writing campaign to Washington legislators while she supplemented her own education with self-taught civics lessons.

Grandfather Clay emigrated from Illinois, taking the long, adventurous way by sailing around Cape Horn in 1862 to join his parents, who had left him behind while they traveled overland and made a new home in Garden Valley, Nevada. He met and married Josephine Hunter, daughter of Plum Valley Methodist minister Frank Hunter.[4] They had eight children, including Gertrude Clay of Reno, Nevada. Clay continued as a hydraulic miner until the Supreme Court outlawed that method of mining. He then sluice-boxed along the Yuba River, mining for precious minerals.

Velma's paternal grandfather, Benjamin R. Bronn, traveled to Nevada from Maine in the late 1800s so that he and his wife could establish a new life together. Deanne Stillman, author of *Mustang: The Saga of the Wild Horse in the American West*, noted the family stopped in Ione, Nevada, where Benjamin became the foreman of a silver mine. When the mine went bust, the Bronns loaded a covered wagon that was drawn by a team of four mustangs that Benjamin had tamed. Quoting from an unpublished partial narrative written by Velma Johnston, Stillman wrote, "The children, Ben and Ella, would be lifted into the box-bed of the spring wagon, sleepy-eyed and querulous, as children are when they are faced with the unknown. Grandma and Grandpa would climb to the high seat, Grandma with the infant in her arms."[5]

Travel by wagon was difficult for the displaced New England farmers, compounded by a personal problem: Benjamin's wife had given birth to Joe Bronn in Ione, Nevada, just before the trip. The hardships of the journey made it difficult for Benjamin's wife to provide enough breast milk for the baby. Fortunately, a range mare they caught during the trip also gave birth to a healthy colt, and the mare's milk was able to nurture both the foal and the baby for a short time. The mare was beginning to dry, and the Bronn party realized the mare could no longer provide enough nourishment for both newborns. Plans were made to destroy the colt so the baby would have whatever milk was available from the mare.

The Bronns' misfortune continued. During the night, a band of Paiute Indians approached the wagon while the family slept inside among their food and belongings. Without waking the family, the Paiutes stole the horses and other livestock, including the mare and foal that were instrumental in the baby's survival. The following morning, the Indians returned. After some negotiation, the family paid the ransom to have most of the stolen livestock returned in exchange for some of the sacks of food the Bronns still had in their possession. The Paiutes were pleased with their new colt, but the Bronns were grateful for the return of the lactating mare.

For all her life, Velma proudly boasted that her avocation with the protection of wild horses was founded in 1885 when her father was nourished by the wild mare's milk. Velma never hesitated to enhance the story and told people that she had "wild horse blood" running through her veins.

Benjamin Bronn and family arrived in Grass Valley, west of Reno, but work was not to be found. The family repacked the wagon and continued to Nevada County, California, where they settled on a small ranch and took advantage of the pure springwater that was available and built a home brewery and stage stop.[6] According to local stories, Bronn's wife, a native of Sacramento, served homemade doughnuts to weary travelers who stopped at the halfway house on their journey to or from Reno.

Young Joe Bronn was developing into a young man and frequently visited the new neighbors, Frank Clay and his family; after all, the Clays did have several lovely daughters. He passed over Gertrude "Trudy" Clay and became infatuated with her older sister. But love was fickle, and nothing ever came of the relationship.

As Trudy matured into womanhood, Joe began to take second notice and reevaluated his opinion of young Trudy. Every summer, Bronn rode his horse approximately one hundred miles over the mountains from Reno to San Juan to visit her.[7] He owned what Trudy later described as "a woman-hating stallion" that gave up his fiery disposition any time she was around

Joe, much to his bewilderment and frustration. With the steed helping in the courtship, Joe Bronn could no longer ignore the attraction of Miss Clay or the realization of how integral the horse was to the family.

When the Clays moved on to Marysville, California, in 1910,[8] Joe could not forget their young daughter. On Christmas Day, twenty-six-year-old Joseph Bronn married sixteen-year-old Gertrude Clay. The newlyweds took a wagon train across the Nevada border and settled outside Reno to raise a family. The fiery stallion resumed his "woman-hating" attitude as soon as they settled in and never allowed Trudy to get near him again. As she recalled, "I guess he thought things had gone too far, when he found there would be a female around all the time."[9] There on the Painted Rock Ranch on March 5, 1912, Velma Bronn, the oldest of three daughters and one son, was born.

A few years later, Joe Bronn introduced his three-year-old daughter to the view from astride a horse's back.[10] She stayed for a moment before the horse kicked up his heels, and Velma found herself looking up at the underside of the horse.[11] Despite the well-intentioned but painful way Velma's father introduced her to the horse, father and daughter shared a respect for the animals. "I am a mustanger's daughter," wrote Velma to a friend, "and the one I got bucked off of when I was only three years old had been caught by my dad by running him into a box canyon on his own mount. In those days they were so plentiful that it was considered a fair challenge to try to get them. Nowadays they are so scarce that chances of capturing any from horseback are much slimmer."[12]

Joe Bronn was able to show Velma that a relationship with a horse could be developed through cooperation and understanding. Maturing as a western businessman, Joe Bronn became the owner-operator of the Mustang Express, a horse-drawn freight liner that used hardy mustangs to keep him in business. Periodically, he rode with several of his neighbors and lassoed a few wild range horses roaming near the ranch. The more wily and powerful horses escaped; Joe captured and gentled the young or less elusive horses. "I don't like that word *broke*," Trudy Bronn once corrected me during an interview. "We *trained* a horse; we didn't *break* it!"[13]

Under the watchful eyes of his children, Joe Bronn took the wild horses he personally captured off the range and slowly developed a relationship of trust that was based not on dominance but on respect. If the horse did not want Joe to come closer, the horse made it known and Joe respectfully backed off. The next time, he pushed the comfort zone a little more, gradually shortening the distance between them. Once able to approach the horse, Joe then slowly introduced the horse to the harness and then the wagon, gradually gaining the trust of the horse until the two became a team. Young Velma probably did not realize it then, but she would use the same technique as she earned the respect of formerly wild and uncooperative administrators.

AFTER SPENDING SEVERAL WEEKS with Velma, Marguerite Henry wrote an undated press release for her publisher, Rand McNally, that described Velma's childhood years. As a five-year-old, she was already "Pa's Pardner," helping her father keep the team harness clean and the brass shiny. Velma told Henry:

> At night, I'd wash up for supper along with the teamsters. It was fun because of the crazy mirror tacked on the side of the barn. It had a jagged crack as though lightning had struck it, and I'd stand up on the wash bench to dry my face and laugh at myself. It was like going to the mirror-house in the amusement park. One half of your face set up higher than the other. I'd make faces and laugh until I had to give up my place to Pa or one of the teamsters, who didn't think it was nearly so funny.[14]

The joy of the interview softened without emotion as Velma continued her story. "One day when I was five-and-a-half, I woke up screaming in pain. I knew I was in my own bed but it wasn't morning because the sun was streaming in the west window. And there, sitting on the edge of my bed, was old Dr. Whitcomb with his white dusty hair and his black rusty suit. He was trying to move my head, but it wouldn't move." The doctor feared she had polio.

Each morning, Velma left the ranch to attend school. Most young girls look forward to a year of grammar school where they will reunite with old friends and meet new ones, building relationships with someone other than family members and ranch animals. Velma's first school year was tainted by the dismal prospect of spending half of it as a curiosity.

Trudy Bronn had been silently listening to Henry's interview. She cleared her throat, and her voice exposed her stoic sadness. "We tried to do everything we could for Velma," she began, "so we sent her away to a hospital for crippled children in San Francisco. And the last thing I told that little tyke of mine was, 'You'll like it there, honey. There'll be other children like you.'"

"But I didn't like it," Velma interjected. "And there weren't other children like me. The others could race down the halls on crutches. But I was in jail."

She was the victim of polio, and the doctors in a San Francisco hospital put her in a half-body cast from her hips to the top of her head. Holes were cut for her mouth, eyes, and ears, and a little hole accommodated the blunt end of her grandmother's knitting needles to scratch her head. The needles were sent with some yarn to keep Velma's hands busy. Velma's disease was something the entire family would have to accept and seek a positive resolution to overcome its social effects.

Henry's press release, "In Her Moccasins," continued the story. At first Velma did not mind the cage too much because she was excited by the prospect of emerging tall and straight and beautiful. But then she began feeling smothered. The prison was crushing her. In the dark of night she would fill her lungs, hoping to crack the cast and escape to freedom. When this failed, she tried to claw it open with her fingernails. But it was strong as steel. She was like an animal in a trap, hurt and afraid.

Weeks went by, then months; spring came again and with it Velma's freedom. When the cast was removed she looked forward to being able to bend, walk, and run like the other children. Before the Bronns took Velma back to the ranch, though, the family removed all the mirrors from the house. When she found a piece of broken mirror, her reflection looked like the cracked mirror on the barn—the two sides of her face did not match. Due to the ignorance of the medical practitioners, her body had gone through the contortions of the disease as her face stuck to the plaster, leaving the symmetry of her face vertically off-center by a full inch. The cast distorted her lower jaw in a way that prevented the development of her chin. Confronted with a life of permanent disfigurement, the young Velma decided to take adversity and put it to good use. With the support of her family, she found strength in this misfortune and was able to develop a remarkable ability to adapt to adversity.

For the next five years, Velma described her life as "agony," as she was unable to step up or down even a small height without help. When her hair was combed, someone would have to hold her head rigid while another carefully brushed her hair. Gradually, she was able to move without screaming and adapt to the pain during her illness.[15] She described the five agonizing years she spent as a polio victim in a letter to a friend many years later as "the long period of getting used to being different than everybody else. The twisted back, the face, neck and shoulders askew; and all that goes into a condition such as this." The good days were at best uncomfortable, and the bad days were simply painful. She used traction at times when nothing else helped, and no matter what, she kept moving, regardless of how uncomfortable it was, for the doctor advised that it was the only way to avoid becoming immobilized: "Hence the horse backing and other exercise—out of which has emerged quite a wonderful life—wonderful that is, when I learned to whip my gremlins."[16]

Though concerned for her daughter's mental well-being while Velma learned to adjust to her physical disfigurement, Trudy Bronn also admired her daughter's strong spirit: "I think it's marvelous that people could do that because there are so many people that just let an illness of some kind just knock them—not even try to make something out of themselves. And Velma was determined—she just had too many brains to not use them."[17]

Children can be cruel to someone with a handicap or disfigurement. To keep busy and away from her private fears and the taunts of other children, Velma spent her free time studying, working with the ranch animals, and creating arts-and-craft projects. When she was in a reflective mood, she wrote inspirational thoughts, but invariably her prose turned into poetry. Meticulous little sketches, usually of free-roaming horses, adorned the pages of her notepad as well.

Many preadolescent children find consolation through the warm brown eyes of a horse and that nonjudgmental compassion that develops between horses and people. For Velma, life on a ranch provided the necessary therapy and impetus for wanting to reward the relationship that helped her adjust to her new physical and emotional life. "I had to face people," Velma told Herman Weiskopf of *Sports Illustrated*. "When I'd see kids I'd ask, 'What're you playing? That looks like fun.' They'd let me join in. I know my face is not pretty, but now when people stare at me I know they can't help it and I smile at them. And, you know, they smile back."[18]

Her health problems frequently kept her out of school. When she returned to the sixth grade, her medical absences put her into the lower half of the class, while her friends were in the upper half. She wanted to be able to go on to junior high school with her friends, but in order to do so, she would have to take twice the sixth-grade workload to catch up. The principal thought the extra workload would further endanger her health. Without the knowledge of the principal, Velma studied the two levels of schoolwork at the same time. At the end of the school year, she asked the principal to humor her and allow her to take both levels of examinations that would be necessary in order to graduate and move on to junior high school with her friends. Permission was granted, and Velma Bronn passed the exams with the highest score of the entire class.

But tragedy was not about to give up its relentless attack on the Bronn household. Velma's brother, Jack, was not able to follow Velma far into adolescence, as spinal meningitis took his life on August 2, 1927, at the age of thirteen. His obituary stated he broke his hip at the age of three, "which left him a cripple, and his health was believed to have been affected by his injuries."

When Trudy Bronn was asked how she could deal with the loss of Jack so soon after bringing Velma home from the hospital with the aftereffects of polio, she collected her thoughts before describing her one strong philosophy in life: "to be honest, and stay as happy as you can. I think that's the most important thing I found out as you get older—not to remember the sad things, but remember the happy things, because there's a lot of happy stuff that goes on in your life."[19]

When Velma was not spending time with the ranch animals, she was immersed in library books, expanding her world beyond the fence lines of the Bronns' Nevada ranch. Spending time in the library was not always an exercise in isolation. At the traditional romantic age of sweet sixteen, she described her summer vacation as "one star-studded summer of a hopeless case of hero worship and undying love of an adult male, aged twenty-one." She frequently visited the library to "feast my eyes on this object of my affection."[20] The unnamed recipient of her visual affection was an avid reader, a trait that prompted Velma to increase her interest in literary self-improvement. Opera became a favorite subject so she could impress him with her newfound sophistication. Nothing ever developed between the two, but Velma did become quite proficient in her knowledge of the fine arts.

Building upon that insatiable curiosity, Trudy and Velma traveled to neighboring states to see places Velma previously only read about in books. Travel brought geography and other academic studies to life, expanded her knowledge of the world around her, and helped her earn a position on the 1928 high school honor roll. Throughout her scholastic life, Velma was one of only a few students recognized by the school for her ability to maintain grade levels of at least 90 percent for three consecutive school years. She also was one of only 16 in her high school class of 133 students whose high academic record enabled her to graduate several months ahead of the rest of the class of 1930.

As Velma's body matured, the damage from polio permanently left its mark. The homemade clothing that Velma designed from the latest fashion magazines she read in the library could stylishly cover her thin-framed physical body, but her face was a different challenge. To compensate, Velma learned that various angles could reduce the perception of her facial deformity—a tilt of the head or a shift in the way she stood. Her biggest allies to her makeover were a cordial personality and a freely offered smile that quickly eased the most uncomfortable introductions with a stranger. For Velma, only her closest friends knew the depths of her shyness, but she also recognized how disarming a comfortable and positive attitude could be to mask whatever demons were left from her bout with polio.

Velma's academic success helped her become an employee at the Farmers and Merchants Bank (later renamed the First National Bank of Reno). Although Velma was quick to grasp the skills required to become an excellent secretary, stenographer, and office administrator, mechanical inventions were her weakness. Velma and manual typewriters were never friends. Faced with the mechanical monster, Velma attempted to combat her foe while trying to make a good first impression on bank president Harris. "I made so many mistakes that day," Velma remembered. "I was afraid to throw all the ruined letterheads and second sheets into the waste basket to give proof of my inefficiency, so I tucked them all up my bloomer leg and fairly rustled home that night."[21] Her first job was also her last—executive secretary for the bank cofounder's son, Gordon Harris. She stayed with Harris for more than forty years.

When she was not doing battle with the typewriter, Velma became active in the Beta Sigma Omicron social sorority and attended many of their dances at the Riverside Hotel. More peaceful hours were also spent with friends at the weekly meetings of the Thimble Club, where she honed her skills as a seamstress in the late 1930s.

WITH HIS CHILDREN finding life off the ranch more interesting than ranch chores, Joe Bronn found himself without his family workers to help. The Mustang Express became unprofitable with the advent of automobiles and trucks. The Bronns moved to a ranch in Wadsworth, Nevada. Ranching was a hazardous business, and equestrian accidents were part of his job. He was recovering from one such accident when Velma and Trudy Bronn came to visit him in Washoe General Hospital. They were introduced to Joe's roommate, a West Virginian by the name of Charles Clyde Johnston. Charlie, despite his rough exterior, was a gentleman—soft-spoken, witty, and compassionate. Velma's father was a good judge of character and encouraged Velma and Charlie to see a lot of each other. Charlie originally went to Reno for a divorce and decided to stay and learn the ranching trade. The western way of life appealed to Charlie, and his newfound friends made his adjustment easier—and he did like the Bronns' daughter. Velma recounted their first meeting: "It was almost electrifying—and I said to myself, 'That's the man whose wife I want to be!' I did not know if he was married or not, from whence he came, what he did, or what he might do.'"[22]

Several weeks later they ran into each other again. Velma joined another couple for a five-cent beer at a small Reno establishment on Commercial Row. Still feeling the electricity that sparked between them, Velma coyly invited Charlie to join the group. The cold beer stirred their appetites, and the foursome moved on to a hamburger restaurant. Their friends dined on burgers and fries while Velma and Charlie sat in the car comparing their taste in poetry. Months later, Velma learned Charlie was equally hungry but thought her culinary tastes exceeded the twenty dollars in his wallet.

Velma and Charlie appeared together at local square dances or rode horseback through the valleys around Wadsworth. They shared an optimistic outlook on life and an ability to snap back from personal problems, and they exhibited sensitivity for each other. It was inevitable that Charlie would marry Velma. At the same five-cent beer pub three months after their first date, Charles Clyde Johnston proposed to marry Velma Ione Bronn.

Matrimony caused problems for young working females; bank regulations prohibited married women as employees. Breaking from Velma's conservative and traditional beliefs regarding family, Velma and Charlie impetuously stood before the justice of the peace and one witness and were secretly married. Not even Velma's parents shared in the knowledge of their nuptials. The clandestine marriage ceremony was a moot issue, though, because a short time later, Gordon Harris also made a major change in his life.

When Harris left the bank to form his own insurance brokerage, he took his executive secretary with him. Away from the archaic bank regulations, Velma and Charlie pleasantly surprised the family and announced their marriage. At

TOP: Velma Johnston stylishly prepares for a ride from the barn at the Double Lazy Heart Ranch. Courtesy of the family of Velma Johnston.

BOTTOM: Charlie Johnston astride his horse. Velma and Charlie frequently rode in the hills outside their Wadsworth, Nevada, ranch. Courtesy of the family of Velma Johnston.

the home of Velma's parents, the Johnstons repeated their nuptials in a wedding ceremony, witnessed by only the family and a few close friends. "Why Charlie married me I'll never know," Velma said in a *Sports Illustrated* interview in 1975. "He could have had his pick of women. Charlie was big—6'4" and 225 pounds in his prime—and he looked so much like John Wayne. I've always remembered my first dinner date with him—a can of coffee, pork chops, and corn and chestnuts roasted in the coals of our outdoor fire."

During the war, Charlie worked in a magnesium mine in Gabbs, Nevada, and Velma volunteered to help in the small community. When Velma arrived, she spent her first night with another man: because the Johnstons did not have any children waiting for them at home, the sheriff gave Velma the assignment of sitting with the body of a man who was shot to death earlier that day.

The Johnstons lived in a small shack with no running water and a privy in the back. When the mine gave out, Charlie took over the operations of the local bar, the Bucket of Blood.[23] Occasionally, Velma was recruited as a barmaid and blackjack dealer while Charlie tended bar.

The newlyweds registered their branding-iron design with the state brand inspector as a western tradition, but it was never used on any animals. The brand was composed of two horizontal hearts, top to top. When the Johnstons bought the ranch from Velma's parents in 1945,[24] they renamed it the Double Lazy Heart Ranch. Initially, there were few buildings. Joe Bronn and Charlie dug in and erected a barn and installed a stove in a partitioned corner.

The advent of World War II made fresh-cut lumber impossible to buy. Charlie, an innovative craftsman, located three large old cabins for sale and moved them to the sixteen-acre Double Lazy Heart Ranch, a tiny ranch by western standards.[25] He formed the cabins into an L-shaped configuration, made openings for passage between the abutted cabins, added a fireplace, and turned the cabins into a comfortable home. Velma, never feeling her place was exclusively within the confines of the house, joined in to add her touches to the exterior. "Charlie and I built every inch of the Double Lazy Heart," she wrote, "except that I chickened out when it came to helping him shingle the roof. I literally froze to the darned thing, flat on my stomach, and he had to pry me loose to get me back down the ladder."[26] The young couple shared ranch chores—plowing, planting, irrigating, hauling hay, and milking the cow. Velma noted that when she tried the latter, more milk shot up her sleeve or down her cowgirl boots instead of in the milk pail.

Children of friends from all over the state came to the ranch to spend their vacations or weekends. The Johnstons wanted to pass Charlie's heritage, part–Delaware Indian, along to a son or daughter, but it was not meant to be. With no children of their own, the Johnstons' Double Lazy Heart began to look like a dude ranch for young people. Charlie and Velma both learned the character of self-awareness and self-confidence on their own at the same age as those children; for Velma, it was done around horses and within the caring environment of the family. Even though Charlie and Velma did not ride much anymore, they instilled a foundation of responsibility, independence, confidence, trust, and rapport with the horses by turning the children out on horseback without overly protective supervision.[27] If they fell off, the children could come back to the stable, and Velma or Charlie would help them get back on—just as Joe Bronn did after Velma's first tumble off a horse when she was three years old. Velma's respect for the abilities of children remained a foundation for her future work with the wild horses.

Velma and Charlie believed adults owed children something more meaningful than a mechanical pat on the head and an empty smile. The Johnstons tried to instill a sense of faith in themselves supported by the faith adults had in the next generation. In Velma's ideology, it meant making her workload very heavy, but she firmly believed that she could not let them down. She believed that too many children had already been let down by adults.

With the happiness, there was some sadness. After a long illness, Joe Bronn passed away on December 11, 1946, at the age of sixty-two. In attendance were his friends from the Odd Fellows lodge, his wife, his sister, three surviving children, and a grandchild. With the loss of her paternal role model, Velma contemplated the future of her own role with Charlie.

Philosophically, the Johnstons were developing their own legacy. Velma credited Charlie with teaching her lessons in humility, honesty, and compassion and a belief in a divine being. Charlie had no formal religious beliefs; his religion was in his heart, and the outdoors was his church. "I wish you could have known him," reflected Velma in another letter to a friend, "for Charlie was a man's man all the way through, and it took a damned good woman to come first in his life. That's another thing I owe him—the knowledge that I was good enough to be first—always. It makes me walk a little taller."[28]

In the time of the 1960s' "Age of Aquarius," changing roles of gender brought about by women's liberation, and political unrest as the Vietnam War unfolded, Velma and Charlie took time to reflect on their roles in a changing society. Charlie wryly joked he was holding on to the macho image of a western ranch owner when it came to traditional marital relationships. "All wives, children and animals have to be disciplined—but not brutally."[29]

For Velma, she was comfortable with what were the traditional roles of women in postwar America, despite what would later become her national leadership role as a wild horse advocate. "I'm just a lowly housewife who has lived and loved in Nevada," Velma wrote to a friend. "My main purpose in life is to rest my weary husband's head on my shoulder when he comes home each night from the business of earning a living. I really like being a dame, with all the little fussinesses that go with it—car doors opened, coats held, cigarettes lighted, and a shoulder to lean on. How I ever became a crusader only the Good Lord knows." She went on to confess that it was a challenge for people like her who were born under the sign of Pisces: "They are destined to live two lives in one—that of being as feminine as she wishes, and that of 'being one of the boys,' goodness knows, my life is just that."[30]

Like all couples, the Johnstons occasionally had disagreements, but arguments were rare. Instead, they found each day a new experience and turned disagreements into learning periods of growth. Velma freely gave Charlie credit for teaching her the infinite patience to reach toward goals previously unavailable to her, but they both knew that the foundation of those traits was firmly entrenched through Velma's upbringing and in her ability to scale adversity.

Both Charlie and Joe taught her stoicism to take disappointment with a smile, the wisdom to accept the next best thing when the best was unattainable, and the importance of always being fair in both marriage and relationships with others. "Charlie gave me faith in myself because he had an unshakable faith in me and let me know it," Velma explained.[31] The Johnstons settled into a comfortable and loving marriage, content with their ranch life and armies of laughing children who reveled in the tranquillity of the Double Lazy Heart Ranch.

But even the most idyllic environments cannot replace some images. Velma owed so much to the horses in her life that had helped her through the most difficult times. She had the horses when she was alone, and she knew that someday she might have to consider making a solo journey as part of the payback for the character building they had brought to her. She just did not realize how soon "payback time" would enter her life. And then there was that memory of a horse trailer that she saw on the way to work one beautiful springtime morning in 1950.

ROUNDING UP NEWSPAPERS
AND POLITICIANS

There is an adrenaline rush while astride a good cow pony in pursuit of a wild horse at full gallop. Timing is critical, as the rider must anticipate each evasive move of the fleeing horse. The cowboy must match the rhythm of the mustang and position himself close enough to dally a lasso against the wind and over the outstretched neck of his intended target.

For Velma, her chase would also have to be at full gallop, dodging evasive bureaucratic moves and maneuvering her campaign close enough to bring her cause to her intended objective. The world of catching a wild horse was changing. Gone was the respect for the relationship of horse and rider. A new motivation for catching wild horses was developing on the western rangeland.

Even though Velma's father gathered wild horses in the late 1800s and early 1900s using the traditional method of catching a few of them by roping them from a saddle horse, she got a new lesson in contemporary mustanging from eyewitnesses. When Velma began looking into the reason wild horses were being transported to slaughterhouses under inhumane conditions, she went straight to the source. Using the socially disarming techniques she learned from her experience with polio, she got to know some of the people involved in the industry.

On one occasion in 1952, Velma entered the BLM office in Reno to inquire about local wild horse roundups. "Mrs. Johnston," the BLM employee confided, "we do not advertise these roundups, for if the people knew about them, they would not stand for it. How did you find out?"[1]

Much of Velma's information came through "outfielders" (as she described the whistle-blowers)—people who often worked for the government or even the slaughterhouses. One transportation driver took the time to introduce himself to Velma with a dire plea to keep his identification confidential. She nicknamed the foghorn-voiced informant "Zeke" and learned to rely on the accuracy of his information about pending roundups.

One evening, just as the Johnstons thought they were settling down to a quiet evening at home, Zeke called. He described two men on horseback, positioned behind juniper trees on the public lands outside of Reno. An airplane pilot working with them hazed a band of wild horses toward the mounted horsemen. Shotgun pellets blasted out of the aircraft, peppering the wild horses to keep the frantic animals moving toward the concealed horsemen.

Zeke described the condition of the horses when they were hit with buck-shot: most of the shot penetrated their hides, and the horses arrive blood-ied at the rendering works. He explained that the animals were terribly mis-handled, with rope burns on their badly swollen legs until no hide remained. When a horse was tied down, he said, it would often thrash, flailing against rocks so badly that it was blinded.

In rapt silence, Velma listened as Zeke described how the horses were bound with a rope until the transport trucks arrived (sometimes a full day later). Zeke paused in his story to be sure Velma was keeping up with him. She took a thoughtful breath and asked who was conducting the roundup. "Lazy cowboys that won't do anything else," Zeke replied.

It wasn't long before word of mouth expanded Velma's network of out-fielders to recreational users of the public lands. Casual riders visiting Nevada's barren but beautiful backcountry provided insight into how wild horses that didn't make it to the corral traps were left by the mustangers to die. She listened to eyewitness accounts of hikers who found a rope around a leg of a horse carcass; at the other end of the rope was a section of a train-track rail. The horse dragged the rail from a spring almost ten miles away, and the animal fell from hunger and thirst when the steel caught between two large sagebrush plants.

Sometimes the phone calls at home or notes slipped under the door at her office from Zeke and other outfielders described roundups that were still under way. To horsemen like Velma and Charlie, it was incredible that peo-ple would treat horses the way the outfielders described, and the Johnstons wanted to see the situation for themselves. One day a roundup was practi-cally in their backyard.

As the sun was setting one mid-March Sunday evening, the Johnstons drove their pickup truck to the Wilson Ranch in Fernley, Nevada, eight and a half miles east of the Double Lazy Heart Ranch. Charlie parked his truck on the public road just five feet from a corral of wild horses brought there a few hours earlier. Velma climbed into the truck bed and began photographing the thirty wild horses that were in the corral and forty more in an adjoining field.[2] She hoped her inexpensive flash camera would record what they saw.[3] Every injury commonly inflicted during the airborne roundups that Zeke witnessed was evident on these wild horses. The horses were exhausted, and there was no food or water for them in the corral.

Parked nearby was a large livestock transport truck and trailer, waiting to load the wild horses for their trip across the state line to a California slaughterhouse. When the popping flashbulbs of Velma's camera alerted the three men standing nearby, they ran for the privacy of a ranch house out of range of Velma's camera.[4] Just then an empty livestock transport truck rattled down the dirt road to the ranch.

Velma scrambled to the roof of the Johnstons' pickup and lay flat and still. Scarcely breathing, she screwed a flashbulb into her camera and watched as a large livestock truck turned down the narrow road and backed up to the corral. Velma and Charlie heard the tailgate slam onto the ground and the guttural voices of the men. A lasso swung out and looped a crippled mare in the corral, tumbling her head over heels as the men dragged her into the truck. Velma recognized her money shot, stood up, splay-legged to maintain her balance, and snapped a picture. She reloaded for another shot as a second lasso flew out again but missed its mark. The driver of the livestock truck saw the camera flash and whipped the trailer around without raising the tailgate ramp and headed directly for the Johnstons.

Velma braced herself for impact. As the truck's headlights illuminated them, Velma looked down and saw a glint of metal in Charlie's outstretched hand. He had his .38 revolver pointed at the men. The driver also saw the same glint of metal and made a sudden sharp turn, barely grazing the Johnstons' bumper, gunned the engine as he tried to shift gears, and hastily left the scene.

THROUGH THEIR CIRCLE OF FRIENDS in horse clubs, Velma and Charlie knew of Lura Tularski, a columnist for the *Nevada State Journal*'s "Saddle Chatter." Shortly after the Johnstons' brush with the mustangers, Lura learned the Reno office of the Bureau of Land Management had granted permission for two fliers from Idaho to gather wild horses on the public lands in Storey County, Nevada.[5] The pilots filed the appropriate paperwork with the Storey County commissioners and paid the necessary fees to hold the roundup in early June 1952. Velma took it upon herself to go directly to the Bureau of Land Management office to learn the details about the proposed roundup. There she met Dan Solari.

Velma took careful notes as Solari explained that hundreds of wild horses were destroying the habitat on a ranch near her own. It became clear that his preference was that all the horses should be removed from the public land. Velma respectfully kept silent, focusing her attention on her notepad while she transcribed the conversation into shorthand notes. During the conversation, Solari accidentally tipped her off that the county commissioners proposed to "quietly" approve the airborne roundup application at a meeting the next night at the Virginia City courthouse.

At the appointed time, the crowded hearing room heard the chairman gavel the meeting to order. There were two factions represented that night. The actual applicants were Storey County sheep ranchers and several representatives from a commercial rendering plant. Approximately fifty wild horse advocates who were there to support the horses that Velma later described as "the Wild Ones" outnumbered them.[6]

Velma knew she was walking into a room full of antagonism that reminded her of the early-day range wars. Her stomach was churning, and she wondered if her knees would ever stop trying to buckle. She reluctantly admitted there were other occasions when butterflies in her stomach attempted to destroy her facade of confidence. Velma recognized that many of the characters she was confronting already spent their lives capturing and transporting wild horses and would stop at nothing to maintain that avocation. Charlie's .38 was a close companion, and she confessed that she would use it to protect herself—that part of her was not a "feminine female."

The ranchers began the hearing by stating it was their legal right to conduct the roundup and process the horses through the slaughterhouse. The opposing point of view came from what the *Reno Evening Gazette* described as the local "spare the horses faction," led by postmaster Edward A. "Tex" Gladding and Jack Murray, a Comstock businessman. Gladding and Murray both raised saddle horses and insisted there was insufficient proof that the rangeland was overcrowded. Also attending were Charles Richards and R. J. Flick as spokesmen for the Nevada Humane Society. Not used to public confrontation, Velma and Charlie sat quietly on the side of those opposing the roundups.

Gladding captivated the hearing with colorful details about some of the roundups he observed—fliers jockeying down canyons, eventually running the horses onto the flats, where they were shot from the air as if in a shooting gallery. He said there once were thousands of wild horses in Storey County, but now he estimated only sixty were left. His anecdotal observations supported what Velma had learned a few days earlier during her conversation with Cliff Gardner, regional chief of the Nevada Division of Range Management. His records indicated that seventy-five thousand wild horses had been removed from Nevada rangelands by the time of the hearing.

After a break, the commissioners reconvened, and not only was the application to use aircraft to round up the wild horses denied, but the commissioners promised to formulate a resolution to dispose of future such applications. Later that month the county commissioners passed a resolution that brought an end to the driving or stampeding of wild horses in remote portions of Storey County through the use of airplanes or other aircraft.

Velma knew the resolution applied only to Storey County, though. Operators could legally run horses across the county line and then take up the chase as before. The local ordinance was a small accomplishment but spurred efforts to create similar measures in counties throughout Nevada.[7]

The county resolution introduced Velma to the notion that a grassroots effort could reverse the legislation that had been removing large quantities of wild horses for commercial exploitation and in what many people believed was an inhumane manner. She was further encouraged by *Territorial Enterprise* editor Lucius Beebe's follow-up editorial. Beebe expressed his disdain that the sheep ranchers claimed the public land was their own and the horses had impaired "their" land. He wrote that the grazing lands were practically unlimited in western Nevada, and there was an absurdly small number of horses. The claim that ranchers "owned" the land they merely leased was based on false information. Velma glowed with renewed enthusiasm when she read the concluding sentence of the editorial endorsement: "The wild horses, harmless and picturesque as they are, are a pleasant reminder of a time when all the West was wilder and more free, and any suggestion of their elimination or the abatement of the protection they now enjoy deserves a flat and instant rejection from the authorities within whose province the matter lies."[8]

While Charlie stood by in a supporting role, the others in the "spare the horses faction" began to recognize that Velma was doing more than sitting quietly on the sidelines, wringing her hands over the fate of the wild horses. She was able to chip away at her childhood shyness and employ the gentle but assertive research skills her father had taught her. Charlie also taught her similar skills while they were gathering information about the wild horses. Her quiet demeanor and fairness earned the respect from even her most hardened opposition. After the hearing in Storey County, the "wild horse faction" asked Velma to become the spokesperson for the wild horses. For a woman who used to feign sickness and stayed home from school because she was afraid to give a speech in front of her classmates, Velma now saw a few more layers of her childhood demons flake away. With a straight-forward approach, Johnston brought the wild horse and burro atrocities before the public.

Velma recognized that at one point in time in Nevada, reducing the bands of wild horses was necessary. She also believed, though, that removing them could have been done in a much more humane fashion. "Now that the exploiters have made their money, and the herds are reduced so much, we hope to make it impossible for a repetition of this exploitation and the cruel-ties that go with it." In fairness, she stated, most of the cattle and sheep men she talked to were not aware of the "methods of operation of these horse-meat peddlers, and I do not honestly believe that they will uphold a practice too revolting to the sense of decency of the majority of the people."[9]

Charlie Johnston saw his wife emerge as an advocate for the wild horses when she returned home from the Storey County hearing. He took her aside for a little spousal advice. She may have won over the room full of men who subscribed to the rigid gender norms of the 1950s, Charlie warned, but her opponents would now try to undermine her campaign by discrediting her as an "overly emotional female." Instead of playing strictly on the emotions of horse lovers throughout the country, she realized the appeal of the wild horses and burros had to stand on its own. She had to make documented, objective evidence the principle of the campaign—not emotionalism.

In this campaign, Velma was trespassing in the male-dominated world of range conservation almost a decade before Rachel Carson broke ground with her book *Silent Spring*. Like Carson, Velma kept to the issues instead of venting emotional tirades. "Because I am a woman," she reflected years later in a letter to a friend, "I cannot afford to indulge in anything bordering on the sentimental. . . . There isn't a thing wrong with emotion . . . but when a woman begins on it, fighting a man's battle in a man's world, she has three strikes against her to begin with."[10]

By fighting with what Velma described as "a velvet glove covering an iron gauntlet," her levelheaded approach to range management continued to earn her many new supporters. It was her husband, whose heritage was part–Delaware Indian, who gave her a little Native wisdom that separated her from the other animal advocates. "Whenever I came to a sudden critical decision," Velma reflected, "I would first walk in that person's moccasins for one moon before making up my mind."[11]

Velma learned the way to change the system was to work from within it. The persecution of the wild horses and burros had been going on for several generations. It would take her several decades to change it. To her, the wild horses were an integral part of Nevada's history, but she also recognized the contradiction that was inherent in that heritage. She was concerned the wild horses and burros would disappear from the western public lands, but she realized the large populations of horses in the past might have contributed (along with the livestock on open ranges) to the current overgrazed state of the Nevada rangeland. Range management of all users of the public land had to be part of the foundation of her advocacy of the wild horses and burros.

Part of working within the system meant engaging with local and state authorities. In another letter to a friend, Velma wrote, "I have many times wished that the average citizen would realize just how important his opinion is to his elected officials, not just about horses, but about all our social problems that afflict this great nation. I am sure it would change the apathetic attitude toward an apathetic constituency." She was sure that if officials learned that voters were "interested to the point of taking pen in hand," they would respond on behalf of their electorate.[12]

The Storey County hearing prompted local newspapers to report on the change in the county regulation against wild horse roundups. The news was picked up by Tularski's "Saddle Chatter" column and repeated in the Reno and Las Vegas newspapers. Velma's name became synonymous with the "save the wild horses" faction. Every day the mail carrier jammed the Double Lazy Heart Ranch mailbox to its capacity with inquiries of how to help. Velma personally answered each letter with a request for the writer to become more involved with the legislative process in their own counties where other commissioners were considering roundup applications.

Encouraged with the support the wild horses were earning through the press and word of mouth among the various Nevada horse clubs, Velma brought her campaign to the State of Nevada. Commissioners from various counties had duplicated the Storey County wild horse ordinance. Now it was up to her to unite the entire state in banning motorized and airborne round-ups on state land. In October she was reintroduced to Charles L. Richards, former Democratic U.S. congressman, retired Reno attorney, and the representative of the Nevada Humane Society at the Storey County hearing where Velma started her legislative campaign for the wild horses. Together, Johnston and Richards began drafting a state legislative bill based on the Storey County ordinance.

When the state bill was introduced in 1953, it abruptly died in the senate committee without ever reaching the floor for a vote. Senator William Craig Gallagher (R–Ely) made it clear to Velma that if the bill reached the state senate, his sympathies would favor the cattlemen in his district. He said the horses were destructive and a nuisance and should be disposed of in the most practical manner, regardless of suffering or pain to the animals. "It would seem," Velma wrote, "this is no longer an issue of preserving the ranges for the sheep and cattlemen, but has become a matter of purely commercial slaughter, for a financial gain of the few, at the expense of the many."[13]

Richards enlisted the assistance of state senator James Slattery (R–Storey County) and began to rewrite the language for another state bill on behalf of the wild horses. Richards recognized the livestock industry's influence on any legislation that intended to protect the horses. To circumvent future attempts to block legislation, Richards proposed to build a legal foundation by requiring senators with a vested interest in the livestock industry to recuse themselves from voting on the measure. Unfortunately, Richards passed away on December 22, 1953, before the legislature reconvened. Velma decided to step forward and become Richards's ghostwriter by returning to her familiar second home at the local and university libraries.

After Velma struggled with how to begin the bill, (according to Marguerite Henry's biography of Velma, *Mustang: Wild Spirit of the West*), she decided to put her notes aside and rest her eyes.[14] She fell asleep on her couch and dreamed of the late attorney Richards dressed as Thomas Jefferson and reciting the Declaration of Independence. Bolting awake, Velma grabbed a pen and wrote, "We the People . . ." Within ten minutes she had the first draft of the state law she wanted: "We the People, say it shall be unlawful for any person to hunt wild horses, mares, colts, or burros by means of airborne vehicles of any kind, or motor vehicles of any kind. It shall also be unlawful to pollute water holes in order to trap such animals."

The foundation of Johnston's wild horse and burro program was like a three-legged ranch stool. She wanted to preserve the heritage of the wild horses and burros, protect them from inhumane roundups, and manage them in a way that would equitably protect the public rangeland. She bristled when special interests wanted to take advantage of her proposal of a tripartite management solution at the expense of the wild horses or burros. She believed there was a major difference between "control for range maintenance" and "exploitation."

Velma was the first to admit there were three sides to the situation, the first two being the cattle- and sheep men who desired protection of their ranges and Velma's faction, which wanted the protection to be carried out humanely. The third side, she said, was "made up of certain individuals who are engaged in the horse-meat business, and who are carrying on the commercial slaughter of the horses, under the excuse of clearing the ranges of the menace of the wild horse. . . . It is so contrary to the laws of human decency by which we live."[15]

Senator Slattery lived in the same canyon shared with the Johnstons. After penning her rough draft of the state legislation, Velma delivered it to his home the next evening. The senator was already aware that his neighbor was developing a stubborn determination to see state legislation to protect the wild horses. After reviewing her draft of the state bill, he recommended that Velma "storm the media" to help get the bill passed during the next session.

Velma's manual typewriter clacked away at the Double Lazy Heart Ranch until she had letters written to every Nevada newspaper editor, but only one Reno columnist picked up the story. That was enough to garner the attention of the CBS Radio Network's *Sunday Desk,* and Velma had an opportunity to bring the story of her statewide campaign to a national audience.

Newspapers began to publish letters to the editor from Velma and even the ones written by her growing army of supporters. Lucius Beebe of the *Territorial Enterprise* in Virginia City again took an editorial stance on the statewide wild horse bill. Beebe could not imagine any legitimate point of controversy to the bill, "since the only opposition it can conceivably provoke is the opposition of greed, brutality, and a total contempt for the best over-all

To capture wild horses, mustangers would often lasso the animals from pickup trucks and then tie tires around their necks to exhaust them. Velma Johnston sought legislation—first at the state level in Nevada and eventually at the federal level—to protect the horses from such tactics, which she considered inhumane. Photo courtesy of the Gus Bundy family and Special Collections, University of Nevada, Reno Libraries.

interest of the public." Beebe reminded readers that historically, Nevada had been "blind to all the advantages in the preservation of its natural and historical resources and assets. Protection of the wild horses can, in some small measure, aid in refuting the belief that Nevadans are more deeply devoted to a fast buck than to their impulses toward humanity and decent human conduct."[16]

Support letters began pouring in to the Nevada Senate. One lawmaker approached Senator Slattery and asked, "Who is this Mrs. Johnston? She must know everyone in the state!" With the letters of praise came letters of hostility, too; naturally, those were often unsigned. "I don't mind the signed letters," she wrote to a friend, "but the guy who dips his pen in the poison and writes everything but his name, hiding behind anonymity, the spineless creature, infuriates me. Every guy you see thereafter becomes suspect, particularly if he is sort of paunchy, with a huge silver belt buckle adorning that paunch, dressed in fancy boots and a Stetson."[17]

One of the most unusual letters the Johnstons received was from someone who claimed to be a tribal chief of the Sioux Indians. It was full of extravagant praise and offered the letter writer's support in a unique way. Referring to the Johnstons' stand at the corral of captured horses, the chief wrote, "Oh girl, if I could have been there with a good band of Sioux Warriors, armed with 30/30 rifles, we would have killed us some two-legged skunks."[18] Charlie, with his Delaware Indian heritage, enjoyed a good laugh as he warned Velma to watch her step or she may be held responsible for causing another uprising of the Sioux Nation.

Velma and Senator Slattery crafted a bill that was intended to cause economic hardship for the "killer buyers" by removing the cost-effective use of motorized vehicles to gather the animals on state land. It did not come to anyone's surprise that a bitter campaign developed among the vested interests that would be affected by the bill. Mustangers, slaughterhouse owners and workers, some ranchers, and anyone who benefited from the exploitation of wild horses took notice of this "little old lady" and began to lobby their state legislators against her.

Senate Bill (SB) 29 was introduced on February 2, 1955, by Senator Slattery and transferred to the Public Morals Committee for discussion. Chairman Walter Whitacre killed the bill in committee with recommendations that a new draft be written that could survive the expected opposition.[19] Velma Johnston enlisted two gentlemen for additional support—one closely aligned to cattlemen and the other a member of the Reno White Hats, a well-respected community-service horse club.[20]

While Velma expanded her core of supporters, the *Nevada State Journal* responded to the news that Senator Slattery's bill had failed to leave the committee: "Let's for once, not let these wild animals die in agony and torment because we let the bill to protect them die in committee without ever getting it out of the Senate or Assembly floor as in past sessions." The paper cautioned:

> If we can let wild creatures die in agony and torment, and "viva la commercialism" is the order of the day, we're losing a real part of our human dignity. The United States has laws, enacted by the will of a majority of the people, protecting the bald eagle, a bird of not much practical use to anyone, but the symbol of the history and strength of these United States. By the same token, why cannot we in Nevada afford some protection to an animal, which, more than any other, symbolizes the history, the strength, the progress of Nevada and the west—the wild horse?[21]

A new bill was written and presented to the Nevada General Assembly, and again the bill was sent to the Public Morals Committee for discussion. Velma did not let up and continued to gather supporters. Cliff Gardner, senior state brand inspector and ranking state officer in charge of livestock movement and sales in Nevada, expressed his concern that wild horses were disappearing from the state's rangeland: "The wild horse of the Nevada desert, as much a part of the state's tradition as silver and six guns, probably will become extinct before the end of 1957." Gardner had no authority to prevent the legal and humane slaughter of wild horses, he noted. "We can only enforce the existing laws and hope that a few of the animals will manage to survive the drives being conducted by the horse harvesters. We are preparing to crack down on violators, but we are powerless to prevent the horses from being driven to extinction."

To the Johnstons, it seemed like the bill was stuck in committee forever. One day, though, Velma was tending to the horses back on the Double Lazy Heart Ranch when Charlie called her into the house to take a call from Senator Slattery. He was cordially inviting them to come to Carson City, where the Public Morals Committee would finally discuss her wild horse bill.

With great anticipation, Velma walked into the state senate chamber. As the hearings progressed, she watched as the committee agreed to give Senate

Bill 133 a "do pass" recommendation, with the caveat that the act could not conflict with any federal law or regulation governing the hunting or driving of wild horses with airborne or motorized vehicles. On advice from counsel and to prevent the measure from dying in committee, Velma and her supporters agreed to allow the addendum.

Section 16 of the federal Taylor Grazing Act already reserved the power and authority of any federal law to take precedent over state legislation. Johnston accepted the consolation that losing a slice was better than losing the entire loaf. She agreed to the amendment because she recognized that Nevada's state-owned public land was significantly smaller than the acreage of federal public land. The state wild horse bill would have no effect on the forty-eight million acres of federal land that made up 67 percent of Nevada's land base.

SB 133 passed out of committee and was sent to the senate floor, where it was unanimously passed. After a stormy debate in the assembly, where several representatives attempted to change the bill, the state representatives finally agreed with their peers in the senate. On a vote of thirty-two for, ten against, four absent, and one abstention, Velma Johnston had her state legislation to protect the wild horses and burros on Nevada state land. On March 23, 1955, Governor Charles H. Russell signed the bill into law.

After the excitement wore off, Velma became reflective. The passage of the county ordinances and the state law was a formidable accomplishment, but she also recognized she would have to set her sights on federal legislation. Just as the mustangers moved their operations to other jurisdictions when the county and state laws were passed, Velma knew that most wild horse operations were now being conducted on federal land.[22] Before the Nevada state bill was even put into effect, she began to contemplate the challenges a federal campaign would pose.

Velma knew that if the effort was to succeed, she would have to bring the American heritage of the wild horse to the attention of the national public and invest that public in their plight. It would be a tough sell, even she admitted, as "mustangs would not, in many instances, measure up to accepted standards of equine beauty."[23]

As other western states contemplated similar laws of protection, Velma knew too that the vast western rangelands were difficult to police against isolated acts of animal cruelty and abuse of rangeland conservation. Ulti-

mately, it would be better to work out a control plan so the horse populations never reached a point where their numbers would be another excuse
for wholesale hunting.

Furthermore, there was a general lack of scientific knowledge to repudiate
or justify the allegations that wild horses were injurious to the range. Velma
reasoned that the horses' being classified as "feral" or "exotic" discouraged
range scientists from expending research effort on issues involving mustangs, despite the vast ranges, large herds, and economic impact involved.

BEFORE SHE BEGAN the next phase of her campaign, Velma and her family had an opportunity to laugh about their arrival at the senate chamber
room for the hearing. As she entered the room, she caught the glare of Dan
Solari, the BLM official who had arrogantly expressed his disapproval of wild
horses but accidentally tipped her off about the Storey County commissioners' meeting several years earlier. Solari also remembered that encounter. In
a loud stage whisper to no one in particular, he sneered, "Well, here comes
Wild Horse Annie herself!"[24]

When recounting that memorable day in the state capitol, Velma chuck-
led, because Solari could have committed verbal suicide when he made his
derisive comment. As soon as Solari spoke, Charlie walked into the room, a
few steps behind his wife, and returned the glare of the discourteous public
official. In return for the new moniker that was bestowed upon her, Velma
dubbed Dan Solari with the nickname "Dante Solari."[25]

As Velma wrote to a friend, "For some reason, even the proponents of the
bill began calling me [Wild Horse Annie], most respectfully however, and the
name has stuck." After that hearing, Velma B. Johnston insisted her friends
continue the nickname as a reminder that her pathway would be filled with
many people like Solari. "Whenever I am interviewed and asked which name
I prefer," Velma responded to a letter writer, "I always answer 'Mom and Dad
gave me the name Velma. My husband bestowed upon me the name Johnston, but by golly I earned the Annie.'"[26]

To her family, she was still known as Velma. In her business environment,
she was still known as Mrs. Johnston. But the growing number of friends
(and foes) freely accepted her request to call her just "Annie." It was a new
moniker that transformed the quiet secretary and ranch wife into a national
advocate and conservationist.

THE FINAL DAYS OF
LEGAL MUSTANGING

Most people would have been satisfied with a series of county ordinances and a state law on behalf of the wild horses. As Velma "Wild Horse Annie" Johnston recognized, though, most wild horses and burros roamed on federal land, outside the jurisdiction of county and state officials, and she knew the Nevada ordinances and law were just a "foot in the door." Range-management issues and wild horse and burro protection were more complex on a federal level.

Throughout the years 1950 to 1955, Annie's introduction to the wild horse controversy involved civil discourse among her neighbors on county and state levels. The Nevada newspapers were gentle to this compassionate local horsewoman; her propensity for flawless documentation earned respect among the staid journalists. With the move to a national stage, Annie faced new opponents who did not like wild horses as well as well-intentioned advocates who brought their own personal and organizational agendas to the debate.

Roundups on federal land were legal under the Taylor Grazing Act. Applications filed with the county commissioners were published as public notices in small-town newspapers. The formality was usually overlooked except by Annie's growing posse of outfielders who carefully read the local papers, sometimes monitored the roundups, or inventoried the condition of the gathered wild horses in local holding areas or stockyards.

Not all opposed the roundups on federal land. While some of the stockmen of Joe Bronn's generation expressed concern that their heritage as ranchers was being tarnished by the actions of exploiters of the public lands, to these gentlemen there were also philosophical gray areas to the debate over the economic value of the wild horses versus the benefits of their roaming on public land. Ranchers described how wild horses "paw" the edge of the water holes, making pools of water from the mud created by other animals that only wallow in the water hole. During the winter, wild horses were seen exposing sparse vegetation that was under the snow or breaking ice to open frozen water holes. Moreover, because the horse's digestive system is incomplete, grass seed consumed by the horse passed unharmed through the animal and was deposited along with natural fertilizer, effectively reseeding the public rangeland.[1] In other livestock, the digestive system destroys the grass seed.

Annie was initially open to discussions about alternative management of the wild horses. *Only if* legitimate and accurate scientific range management indicated the horses, burros, or livestock were doing long-term damage to the rangeland would she consider that wild horse (and livestock) reductions be implemented. In a conversation with Walter Whitacre, chairman of the Nevada Public Morals Committee, she temporarily acquiesced that excess horses should be dispersed by the same government wildlife agencies that had successfully controlled the deer population in the state. If that meant shooting some of the horses, at least it would be more humane than using motorized vehicles to chase the horses. "I have never advocated a completely 'hands-off' program," Annie explained, "for I realize that in time the numbers might possibly increase to their own detriment insofar as their physical condition is concerned, and an over-abundance of anything is not good."[2]

She went on to state that the ranges must also be carefully managed. Annie said the public would be more understanding if range clearance of wild horses, cattle, and sheep was done for the purpose of rangeland preservation and only if it was supervised, humanely carried out, and intelligently planned. Instead, she said, it was being done at minimal expense through what Annie believed was inhumane private commercial exploitation. To Wild Horse Annie, that was the line drawn on the prairie that established her federal campaign. Since livestock owners and the government land managers were not willing to recognize their responsibility for range management, she took that option off the table, and it was never raised again.

WITH ONLY ANECDOTAL INFORMATION AVAILABLE about the quantity of wild horses roaming the public lands, Wild Horse Annie needed to establish a baseline of population information. Earl Thomas, acting director of the Bureau of Land Management, provided her with an updated estimate of wild horse numbers in 1958. After canvassing the BLM's fifty-nine grazing units, Thomas estimated twenty thousand head of "unclaimed and abandoned" horses were grazing on federal land; he was careful to avoid the terms *wild horses* and *mustangs*. He also reported the Bureau of Indian Affairs estimated an additional forty-five hundred to five thousand horses grazed on federal reservations. The U.S. Forest Service disclaimed knowledge of any "abandoned and unclaimed horses" on its land.[3]

E. R. Greenslet, Nevada state supervisor of the BLM in Reno, stated that during a four-year period in the early 1950s, the BLM authorized the removal of more than one hundred thousand "abandoned and unclaimed" horses from Nevada federal ranges. Branded horses were turned over to the owners, who could then sell the animals. Unclaimed horses were given to the pilots, who could sell their share of horses as compensation for their work.[4] "The practice of abandoning horses (which I cannot believe would account for the numbers that have been captured), would appear to me to be a matter of following the course of least resistance," Annie once wrote, "for the owners know full well that the ready and highly lucrative market for the animals for use as pet food will sooner or later attract exploiters who will dispose of the animals for them." Mystified as to why this roundabout course would appeal to anyone, Annie was sure there could be "no justification for the manner in which these animals are captured."[5]

The baseline of wild horse statistics was established through the anecdotal observations of nineteenth- and early-twentieth-century journalists and authors. Early-twentieth-century writers claimed one to two million wild horses roamed the West. The "off-the-books" roundups of wild horses, authorized roundups scheduled by county commissioners, and questionable livestock gatherings to recover the progeny of horses that left ranches for the wild bands contributed to dramatic changes in the estimation of the wild horse population. Wild Horse Annie's national attention to the wild horses and burros prompted some BLM offices to falsely claim they had no "wild" horses in their jurisdiction in order to avoid additional outside scrutiny. With the increase of commercial and recreational roundups and the development of Wild Horse Annie's campaign, the official government estimation of wild horses dropped to some seventeen thousand wild horses.

The BLM could have used aircraft to conduct more accurate census counts at the same time each year. Some BLM wild horse specialists proposed counting wild horses immediately after a snowstorm. Trails in the fresh snow made it easier to locate and more accurately count each horse. The specialists proposed using a grid system to ensure accuracy. These concepts were never implemented throughout the western states, and no reliable wild horse population figures were available during Wild Horse Annie's campaign.

The number of wild horses removed from the public lands could have been more accurately documented. Each state hosting wild horses also has a state brand inspector. While each state may have minor variations, the fundamental regulatory responsibilities include:

recording and administering livestock brands

inspecting livestock and verifying ownership before sale, transportation beyond seventy-five miles, transportation out of state, or slaughter

inspecting and licensing packing plants and livestock sales rings and inspecting all consignments before sale to verify ownership

preventing and returning stray or stolen livestock and investigating reports of lost or stolen livestock

It would have been a relatively simple task to compile brand-inspection documents and determine a fact-based study of the number of wild horses and burros removed from the public lands if the removal of horses and transfer to private or commercial use were legally done. No such analysis has ever been conducted.

As the public became more aware of Annie's campaign to preserve, protect, and manage the wild horses, the number of reports of wild horse roundups exponentially increased. Annie's legislative victories on county and state levels threatened those individuals whose mustanging enterprises were being pushed into a figurative corner on the federal public lands. With no national legislation to protect the horses, individuals used the loophole that they were gathering their own domestic horses and said it was "unfortunate" that several bands of wild horses got caught in the process. Under the protection of the Taylor Grazing Act, the Bureau of Land Management condoned the roundups. All expenses were paid from the sale of the horses to slaughterhouses.

The formation of the Bureau of Land Management in 1946 provided an alternative for western ranchers to apply for secure employment. Young men returning from the war could trade long, cold hours on the ranch for a warm office, providing personal insight into the ranching community. The independent lifestyle of the western livestock operators was contrary to the culture of eastern legislators and administrators. Having federal legislators in the East mandate the management of wild or unclaimed domestic horses on the public lands was not a responsibility desired by the Bureau of Land Management in the West. Many land-management employees had little regard for the wild horses—except as a little unreported personal income.

The local districts of the Bureau of Land Management, many of whose members were from ranching backgrounds, supported those individuals who gathered wild horses with the aid of airplanes. Without the oversight of law enforcement to ensure the roundups were humane, the BLM merely granted the permits to public land lessees who then employed wild horse hunters to actually conduct the roundup. If "accidents" took place while gathering the horses and some of the wild horses were injured, it was just part of the process.

Annie did not give up on alerting the local newspapers about what was happening on the public lands. Those stories were then picked up by the wire services that fed them to national and international news outlets. Annie's campaign generated hundreds of letters, reflecting the public's indignation toward those who exploited the wild, free-roaming horses and burros of the American West. The public wanted to know what could be done to enact federal legislation to protect the mustangs. Letters of personal support were postmarked from Portugal, Spain, the Belgium Congo, Brazil, Poland, Puerto Rico, the Philippines, Yugoslavia, England, Canada, Mexico, Argentina, Cyprus, and even the latest American state—Alaska. To each inquiry, Annie sent packets of background information at her own expense to ministers, housewives, students, teachers, sportsmen, the nuns in a convent in the East, and even a blind man who read "Mustangs' Last Stand" in the December 1957 Braille edition of *Reader's Digest*.

Schoolchildren took interest in "saving the wild horses" and were particularly excited that "Wild Horse Annie" herself took the time to respond to their inquiries asking how they could help. Teachers seized the opportunity to teach children civics lessons on how laws are passed through the legislature. The children became the enlistees in Annie's "Pencil War" or "Children's Army" with their first letters sent to their elected officials on behalf of the wild horses and burros.

Representatives from Italian and Dutch news organizations arrived in Nevada to get the story firsthand and wrote glowing tributes about "Wild *Pferd* Anna" and critical exposés about the mustang exploitation. European writers who grew up with the books of Karl May and his romanticized image of the American West rekindled that excitement for a new generation of

Wild Horse Annie posed for a publicity photograph with her horse Hobo and one of the Johnstons' cocker spaniels, Daiquiri. Autographed photos were sent at Annie's expense to any schoolchild who requested one. Author's collection.

readers through stories about Wild Horse Annie. As Annie wrote to a friend, "At least my efforts have accomplished this much—mustang fever is raging!"[6]

Through typographical errors and editorial oversights, some of the articles failed to provide an accurate mailing address where readers could correspond with Wild Horse Annie. Somehow the Nevada post offices were still able to deliver the daily sack of mail to the ranch—even those letters addressed only as "Mustang Annie, somewhere in Nevada." One letter was directed to "Velma Johnston; Mustang Ranch, Nevada." She laughed about that, insisting that if the correspondent ever met her, he would never mistake her for one of the young working girls at Nevada's famous brothel of the same name.

In one of the lighter moments in her correspondence with the Washington, D.C., Bureau of Land Management, Annie reminded them about the postal mix-ups between her organization and the Nevada brothel. She described receiving a letter from a woman who planned on taking her young daughter to Reno in a few weeks and would like to tour the "Mustang Ranch" with owner "Wild Horse Annie." The woman's letter arrived the day before their arrival in Reno, leaving Annie with little time to delicately explain to the young lady and her mother the finer differences between Annie's operation and that of the other fillies. Even the Reno Chamber of Commerce had to carefully sort its mail inquiries to determine which "mustangs" were being addressed.

ON FEBRUARY 28, 1958, Annie finished compiling her reports for the proposed federal legislation and sent a package to her local federal representative and personal friend of the Bronn family, Walter S. Baring (D–Nevada).

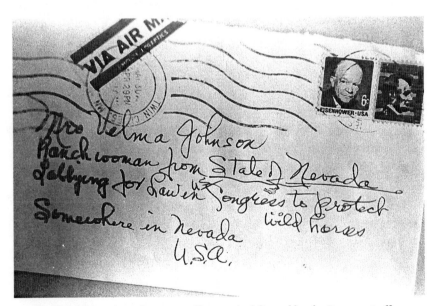

A vaguely addressed envelope was still properly delivered by the Reno post office. Velma Johnston Collection, Denver Public Library.

Annie's cover letter was professional in nature and requested the enclosed information be used to obtain federal legislation for what Annie described as "the protection, control and rehabilitation" of wild horses and burros before they were eradicated for commercial purposes. Representative Baring composed a bill, based upon the Nevada state bill, to ban motorized and airborne roundups of wild horses and burros on federal public land. It was introduced to a subcommittee for review during the midsummer, but stalled before Congress adjourned.

The June 1958 edition of *True: The Men's Magazine* was then circulating the country with "Mustang Murder" as one of its feature stories. In addition to the riveting text, six photographs of an actual wild horse roundup were included. Gus Bundy, a well-known Nevada photographer, took the photographs during the same 1951 roundup photographed by *Life* magazine.[7]

In January 1959, Representative Baring tried again, with additional information provided by his constituent and chief researcher. Included in the packet to Annie's legislative friend was new information gathered during the past year. She enclosed a letter from the chief of the Information and Education Division of the State of Idaho Fish and Game Commission, claiming one part of Idaho once had a few bands of wild horses, but they were no longer present in the state. Any so-called wild horses would actually be domestic horses that strayed from the ranch. Annie noted that Idaho had been one of the largest exporters of horses to the pet-food canneries. In her report to Representative Baring, Annie explained:

> Be they range horses or be they mustangs, there can be no justification of the brutality and ruthlessness with which the roundups and subsequent handling of the horses is carried on, and any official or bureau who condones the practice—or shrugs it off as being the rounding up of abandoned horses—is as guilty as those who are actually carrying on the operation. It is quite apparent that because of the increasing tendency toward the monopolistic use and abuse of our public lands to the exclusion of all forms of animal life not commercially profitable to private interests, and because commercial exploitation of the mustangs and burros for pet food has provided such an expedient means of range clearance, both from a user and management standpoint, we must expect strong opposition to any plan that will interfere with this convenient arrangement.[8]

A month after the revised bill was reintroduced, Annie learned of another roundup conducted just a few miles from Reno. A Wyoming operator gathered twenty-five wild horses on public land leased by a prominent cattle rancher. According to a witness to the roundup, it was "the worst cruelty" he had ever seen.[9] The operators were caught, but the sheriff could not arrest them because the BLM had issued a permit to gather the horses on federal land in order to protect the range grasses. Of the horses, a few had old brands, but others were branded *after* capture.[10] Considering there were so few wild horses in the area, Annie was incredulous that the purpose of the gathering was to clear the public land for range-restoration purposes.

Annie and Representative Baring knew that the mustangers, in cooperation with the Bureau of Land Management, were stepping up their efforts to clear the public lands of wild horses and burros. Some of Wild Horse Annie's sagacity rubbed off on Representative Baring, and he increased his efforts for the passage of the federal law.

The spread of media accounts of the wild horse campaign and the national reputation that Velma Johnston was earning as "Wild Horse Annie" caught the attention of the Massachusetts Society for the Prevention of Cruelty to Animals. The organization was founded in 1868 and is the second-oldest humane society in the United States, formed two years after the American Society for the Prevention of Cruelty to Animals. Now called MSPCA-Angell, the organization is a nonprofit organization involved with animal protection and adoption, advocacy, humane education, law enforcement, and veterinary care. The MSPCA magazine, *Our Dumb Animals,* introduced members to the cruelties of wild horse roundups and the work Annie was doing on their behalf.[11] Response was so encouraging that the organization made preservation of wild horses its legislative project for 1959.

The livestock operators, slaughterhouses, rending plants, and even the private employees of the BLM were prepared to rally against any effort to nationalize the protection of the wild horses. However, congressional support for Representative Baring's H.R. 2725 from Annie's followers throughout the rest of the country balanced the western livestock opposition.

The Bureau of Land Management hastily attempted to argue for an amendment, allowing them to use airborne and mechanized methods to capture the horses. Annie quickly countered that the proposed amendment would once again give federal approval to the airborne roundups the legislation intended to stop.

Congress finally scheduled a hearing in mid-July 1959. Velma B. "Wild Horse Annie" Johnston, the frail secretary from the little-known hamlet of

Wadsworth, Nevada, was invited to testify in Washington, D.C. The story of Annie's arrival in the nation's capital was in nearly every major newspaper and on the front page of many. Congressman Baring and his administrative assistant met her at the airport. For the next week she was wined and dined by members of Congress and their wives and, as Annie described them, "by civilian brass enough to dim the eyesight."

One morning during her visit, she was the focus of a two-hour news conference led by ten members of the leading news media in the United States who bombarded her with rapid-fire questions. She was also subject to an unrehearsed thirty-minute coast-to-coast television interview. Little did she expect to receive a "hero's welcome" when she visited the nation's capital, but she felt that this episode would be written in the annals of history, and she was proud to have been a part of it.

Her Washington visit continued with after-dinner speeches to congressmen and senators and interviews with every magazine writer who could crowd into Congressman Baring's office. Annie found the scene pure pandemonium and wondered what legislative work other than "Wild Horse Annie activities" could possibly be accomplished that week. For Annie, it was an experience that brought her face-to-face with what the founding fathers may have meant when they created this "government of the people, by the people and for the people." In this prelobbyist era on Capitol Hill, it was one of Annie's finest hours.

Frank Eleazer, a United Press International (UPI) reporter, was given an assignment that must have broken the monotony of his Capitol Hill beat in Washington, D.C.: go interview the woman known as Wild Horse Annie. With only the images of Calamity Jane and Annie Oakley as a reference, he was prepared to make light of his rendezvous with a woman who dared to travel east from her Nevada home. Making arrangements by phone, he reportedly instructed Annie, "Ham it up. We want to see you in your guns and western outfit."[12] His wire-service story reflected his surprise:

> WASHINGTON (UPI)—Wild Horse Annie was here at last, and word spread across the Capitol range like wind whipped fire through sagebrush.
>
> Was this the Wild Horse Annie who single-handedly cowed the cowhands, outdrew the gunslingers, and hogtied the Nevada Legislature in the interest of saving the vanishing cayuse from the can?
>
> It was indeed, it was Wild Horse Annie, the nemesis of the dog food and glue

factory moguls, the terror of the burro bootlegger, the heroine of the mustang's last stand.

I buckled on my fountain pen and galloped through the Capitol canyons to the office of Rep. Walter Baring (D–Nevada) where Annie had agreed to have a few words with a posse of pressmen. I was feeling uneasy about my citified suit and bow tie, and the fact that I wasn't packing a gun. But Annie, it developed, wasn't holstered up for the rendezvous either.

I thought for a minute I had fallen into the wrong company.

Here was a slim little lady in a crisp linen sheath, kind of a blue-green, with stiletto heels, who laid aside her white gloves and white bag to shake hands. My "hi-ya pardner" died in my throat. "How do you do, mam?" I managed instead.[13]

Other papers took the news of the wild horse and burro legislation more seriously. The *Kiplinger Washington Letter* and the *Christian Science Monitor* remarked that Congress was startled by the unusual amount of mail they were receiving in support of the wild horses.[14] The Associated Press reported that congressmen hoped the matter would be settled soon because of the overwhelming heartfelt response from their constituents. Representative Jim Wright (D–Texas) confessed in his newsletter about the deluge of letters, "Am I going to be susceptible to pressure? You bet your boots I am."[15]

On the morning of July 15, 1959, Annie finally testified before the seventeen members of the House Judiciary Committee. Drawn by publicity, spectators filled the chamber and the press gallery as Annie related the story of the slaughter of the wild horses and burros and fielded questions. She came right to the point and told the legislators that she had a response to those who wanted to exploit wild horses and burros: "Of all living things that have played their part in the development of this country, except man, the horse has played the most prominent and beneficial role. The real need for his strength, speed and endurance is past, but as nothing else can, he portrays the West as all people like to think of it; he is a symbol of wild freedom to us all—a challenge to conquer him but not to destroy him. Surely he has earned his right to survival."[16]

Annie explained that horses generally do not graze where domestic sheep or cattle may compete except under adverse conditions. She said if the range was as poor as the land users described, the ranchers had themselves to blame. Annie said she had proposed a program of control, rehabilitation, protection, and preservation, but had gotten nowhere. She observed that none of the governmental agencies wanted to take on the responsibility of developing a program that would incorporate her proposals. Other agencies suggested that setting up wild horse preserves would be another alternative. Annie had considered that option, but thought the opposition against the idea would be too strong.

This was a critical junction where Wild Horse Annie's advocacy, the Bureau of Land Management's stewardship, and the public-lands lessees collided on philosophical principles. Annie proposed that Congress reexamine the range-management policies that were originally established by the ranchers for the benefit of the ranching industry. Annie's objective was to ensure that wild horses and burros would not be used as scapegoats while the livestock industry overgrazed their allotments and then blamed the damage on the wild horses and burros. For the wild horse and burro program (and public-range management in general) to represent all aspects of the federal land, a serious review of public-land conservation needed to replace the mandates established by special interests.

Congressman Walter Baring and Velma "Wild Horse Annie" Johnston review the wild horse legislation in a publicity photograph in the congressman's Washington, D.C., office. Author's collection.

One of the most critical issues still impacting the wild horses and burros was written in the form of a legislative ruling that defined the animals for the first time. On August 11, 1959, Report no. 833 of the House Committee on the Judiciary finally defined wild, unbranded horses, mares, colts, or burros running at large on any of the public lands or ranges: "The word 'wild' referred to horses or burros existing in a wild or free state on public lands. The language is broad enough to apply to any horse or burro existing in a free or wild state on public land or ranges, and this plus the requirement that they be unbranded is sufficient to differentiate these horses from horses whose ownership can be traced to some individual. It should be noted that this classification does not rest upon the origin of the horses in terms of bloodlines or similar technical limitations."

The wild horse bill passed the House without debate on August 17 and then likewise passed the Senate on August 25. On September 8, 1959, President Dwight D. Eisenhower signed Public Law 86-234.[17] Today, the federal law is popularly known as the "Wild Horse Annie Act of 1959."

ANNIE'S APPEARANCE IN WASHINGTON increased her workload. After her impromptu press appearances and public speaking engagements, Annie left her hotel with more than a satchel full of range-management documentation. Her flight home was spent sifting through the paperwork in the company of her cigarettes, an adult beverage, and the quiet of the airplane, away from the persistent telephone calls.

Exhausted by her eight-day emotional and physical legislative marathon, Annie had little time to relax. Despite how much her opponents misread her intentions, Annie continued to make them very clear to the press and legislators. Considering the growing number of legal and illegal roundups, it was imperative that the last herds of wild horses be immediately protected. At the same time, Annie also called for a management program to control their numbers "so that never again will there be an excuse for such a mass extermination program as has been permitted in the past few years."[18]

Annie described her victorious trip to Washington in a letter to a friend. She explained that the U.S. Department of the Interior had fought her every step of the way, presenting their own internal experts to rebut Annie during the congressional hearings. "I whipped them in their own backyard!" exclaimed Annie. "What an experience!"[19] She reflected on an idea that began in "a tiny courthouse in a dot on the map of this great country" and grew to Washington, D.C., where she was able to personally present her cause to national lawmakers. Her storybook course took seven years and three months, propelled by a growing core of supporters who provided public pressure to the lawmakers on Annie's behalf.[20]

Tularski's "Saddle Chatter" column in late December 1959 was Velma's Christmas present when Lura bestowed the title of "Most Outstanding Horsewoman of the Year" in print. When Annie opened the Nevada newspaper, she blushed as she read:

> I bestow this title upon Velma because of her tenacity of purpose and courage in the long (ten years) struggle to final success in getting a bill passed into a federal law. . . . Not only has her mighty effort prevented man from having opportunities to practice cruelties on our feral horses, but has inspired persons all over the world to renew their faith in a democratic government where anyone may have his day before the greatest tribunals of the nation and where that same anyone may be listened to with respect and if a case is well prepared and presented have hope the injustices will be corrected.

Congressman Baring had one more memento waiting for Wild Horse Annie—the pen used by President Eisenhower to sign the bill into law. She described the gift to a friend: "It is quite an ordinary looking pen, really, but if you look at it closely, as I have, you will see that instead of the customary plastic composition, it is made of stardust and dreams come true; its shiny finish is not black at all, but is glowing with the red, white and blue that is America; the faint trace on its point is not ink, but a special formula containing the warmth and humanness and courage of its people."[21]

For Annie, discussions like those she engaged in with the Judiciary Committee provided her with the recognition of what still needed to be done on behalf of the wild horses and burros, despite her doctor's concern for her health. She was still recuperating from the strain caused by several years of state and federal legislative wrangling. In vain, her doctor ordered Annie to rest. Even though she believed the law was a step toward reducing some of the mass roundups, the doctor's orders had to wait—there was still a lot more to be done on behalf of her "wild ones."

Requests for Annie to make personal appearances sent her crisscrossing across the country. Three days after the passage of the federal law, Annie flew to Boston to receive the MSPCA's Angell Memorial Humanitarian of the Year award. The gold medal had been awarded only three times during the organization's ninety-seven years—and Annie was the first woman to receive the honor.[22] Her acceptance speech reflected the glow she still felt after her victory in Washington, D.C. "How does it feel to touch a star?" she asked the audience. "It feels real good." Annie described the combination of feelings— the exhilaration celebrating the successful completion of a difficult job, her gratitude for the support of so many people throughout the country, and the relief that her long, hard fight was finally over. To Annie, it was an opportunity to fight for something she believed in and bring that campaign directly to national lawmakers.

It would have been easy for her to share the accolades with her husband, but she knew it was the many hundreds of letters of support and motivation that she received from supporters throughout the world that also helped the campaign. Annie continued to acknowledge the courtesy, kindness, and consideration that were shown to her by every elected official she met during her visit to Washington. Even the local and national press received Annie's appreciation for the coverage that provided support for her efforts. She concluded that in the fight to right the wrongs done to those in the animal world, a sense of peace came with knowing that one small part of this earth was a little better off.

Charlie stayed in the background and let his wife take all the well-deserved credit. He knew she had finally overcome her shyness and would be able to carry through on her own with their mutual dream to save the wild horses. Whenever Velma wanted to quit, it was Charlie who gave her the emotional push to keep going. Many awards and congratulations were yet to be bestowed upon his wife as Wild Horse Annie. Charlie could rest in the knowledge that her childhood demons were gone, but neither of them knew what new demons would be waiting for them.

The 1960s was a decade of changing public attitudes, social changes, and rising political awareness. But it would be personal challenges away from the national limelight that had the greatest impact on Annie and Charlie.

GOING IT ALONE FOR CHARLIE AND THE HORSES

The quiet of the coach seat in the smoking section of the return flight from Boston to Reno was the first time in years when "Annie" could put aside her public personae as "Wild Horse Annie" and return to being "Velma" to her family. Sipping on either a martini or a highball and puffing on a Virginia Slims menthol cigarette, Velma reflected on the past week of events in Washington and Boston. Nearly a decade of diplomatic wrangling to herd government bureaucrats and challenging the ideology of the ranching community, and the sometimes naive, sometimes compassionately savvy wishes of the public, took Velma on her first trip outside her western home. She thought back on the trip as some of the happiest moments of her life.

In the peace of the airplane, Velma reflected on how she would celebrate with Charlie at their Wadsworth ranch. She remembered the horseback rides together along the Wasatch Mountains and the quiet evenings in front of the fireplace. Her jubilation faded quickly when the plane landed. Charlie was not among the well-wishers greeting her return.

His health was not good. While Velma prepared to fly to the East Coast for her legislative marathon in Washington, he put on a convincing act of good health until his wife was on the airplane. Charlie then went to the doctor to get a diagnosis of one of his problems—a serious case of shingles of the optic nerve.[1] He was suffering for days before she left, but would not tell Velma. He knew she would not leave under those circumstances. "He had waited almost too long to go," Velma wrote to a friend, "and the doctors have been battling to save the sight in his left eye, and to keep the condition from breaking out on the right side as well."[2]

The eye condition did clear up, but Charlie's sight was the least of his medical problems. Velma's Virginia Slims and Charlie's unfiltered Salem cigarettes led to a new medical battle. This time, Charlie was diagnosed with bronchial emphysema. With all the chores to do around the barn while his wife was away, Charlie spent much of his time doubled over in coughing spasms that left him gasping for breath.

When Velma returned home, she was ready to put the wild horses on hold so she could tend to her husband's medical needs. Charlie insisted she continue to at least field phone calls on behalf of the wild horses; he knew his wife could never completely ignore them. It would be unfair to Charlie, Velma, the thousands of their supporters, and especially to the wild horses and burros.

On the Double Lazy Heart Ranch, the steady hum of a tractor could be heard. A kindly neighbor mowed the hay so the Johnstons would have feed for their animals during the winter. Charlie could no longer perform the normal ranch chores, and Velma's full-time job limited her "free time" to evenings and weekends. A growing revelation kept surfacing in Velma's correspondence to her friends. "A week of daily commuting, plus all the worry, and keeping things going on an even keel here, has proved what I've always known—that this special Utopia of ours could be a real nightmare without him."[3]

Velma's favorite horse, Hobo, was sent to a stable located along the Truckee River; their other horses, Roxy and Charlie's half-mustang Ranger, went to California to stay in a stable owned by Velma's sister. For years, Velma sent a picture of herself on Hobo to all those who requested an autographed picture. Years later she told me it was not her favorite picture. When a Dutch photographer prepared to photograph Velma astride Hobo one cold January morning, no amount of grooming his shaggy winter coat could make his hide look sleek. Hobo's attitude was equally unmanageable while the photographer clicked on. Hobo was about to unload Velma and head in a different direction in a stubborn battle between the half-mustang and his wild-horse matriarch. "The photographer caught us at our stubborn best," she explained of the photo shoot.[4]

To keep Charlie company, the Johnstons acquired a light honey-colored mix-breed cocker spaniel from the local animal shelter. Another cocker would soon be added to the menagerie; at one time, there were five cocker spaniels curled between the fireplace and the feet of their human companions.

She had nearly lost Charlie several times during the past few years, but their mutual sagacity pulled him through each time. Charlie was too tough to die, and Velma was too ornery to let him go. They made the best of things by sharing those times when Charlie was having "good" days. Velma caught up on her personal correspondence while Charlie napped on the couch with their cockers lying in various positions on the floor near him, lost in canine slumber.

With great sadness, the Johnstons realized they should leave the Bronn family property to someone who could do the maintenance necessary to keep the Double Lazy Heart Ranch in shape. A California businessman placed a bid on the ranch and allowed the Johnstons to stay on as caretakers while Velma and Charlie had a small ranch home built closer to Reno. The new homestead was approximately twenty-six miles west of the old ranch, but it brought Velma back to the town where she was born and worked most of her life and where her mother still lived. The new Johnston home was located on a hill overlooking Reno and Sparks. They awoke to the morning light on the Sierra Nevada, while the neon lights of the gambling casinos and resort hotels provided a fairyland of artificial beauty at night.

Velma shared her ideas on how they could make the transition from their old place to their new home. They would create a "Double Lazy Heart Room" where they could retreat to the time they had enjoyed the informal atmosphere of the ranch despite their new residence a short distance from downtown Reno.

With the assistance of three husky young men who used to visit the ranch, the Johnstons were able to put in a new lawn and added a few personal touches to the landscaping.[5] When Charlie felt well enough, he pruned a few trees on his own, while Velma immersed herself in gardening. "I'd rather garden than do anything I know of. If there's anything in reincarnation—I hope that I'm a gardener the next time around!"[6]

Charlie's health remained a great concern for his wife. When his illness stabilized, Charlie was able to move around with the aid of a respirator. On his bad days, his emphysema kept him restricted to a wheelchair during the day; walking would have exhausted whatever oxygen his scarred lungs could absorb. Three to four times a day he adjusted the valves and gauges connected to the bottles of oxygen. When Velma switched tanks, she had to be extremely agile because even a moment off oxygen left him gasping for breath.[7] Each day bottles of oxygen were delivered to the Johnston household with the same regularity the milkman delivered milk for other people.[8] "It's an overwhelming thing," she wrote, "to realize that a human life is depending on that small plastic tube that leads from a tank to a mask, which he wears over his nose and mouth."[9]

For five months Charlie also fought constant severe headaches, the result of an old skull fracture. It was only the nerve-blocking shots administered by his doctor into the base of his skull that brought him even temporary relief.[10]

Her own stress level also taxed Velma's health. She developed an allergy to the antibiotics prescribed to combat a respiratory infection and broke out in hives that left her "sore as a boil all over—Surely wish I were rich instead of famous. I'd hide out someplace for six months and do nothing but sleep and rest."[11]

In the quiet moments at night, they spent time talking about Charlie's medical condition. They both knew their days together were running short. Velma remained stoic, putting on a smile as Charlie expected but kept blinking back the tears that reflected her true feelings. It was his personal courage that had inspired Velma since she began her campaign on behalf of the wild horses they both loved.[12]

Velma told people at work she was learning to "roll with the punches." But at home while Charlie napped, Velma let the clacking of the typewriter mask the sound of Charlie's labored breathing as she wrote to close friends about her inner feelings and described the awful eleven and a half months while Charlie was slowly dying.

Charlie and Velma performed a family drama of tranquillity, each trying to protect the other's feelings, and each knowing that the morning sunrise could possibly be the last one they had together. Velma dutifully planted tulip bulbs throughout the yard, while Charlie watched approvingly from his window. They both knew he would never see them bloom.

When each breath brought searing pain to Charlie's lungs, he pleaded to have his wife bring his loaded .38 revolver to his bedside. It was the same gun he used to defend his wife while Velma stood on the cab of the pickup truck. Now he wanted to save them both from any more misery. It was one last request his wife could not fulfill. Instead, Velma engaged in gay chitchat at his bedside until he fell into a labored, medicated sleep.[13]

Finally, Charlie was taken by ambulance to the hospital one last time. Velma's new responsibility was to order massive doses of medications when he needed them during his final days. She could not give him the loaded .38 but was able to give instructions to the medical staff to withhold the intravenous feedings that would have only prolonged a life that could not be saved. "The long, sad road of suffering ended for my husband on March 1st, when he passed away quietly in a coma," Velma wrote to a friend two months later.

"Thank God, I was there at the end. I had so feared that he would die in the agony of suffocation, but we were spared that. Just before he went into a coma, about eighteen hours before his death, he motioned me to his bedside, put an arm around me, and ran his fingers through my hair, as he so much loved to do. He could not talk by then, and it was his goodbye to me. I kissed him, he smiled, then closed his eyes and did not open them or move again."[14]

As Charlie's breathing became shallower and shallower, Velma intentionally did not press the buzzer to summon a nurse to give a shot that would have postponed the inevitable. As their twenty-seven years of togetherness transitioned into a memory, Velma vowed that never again would anything hurt her more than "the sheer hell it was during that awful time" as Charlie succumbed to his weakened lungs. Her memories of them together were the legacy of courage that Charlie gave to his wife.

At the grave site, Velma sat with her mother and family. When the flag of the United States was taken off the simple casket, she stared at it, focusing on the special three-cornered way it was folded, thinking about where those stars had taken her during the past decade. As she reflected through letters to friends, she sat there, recognizing she had to make choices about what to do with the rest of her life. She recognized that Reno was full of lonely women left by quickie Nevada divorces or through the death of their spouses. Within a week of burying Charlie, she was invited to join what Velma described as "the daily congregation of secretaries whose five o'clock meeting at a local lounge had become a ritual." She declined that pathway.

The wild horses and burros were the cornerstone for Velma. By a strange course of events in 1950, they drew her into the world of inhumane commercial exploitation of horses. They provided a means for Velma to develop a sense of self-esteem that brought her before county commissioners, state legislators, federally elected officials, and the national and international press corps. But more important, the wild horses were the common glue that gave Velma and Charlie something they could accomplish together.

"It is a loving living memorial to Charles," Velma wrote. "He once said to me 'Saving the horses, honey, will be our gift to future generations of kids in America.'"[15] What they thought would be their gift to those children took on a special significance after Charlie died. Her long journey from Wadsworth, Nevada, to the nation's capital could not have been done without the support of many people.

Velma's friends and family told her that "time" would eventually give her the strength to renew her life. In the quiet of her home office, Velma used her typewriter to reflect on her feelings in a letter to one of her many correspondents who expressed their condolences. Slowly, her fingers transferred her emotions to the typewriter paper. "Although there is always that ache of loneliness when the sunsets are particularly beautiful and there's no one special with whom to share or a song comes through in startling loveliness; or a bird perched on the window sill asks for admiration; or just plain frustration and rage that could be lightened with just the right touch. The will to go on in spite of everything is stronger than the other emotion, and somehow you just do. Oddly enough, laughter becomes possible again; and lovely memories can be brought out for review without a baptism of tears."[16]

In the quiet of their "house on the hill," Velma spent time reflecting on her life. She never set out to be an international spokesperson for her "wild ones." She never thought she would take on the livestock industry as well as be a cause célèbre among the elected officials in the nation's capital. It was Charlie's support that helped nurture his wife's self-confidence. As she described to a friend, this would have been an opportune time for her to retire, "doing all the tiddily little things dames do"[17]—sewing, keeping a nice home for her husband, entertaining, and baking cookies. But without Charlie, those luxuries would have to wait.

For several months, she refused to accept his death. Velma had mixed emotions, knowing that during the last few years of Charlie's life, she had had to maintain a lie between them. He never knew that the sale of the Double Lazy Heart Ranch never materialized because the state was in the process of turning the property into an interchange for Interstate 80. Charlie thought the ranch had been sold and they had enough funds to take care of his hospital and nursing care, with enough left over for his wife's well-being for the rest of her life.

Mechanically, she continued to maintain their new home and pay off Charlie's astronomical medical bills. After his burial, she refinanced the house for lower monthly payments and tried to begin a new life. The cost of his medical bills and burial left her with a grand total of six hundred dollars in assets,[18] but she maintained the wealth of a close and loving family and the gratitude of many more throughout the country.

Trudy Bronn moved in with her daughter to try to ease the emptiness.

But mothers are inclined to worry a lot, particularly about daughters who meet informants in strange, shadowy places. They also worry when daughters take off into the remote parts of the state to scout for clues that may lead to an arrest in an illegal mustanging operation.

Most of the time Velma fared well, but little things such as the glimpse of a tall man on the street, the sound of a familiar refrain, or even the sight of a particular dress in the closet conjured up the thought of a happy evening together and brought on the sense of loss and futility.[19] When Charlie died, her heart literally faltered. Periodically, Velma's own coronary problems warranted careful monitoring; only her closest friends knew of her developing heart problems.

Gertrude "Trudy" Bronn stands among her daughter's awards and mementos in their Reno, Nevada, home. Courtesy of the author.

In a letter to Pearl "Billie" Twyne, a longtime animal-protection lobbyist in Washington, Velma expressed her personal apprehension. "Damn, . . . for the first time since that awful year I was losing Charles, my heart acted up this past week, and I thought it was going to do me in! I'm better, though awfully weak. I don't fear dying, but all I could think of was how much there is still to be done for the animals! [I] am trying to walk instead of run. But it is hard to say 'no' to the many requests that are made of me!"[20]

Her health gradually stabilized, but the amount of Velma's work grew. Few people understood what kept this wisp of a woman going. Her tongue-in-cheek answer was "a tight girdle and a case of hair spray."[21] The death of Charlie would have provided her with the opportunity to retire from the public arena. She had accomplished what she and Charlie set out to do—move legislation from the county to the state and finally to the federal government, where there was now a law to prohibit airborne and mechanized roundups of wild horses. No one would ever criticize her for kicking back and enjoying "the fancies that little old ladies like to indulge in," as she described them—a little good music, a dream or two by an open fire, and maybe a trip somewhere just for the fun of it. "I've not been anywhere in years that I've not had to work every blasted minute of it," she wrote.[22]

When considering the year following the passage of the Wild Horse Annie Act, it is important to also understand the conflicted feelings Velma had at the time. When she was ready to give up, it was a fan letter from a couple of entertainers who refocused her mission.

Velma's campaign had inspired many people. As her state legislative battle gained publicity in the 1950s, two retired Reno entertainers, John and Helen Reilly, read the *Reader's Digest* article about Wild Horse Annie. John had just purchased a Spanish Barb mustang from Bob Brislawn, the cofounder of the Spanish Barb Mustang Registry in Oshoto, Wyoming. Brislawn was a devoted advocate of Wild Horse Annie's campaign and recommended the Reilly family channel their admiration for the wild mustang through Annie. The Reillys invited Velma and Charlie to their "Life of Reilly" guest lodge just over the border in Badger, California, while Charlie was battling emphysema. "We were just overwhelmed," Helen told me years later. "She was just a tiny, fragile person. Charlie was very ill at the time. They stayed with us two days; they figured this was Charlie's last trip, and they wanted to see all the friends they could in California before returning to Reno."[23]

It was during this visit that the Reillys and Johnstons forged a friendship that would last the rest of their lives. After Helen and Velma talked about the infamous meeting with Dan Solari at the hearing for the Nevada wild horse law, Helen turned to her mentor and said, "I just can't call you Mrs. Johnston or even Velma. Wild Horse Annie just seems to fit. May I call you Annie?"[24] The Johnstons had a good laugh, and the Reillys never called their friend by any other name for the rest of their lives.

The Johnstons and the Reillys talked about what should be done now that the Wild Horse Annie Act of 1959 had passed. Annie was frustrated that "management and control" was not written into the law, but Representative Baring told her to forget about it. "We'll just take one step at a time," as Helen related the story to me. "We are on the right track with our 'management and control' approach!" Annie wrote to Helen Reilly. "There are some who will be critical of us, and they are the ones who can't bear to see anything killed—even though it be for the animal's own good. These are the 'little old ladies in tennis shoes' part of the humane movement. It is an attitude that has to be avoided, and a reputation that has to be lived down, with an objective approach to the whole thing."[25]

Velma told Helen that the 1959 law was the end of it for her because of her own heart problems and the seriousness of Charlie's illness. The Reillys responded that if the work was incomplete, she should continue. The discussion continued for the next few years as Charlie's health continued to weaken and eventually left Velma alone. For now, Velma would put the wild horses aside and spend her time closer to home. But that getaway weekend at the Life of Reilly Lodge would become another critical milestone for Wild Horse Annie and her unwavering advocates, the Reillys. It was the thought of that fortuitous weekend that Velma would return to when the time to rejoin the wild horses was appropriate.

To adjust to her life without Charlie, and to reevaluate her own future, Velma did a little traveling (including a return trip to Washington to see the tourist spots she did not have the opportunity to see in 1959). She also became the founding incorporator of the Reno-based Animal Welfare League in January 1963,[26] where she served two years as president, despite the competition from other humane groups. "It seems quite a discouraging endeavor," Annie shared with the Reilly family, "because there is always so much friction among those who originally got us to try to get something new going. Don't know why humane groups are always so belligerent toward each other! You would think their mutual interest, and the welfare of the animals, would tend to weld them into one united movement. However, no two people, nor no two groups seem to think alike."[27]

Under her leadership, the organization launched a humane education program in the local elementary schools. It was a concept that was planted in her thoughts during her trip to Washington in 1959. She saw the childhood innocence of schoolchildren, unfettered by bureaucratic motivations, economic greed, and a dark disregard for humanity. The hundreds of letters from children were the lifeblood of Annie's ten-year campaign to bring the wild horses and burros from Storey County, Nevada, to Washington, D.C.

Velma and Charlie did not solicit national and international attention; it just seemed to find them. Marguerite Henry was a prolific author of many children's books, all with horse themes. Considering the many letters that Annie's campaign generated during the 1950s and '60s, the story of Wild Horse Annie was an ideal topic for a Marguerite Henry book. In March 1965, Marguerite contacted Velma and proposed the idea. She spent many days with Velma and Trudy Bronn at their home in Reno, pouring over Velma's files and interviewing Velma about her experiences, from childhood to her momentous time in Washington, D.C. Velma and Trudy took Marguerite back to the ghost town of Ione, Nevada, and along the pioneer road where Velma's father was spoon-fed the wild mare's milk.

No matter how many news reports told the story of Wild Horse Annie, it was different when she saw her life from childhood to her current fight for the wild horses portrayed in book form. When Henry's *Mustang: Wild Spirit of the West,* illustrated by Robert Lougheed, was published, it brought Velma's story to a new audience of children. Velma saw the published book and responded with her Mark Twain sense of humor: "It is like being around to read your own obituary and enjoying it very much."

In April 1967, the book won the Western Heritage Award from the National Cowboy Hall of Fame and Western Heritage Center in Oklahoma City. The ceremonies rivaled the Academy Awards, with "Best Movie of the West" presented to *Appaloosa* and best television depiction going to an episode of *Gunsmoke.* Marguerite Henry, the publisher, and the artist received additional awards at the gala black-tie dinner and reception. One thing was missing: Wild Horse Annie had not been invited to the award ceremony.[28]

Five months later, Velma joined the author, artist, publisher, and Representative Baring at the center, where the administrators dedicated an exhibit to Wild Horse Annie. Henry donated the original handwritten manuscript; the artist provided the original black-and-white illustrations. Ford Motor Company, manufacturer of the Ford Mustang, purchased the five additional original oil paintings used to illustrate the book for fifteen thousand dollars and then donated them to the center.

In memory of Charlie and her father, Joe Bronn, Velma donated the silver bridle of her horse Hobo who was featured in the book, the pen with which President Eisenhower signed the Wild Horse Annie Act in 1959, her original notes from which she presented her plea before Congress, and some pictures. In her address at the center's dedication ceremony, Velma noted the beauty of the shrine that was built to honor not only the men and women who settled the West, but those who continued to keep that heritage alive as well. She noted that since the wild horses were such an integral part of that development of the West, it was appropriate that the wild horses also be represented that day. She told the gathering that when Charlie was restricted to their home after Velma's return from Washington and Boston in 1959, they joked about the very same facility. "I told Charlie that we would someday be in the National Cowboy Hall of Fame and Western Heritage Center because of the fight for the wild ones, and he replied, 'Oh, probably so, fifteen or a hundred years after we are dead!' I am glad that I, at least, was privileged to be there for the both of us."[29]

Speaking engagements soon refilled Velma's schedule. Her favorite title for her presentation was "The Fight to Save a Memory." She spent her rare weekends at home making her own clothes, shortening them, cleaning, pressing, and packing for the next appointment. "There are just lots of people who love constant activity and limelight, but I'm not one of them."[30] She felt, however, that she could not pass up the opportunities of personal contact, "because I feel that this whole struggle will be won on the basis of public relations. And if it is possible for me to win people over that way, I can't neglect that possibility."[31]

The emotional shroud of Charlie's death was barely lifted when Velma was shocked back to reality. Local Indians were catching wild horses in the Fallon district of Nevada. The method used in this case involved a hole dug into a trail, covered by a piece of tin slashed from corner to corner. A noose of cable was placed around the tin cut, and the whole trap was lightly covered with dirt. When a horse's hoof stepped through the tin cut, the metal sheet stayed on the horse's leg while the cable stretched tight. If the horse attempted to run or fight, the sharp tin edges shredded the horse's leg tendons.[32] Horsemen, riding in relays, prodded the wild horses toward the booby-trapped path. Out of thirty horses captured by the Indians, seven mares were run to death.

A second roundup occurred after several horseback riders posted the obligatory two-thousand-dollar bond with county commissioners. The relay of riders planned to drive the horses to a point of exhaustion before the animals were shot with tranquilizer darts. In counties where sheep and cattle ranchers dominated county politics, it was likely that most roundup applications would be approved.

In a letter to the executive director of the National Catholics for Animal Welfare, Annie explained her greatest opposition was from the cattle and sheep ranchers. They still claimed the wild horses were depleting the ranges of forage for the livestock. Annie rebuffed that claim and described the habitat for the horses, which was in the remote and barren areas void of domestic livestock. "Supporting the livestock men in this contention," Annie continued, "was the Bureau of Land Management whose ends have been well served by the operation of the commercial exploiters who have cleared the ranges of these mustangs and burros with no cost or effort on the part of the Bureau."[33]

As a tribute to Charlie, Velma left her self-imposed isolation and renewed her campaign to preserve the mustangs. The period of accolades, grief, and mourning was over.

> When Charlie and I were a team, no hill was too high to climb, no challenge too great to tackle. . . . I supposed I am not using good judgment in taking on so tough a fight as this for the second time in my life, with limited time, health, finances, and a decade added to my age, but having spent the greater part of the last eighteen years witnessing the unspeakably cruel destiny of the wild ones, it would not be characteristic of me to turn my back on them until the last victorious plateau is reached. God willing, and with the help of all who love them, may that time not be too far away.[34]

Velma reflected on the time following Charlie's death. She explained to friends that during the years that she continued alone, the wild horses eased any feeling of being isolated in her life because she still felt that Charlie was at her side. "His greatest concern was for me—and his little dog," she wrote. "Somehow, though, you have to go on in the face of heartbreak and the almost unbearable loneliness. And I have found that keeping busy is the best antidote."[35]

It was time to leave "Velma" lounging by that crackling fire with the cocker spaniels at her feet. The wild horses and burros needed "Annie" to continue the legacy that she and Charlie had forged together at the Double Lazy Heart Ranch.

PRYOR COMMITMENTS

Annie did not have much quiet time to contemplate her future without Charlie: she had a full-time job and spent evenings and weekends volunteering for local charities. It was clear that she was not going to heed her doctor's advice to slow down. While the doctor wanted to protect her heart, Annie was focused on protecting her wild ones.

For years Annie was on her own when it came to the protection, management, and control of wild horses. She and Charlie operated their campaign out of their home, keeping friends and strangers updated through correspondence. Newspapers interested in the cause published Annie's letters to the editor and reported her progress. The Johnstons did not have corporate sponsors or foundation grants supporting them. Small amounts of money trickled in from people willing to donate to the cause. There was no nonprofit organization to assist them.

Colonel Ed Phillips of Kansas City, Kansas, followed Annie's progress and organized the International Mustang Club, offering Annie a lifetime membership. Phillips's objective was to solicit the federal government to develop wild horse and burro refuges to protect the animals from the roundups that continued on the western rangeland. If Annie could not protect all the wild horses, she briefly considered saving some of them in sanctuaries. Phillips knew that her reputation to get things done as "Wild Horse Annie" would bring greater credibility to his club.

John and Helen Reilly agreed with the concept and joined the organization, primarily to help Annie achieve her objectives. Leading the club, which had approximately 250 dues-paying members, were president Ed Phillips, vice president Velma Johnston, and secretary-treasurer Helen Reilly.

Without much publicity, the International Mustang Club began making its support of wild horse sanctuaries known to the Bureau of Land Management. If the BLM wanted to clear the range horses and livestock from public lands for range-recovery purposes, sanctuaries were one way to preserve the heritage of the wild horses in their native habitat. The Nevada BLM was the first to accept the administrative challenge.

The 2,209,326 acres of the Nellis Air Force property outside of Las Vegas, Nevada, was a strange location for the creation of a wild horse range. The U.S. Air Force, Bureau of Land Management, and Nevada Game and Fish Commission worked in concert and agreed to establish a refuge in the north-central part of the air force property. The herd was managed by a cooperative agreement between the two federal agencies. Annie was pleased to have the BLM provide a good-faith gesture so soon after the passage of the Wild Horse Annie Act but suspicious too, considering the government's past animosity toward the wild horses and burros.

In 1962 the BLM carved out approximately 400,000 acres of the federal weapons testing, flight training, and bombing range, located within a 900-square-mile area of Cactus Flats and surrounded by low, rocky desert mountains. The BLM designated the area as the Nevada Wild Horse Range—the first of its kind in the country. Administrators claimed the refuge was their response to public pressure from thousands of wild horse admirers.

On the refuge, which is approximately half the size of Rhode Island, officials allegedly counted two hundred horses during the first year. As Secretary of the Interior Stewart Udall explained, "Preserving a typical herd of feral horses in one of the nation's most isolated areas may prove difficult, but we will make the effort to assure those of us who admire the wild horse that there will always be some of these animals." The Department of the Interior stated in a press release that the horses were mixtures of Spanish mustangs, Indian ponies, and stray domestic horses. "Only one generation is needed to change a domestic-bred horse to a wild one," Udall said in the press release.[1]

Annie was particularly encouraged when Secretary Udall stated that this "permanent refuge is the first step to assure that at least one wild herd will be preserved." Annie appreciated Udall's gesture of good faith and told him that she hoped this was only the beginning of her long-range plan to reintroduce the concept of "management and control" that was omitted from the Wild Horse Annie Act. She offered the assistance of the people whom she relied upon for their knowledge of wild horses and burros for a possible advisory board to work out the details for the development of refuges in other states. Congressman Baring shared Annie's jubilation, writing that the secretary had morally obligated himself to following through with Annie's objective.

Publicly, the Bureau of Land Management proposed that the Nellis Air Force range would be suitable as a national park–style attraction that would also provide an opportunity for research and resource-management evaluation. Annie was pleased with this proposal by the federal government, which she hoped would advance public interest in the rehabilitation and control of wild horses throughout the West. She was gratified the momentum had not died with the passage of the federal law, but past experience with the Bureau of Land Management caused her to remain suspicious of the public offer. She retained a naive optimism, however, that a man's word was as good as his bond.

Privately, the BLM clarified that the primary purpose of the area was for weapons development and flight training, not wildlife habitat. In an internal memo, the bureau stated, "The existence of wild horses is a secondary use of the lands."

The air force agreed. Because the refuge was completely within a federal military base, visitor access (except at a proposed overlook) was not permitted for national security reasons. Photographs, even at the public overlook, were also prohibited. Boyd Rasmussen, director of the Bureau of Land Management in Washington, told Annie that with the current world situation, that is, the Vietnam War, public access to air force land would be prohibited.

Then Annie and Representative Baring received a notice from Assistant Secretary of the Interior Glen A. Carver Jr. that further dampened their spirits. Carver stated that the Nevada sanctuary on the bombing range would be the nation's only wild horse refuge. The assistant secretary explained that any expansion of the sanctuary concept for wild horses would be at the expense of the domestic livestock economy and that the Department of the Interior's priority was to prevent severe competition for range forage.

Baring's administrative assistant, Tim Seward, forwarded Carver's statement to Annie with a cover letter expressing the congressman's disappointment. Seward encouraged Annie to stay the course because there was still more work to be done.

The entire idea of establishing a public viewing overlook so visitors could see the wild horses was scrapped by the federal agencies—again, for security reasons. A 1966 management plan was also shelved. When Annie wanted to see what was going to be in the wild horse management plan, she was told that it was no longer available for review—for security reasons.

ON AN ORGANIZATIONAL LEVEL, Annie and Ed Phillips began to disagree over the next steps for the wild horses. As it was unlikely that the secretary of the interior would allow more refuges, Phillips suggested that his International Mustang Club begin looking at private, fenced-in sanctuaries. Annie objected, warning that wild, free-roaming horses restricted to unnatural, fenced-in areas would not sit well with either the public or the horses. She worried the horses would break down the fences, wander into traffic, or get onto private property. There were already too many people who considered the horses nuisances on public lands; having them trespass on private property would further fuel the arguments to get rid of them.

Considering the meager funds and few volunteers available through the International Mustang Club, Annie suggested the club abandon the concept of placing wild horses in private sanctuaries. She emphasized that her concern had always been for the long-term welfare of the animals. She wanted to make sure that responsibility would not end with this group of wild horse advocates but be shouldered by future generations. Until the organization's financial stability could be secured through a major increase in membership, endowment, or some other source of continued funding, Annie would not recommend taking on the care of any specific number of horses.

Annie recognized that a small grassroots, nonprofit organization would not have the financial resources to catch the wild horses, transport them, or establish a staff to supervise their welfare. Nonprofit organizations were fiscally unable to bail out cash-strapped ranches to acquire public and private lands that were shared by wild horses and burros. Likewise, nonprofit organizations were unable to purchase land to transfer "excess" equines to create an artificial wild horse and burro habitat and provide supplemental feeding when necessary, veterinary care, farrier services, and liability insurance.

Annie tried to convince Phillips that they were living in a changing era, when civilization was rapidly encroaching upon open space. Landowners faced skyrocketing taxes and could no longer afford to keep their land, especially if it was not producing revenue. Phillips maintained his perspective that horse lovers could band together to take over the responsibility for the protection of the remaining wild horses and relocate them to protective sanctuaries on private land. Annie was more realistic in recognizing that there was no long-range endowment available to maintain such an idealistic fantasy. The rift between Annie and Phillips brought an end to the group. Annie and her supporters left the organization to form a new one.

DURING THE TIME while she was caring for Charlie and after his death, Annie may have put her campaign for wild horses and burros aside, but it was never far from her thoughts. Her mailbox was full of letters, and phone calls went unanswered from outsiders who did not realize she was still mourning the loss of her husband. There was a part of Annie that was already frustrated with the realization that the newly passed federal horse and burro legislation was not strong enough to make the difference she and Charlie had originally envisioned. Public land users and managers who opposed the legislation were already finding loopholes in the law and playing a "good old boys" game of incestuous land management.

Remembering Helen and John Reilly's offer to create an organization for the Johnstons' use, Annie reassessed their offer to establish a new nonprofit organization. When Helen Reilly visited Annie and Charlie just before his death, she could see that Annie was visibly worn out. Annie even suggested that John Reilly take over for her, but Helen quickly asserted that it was Annie who had the necessary public image and was able to accomplish far more than either John or Helen. Helen suggested that they incorporate, but she was adamant that Annie be the organization's president.

After much deliberation, Annie wrote to Helen to explain why she was willing to get back into the campaign. Even though Charlie never became a public figure in their battle to save the wild horses and burros, he was the core motivation for his wife—her silent partner. With his loss, Annie gradually found consolation in standing alone in the spotlight. The invitations to speak about her decadelong journey on behalf of "the wild ones" kept her too busy to be the office administrator for an organization, though. Furthermore, Annie recognized that although her heart was with the wild horses, without Charlie she would have to keep her full-time executive secretarial job. If the use of her name would help, Annie agreed to be the figurehead for the organization if the Reilly family was willing to run it.

Perhaps too she recognized her own health was nearly as frail as Charlie's had been. Annie shared with Helen her concern that responsibility for preserving the heritage of the wild horses and burros would exceed the lifetime of their human advocates. Publicly, Annie agreed to be the executive director of the new wild horse and burro organization. Privately, she confided in her closest friends that her motivation was to establish a tribute to Charlie. "It is my living, loving memorial to the great guy whose wife I was privileged to be."[2]

The first objective was to find a name for the new organization. The International Mustang Club served its purpose because Annie was gaining international attention, but the "Mustang Club" sounded like a group that went horseback riding on weekends, drove around in sports cars, or flew vintage military airplanes. The creation of a new organization provided Annie with the opportunity to include the similar plight of the wild burros in the name. Finally, Annie and the Reillys decided to be as all-inclusive as possible and registered the name of the nonprofit corporation as the International Society for the Protection of Mustangs and Burros. The initials failed to spell out a meaningful acronym, and even the closest supporters had to memorize ISPMB.

Annie was still not used to being in the spotlight without Charlie. She eventually conceded that her reputation would ultimately help the ISPMB and the goals she shared with her late husband. "As you know, my only concern has always been for the welfare of the animals—not for just this season, or year, or lifetime, but for all time."[3]

Annie questioned how she would find the time to lead an international organization, keep the membership supportive of the campaign, and still hold down a full-time job. John and Helen Reilly had to stand close to be her safety net and provide constructive criticism. "I think you two are the real pulse of the organization," Annie wrote to the Reillys. "I think you have always known that my real value to the organization is the fact that I am well-known throughout the country as 'Wild Horse Annie' and that perhaps the use of the name will help in a small measure. As for the actual operation of the organization, I rely on your good judgment."[4]

THE NEWS OF THE ESTABLISHMENT of the Nevada Wild Horse Range planted an idea of a possible way to resolve an administrative range war among BLM personnel, ranchers, and wild horse advocates in the Pryor Mountains, nearly one thousand miles away on the central border between Montana and Wyoming. The purported origins of the wild horse herd were as colorful as the deep-blue sky and red soil where they roamed. Some believed the horses were the descendants of the nearby Crow Indian tribe. Others claimed they were the descendants of General George C. Custer's horses that ran off following the nearby infamous Battle of the Little Big Horn. Still others maintained they were the progeny of the Lewis and Clark expedition, which also lost some of their horses during their passage through the area.

Among the advocates of the Pryor herd was rancher Lloyd Tillett. Whenever a visitor met Tillett, he was proud to display a small collection of the spines of several of the wild horses that died on the land adjacent to the Til-lett ranch. Bob Brislawn of the Spanish Mustang Registry reviewed the skel-etons and confirmed they each had one less vertebra compared to the Ameri-can quarter horses often used by western ranchers. The missing vertebra was characteristic of the Spanish Barb horses used by the conquistadores. The only pure wild horses in the world are found on the steppes of Mongo-lia and also exhibit the shortened-backbone trait. Tillett was adamant that the Pryor Mountain horse bloodlines and archaeology combined to provide evidence of historic horses of the Spanish conquests and the descendants of the mounts that carried General Custer's cavalry to their final battle. For the residents living near the Pryor Mountain wild horse herd, the equines were a source of community pride and potential tourism value.

In 1964 the BLM announced that the two hundred wild horses roaming the Pryor Mountains would be gathered for auction. Unlike ranchers in other areas of the West, Lloyd Tillett had an admiration for the small herd of wild horses grazing on twenty-three to thirty-two thousand acres and considered their rich colorful history to be an important component of the area's heri-tage. The controversy over what to do with the Pryor Mountain wild horses was brought to the public attention through the television news accounts of ABC News correspondent Hope Ryden, who went on to write *America's Last Wild Horses*, published in 1970.

On September 12, 1968, the BLM director declared the Pryor Mountain horses a "valuable national heritage" and placed them under the protection of the U.S. Department of the Interior.[5] The department presented three proposals for the "management" of the Pryor Mountains Wild Horse Area. The May 13, 1968, edition of *Newsweek* described the proposals as "remove, remover, removest."[6] The first proposal required the removal of all but thirty to thirty-five horses that would eventually be allowed to increase to fifty to sixty animals when the vegetation recovered. The second called for a herd reduction to ten to fifteen horses that would be allowed to double in quantity to compete with the present deer population. The final consideration called for the removal of all the wild horses and the reintroduction of huntable bighorn sheep.[7] Most of the support for the latter BLM proposal came from individual hunters and rod-and-gun clubs that wanted to see bighorn sheep reintroduced as part of the regular wildlife hunting season.

Tillett and other like-minded ranchers who respected the wild horses joined the residents of nearby Lovell, Wyoming, to form the Pryor Mountain

Wild Horse Association to stop the roundup. Lutheran minister and supporter of the association Floyd Schwieger contacted Wild Horse Annie for help.

Meanwhile, with no management plan in place, the Bureau of Land Management was feeling pressure from the Montana Livestock Commission. The ranching organization passed a resolution on December 4, 1967, that included an allegation that supporting unclaimed animals, without a caretaking individual or group willing to take responsibility for them, was contrary to both the policies of the livestock commission and state laws.

In response to requests from others to establish a wild horse refuge in the Pryors, the BLM cited the livestock commission's contention that, by Montana law, someone had to sponsor the horses, and so far no group had volunteered to do so. Wild Horse Annie was surprised that the BLM believed it had to conform to Montana law, since the Taylor Grazing Act stipulated that "nothing in this section shall be construed as limiting or restricting the power and authority of the United States."[8] If the federal government wanted to establish a wild horse refuge under the power and authority of the United States, Annie believed that desire trumped the authority of the Montana Livestock Commission.

To try to settle the impasse, Annie and the International Society for the Protection of Mustangs and Burros offered to sponsor the wild horses, if that was the only way to ensure their future. Annie recognized this stance contradicted the point of view she had expressed to Ed Phillips when he proposed that the International Mustang Club "adopt" bands of wild horses to protect them. She was flexible enough to recognize that temporary emergency measures may be necessary for the overall welfare and preservation of the herd.

The BLM informed her the horses must be branded "for their own protection." However, the moment the horses were branded, they would no longer be protected by the Wild Horse Annie Act, which prohibited the airborne and mechanized pursuit and capture of wild *unbranded* horses, mares, colts, and burros running at large. Once again, the nomenclature of the status of the horses became a sticking point.

As early as 1959, Annie had proposed that the government establish a management and control program for the wild horses and burros while their population was at an all-time national low of seventeen thousand. The root of the issue, again, was terminology. Advocates called them "wild," ranchers called them "domestic or unclaimed," and the government called them "feral." If the horses and burros were ever to be protected from bootleg roundups,

Annie was adamant that the animals be "granted the status of true wildlife" and placed in the custody of a federal agency to protect, manage, and control them. Without that designation, Annie believed, the animals would remain targets. "As the situation exists," Annie wrote to Ernest Swift, conservation adviser of the National Wildlife Federation in Washington, D.C., "the Bureau of Land Management is the sole judge, jury and executioner in its own 'control' program, and this one-sided disposition of the wild horses that belong to all of America is meeting with increased disfavor throughout the country." She knew that the BLM was under pressure from the "livestock dynasty," which always believed "the use of the public lands to the exclusion of every living thing that is not commercially profitable to its own is its God-given right."[9] Annie also recognized that exclusive use of the public lands for wildlife, including horses and burro, would not make good sense either. A compromise between these two extemes was thus the grounds for an agreement between the livestock industry and Wild Horse Annie.

It took nearly a decade before the Bureau of Land Management accepted Annie's challenge to define the animals. BLM director Boyd L. Rasmussen explained that the unclaimed and unbranded horses and burros on public lands were technically "feral" and not "wild," but he acknowledged that the general public considered the animals "wild." Strictly speaking, though, he wrote, "Wild horses or burros as defined by the BLM are any unbranded and unclaimed horses or burros utilizing lands administered by the Bureau."

Annie proposed to the BLM that Dr. Michael J. Pontrelli of the Animal Biology Department of the University of Nevada and two predoctoral students be funded to provide an objective study of the wild horses and burros. She also recommended that Steve Pellegrini, a postgraduate student of Dr. Pontrelli, participate in the cataloging of her research notes and other available information.

ANNIE WAS NOT ALONE in following the Pryor Mountain management controversy. A new organization, the National Mustang Association, established in 1965 in Utah, was also watching closely. Tom Holland, the group's president, was interested because of the potential foundational bloodlines of the Spanish Barb mustangs in the targeted herd of wild horses. The organization was not a registry, according to Ryden's book, but a club for people interested in the "sport" of mustanging—chasing wild horses and capturing them for their personal use. In this one situation, Tom Holland and Wild Horse

Annie were united in questioning what they both believed was a case of collusion between the BLM and the Montana Livestock Commission.

Ryden's *ABC News* reports about the Pryor Mountain wild horses and Annie's stories in the print media brought humane organizations into the fray as well. BLM officials had told Ryden and Pearl Twyne, now president of the American Horse Protection Association, that no traps were being built in preparation for the roundup, but Ryden showed a very sturdy and potentially expensive government horse trap that was nearing completion in the Pryor Mountain range.

In addition, the Animal Welfare Institute and the Humane Society of the United States voiced their support to stop the roundup of the horses. After a series of interventions by federal legislators and a federal court action initiated by the Humane Society, the proposed roundup of the Pryor Mountain horses was temporarily blocked.[10]

BLM director Boyd Rasmussen stated that the land-management issue involving the horses required further study and adopted Wild Horse Annie's recommendation to establish a committee for that purpose. "It is essential," wrote Rasmussen, "that we move ahead immediately to designate these lands to provide federal protection for this national heritage, and as quickly as possible to establish long-term management for both horses and wildlife, including a mule-deer herd."

A seven-member "blue-ribbon committee" of citizens, range experts, and Velma "Wild Horse Annie" Johnston met to work out management details to resolve the Pryor Mountain issue. Montana BLM state director Harold Tysk told the committee that while national attention was focused on the committee, some of the herd was actually "disappearing," with the assistance of unknown persons. On September 12, 1968, before more horses disappeared, Secretary Udall took back control of the area from the Montana Livestock Commission and designated the land for the federal protection of what he described as "this national heritage." Annie summarized the situation in a letter to a friend: "The government thinks it is off the hook with the establishment of this refuge, but it doesn't know that as soon as this one is all tidied up, I intend to get a movement going in another, and another, and another until we get them in all of our Western states. Sneaky, huh?"[11]

Annie's hope was to preserve wild horses and burros in their natural habitat on western public lands. She believed that they, other wildlife, and even livestock could coexist in refuges. The Pryor Mountain controversy was the first opportunity to demonstrate that special-interest advocates of public lands could cooperate on common conservation objectives when it came to range management. It would not be the last time a cry for Annie's help would be heard coming from the Pryor Mountains.

DIFFERENCES OF OPINION

Annie and Charlie were not the first people to become interested in the wild horses, but they were probably the most famous. Since they created an interest in the welfare of the animals in 1950, other wild horse groups were created with their own agendas, but few had an interest in working together on common problems faced by their wards. "I guess as long as human nature is what it is," Annie wrote of these rival organizations, "there will be differences of opinion."[1]

She was cautious while welcoming any well-intentioned volunteer into her camp. While applying all the social graces she learned during her childhood ordeal, Annie was brilliant in her subtle ability to discern between friends and foes, but publicly showed equal professionalism and courtesy to both. Her most challenging test was with people in her home state.

The National Mustang Association (NMA) was incorporated in 1965 in the state of Utah by Tom Holland and, as the organizational paperwork described, "a small group of horse-lovers who are also patriotic Americans and are interested in keeping the traditions of our American heritage for their children and their children's children." The organization's mission statement was "to preserve and protect this rapidly vanishing part of early America—the gallant Mustang—the horse that did so much in the making of our country. Another objective is recreation. Preserving areas where people can get out and really 'rough it,' going on riding trips and round-ups as in the early history of the West."[2]

The organization proposed preserving wild horses through a grading system that confirmed the horses' Andalusian and Spanish Barb breeds (believed to have been descendants of the Spanish conquistadores). Members gathered surplus or inferior stock that were not Spanish Barb horses during social roundups. Auctioneers started the bidding at a minimum of twenty dollars each. The association then shipped "outlaw" horses to rodeos as bucking stock.[3]

When Annie and Tom Holland met in the Pryor Mountains, they discussed how feasible it would be to share in the protection, management, and control components of the wild horse program (the aspect of "control" was absent from the National Mustang Association's objectives). Annie initially thought it would be ideal if they could unite under one particular plan, but she soon learned that some of the association's aims were not compatible with her own organization. She believed she would be remiss in her leadership if her organization affiliated with the National Mustang Association or its president.

Within a few years of the club's incorporation, National Mustang Association board members began resigning. They alleged that Holland was diverting funds for personal use and also shot a wild mare that had recently given birth to a foal so that Holland could pose for fund-raising photographs with the "orphaned colt" that he had "rescued." A former board member attempted to sue Holland, but eventually had to "drop the suit without retraction when he ran out of personal funds to continue the lawsuit," according to Annie's files on the organization.[4]

Annie's biggest concern was with one of the objectives touted by the National Mustang Association. She recognized that an estimated 20 percent of the range horses at the time could be classified as true mustangs. Under the National Mustang Association's criteria, 80 percent would be removed by the association's willing recreational mustangers. The vast number to be removed was deplorable to Annie, but she believed that the historic use of horsemen gathering the wild horses was more humane than leaving shot and wounded horses to die slowly on the range.[5]

It was the "wild horse" roaming the public lands that Annie wanted to see preserved and placed under protective management, not just one or two particular breeds. As the National Mustang Association published more information, she began to question the organization's motivations. Annie strongly believed the sale of rejected horses shipped out to rodeos as bucking stock smacked of commercial exploitation, especially since any of those rejected wild horses could easily be transferred to the slaughterhouse killer buyers, as they were before the federal law was passed.

In reviewing the organization's literature showing members loading horses into transport vehicles, Annie was struck with a reflux of bad memories in a letter to a friend: "Ugh! That truck looks exactly like the one in which those mutilated horses were being transported when I followed it to the rendering works in the very start of the fight. Perhaps that is why I am affected so adversely."[6]

Annie's distrust of the NMA and its president deepened a few years later. In mid-February 1969, a severe winter storm dumped several feet of snow onto the Pine Nut range, southeast of Carson City, Nevada. Robert J. Cordes of the Sheriff's Posse discovered that the storm had trapped a herd of wild horses and believed they were starving to death. He established a consortium of organizations and civic-minded individuals under the aegis of the Pine Nut Range Association and began raising money for a hay lift to the trapped horses.

Local and network television news reporters brought the horses into the living rooms of concerned citizens throughout Nevada and California. Film clips showed the horses pawing the ground where the wind had blown the snow off the barren rangeland. Spokespersons for the consortium privately expressed concern to Annie that representatives of glue factories would be waiting if the government attempted to move the horses off the mountain range. Cordes thought Annie's national reputation could get federal funds to help the hay-lift operation. Annie, however, was not usually an advocate of dropping hay to wild horses. She believed that the animals would start becoming dependent upon the hay bales from the sky and would be less dependent upon their ability to successfully forage for whatever was available in their harsh environment. But in this one case, Annie recognized there was a risk that the entire herd would starve.

By March the Pine Nut situation was unchanged. Additional snowfall had stranded approximately three hundred horses on the mountainside. Annie contacted Bob Minarek of the National Mustang Association to request their financial participation for a hay drop to the starving horses, but the association claimed no funds were available for the relief effort.[7] Instead, entertainer Judy Lynn, private individuals, and even Las Vegas strippers responded to Annie's public request to help and participated in fund-raising events to buy 595 bales of grass hay. Annie contributed four hundred dollars herself, approximately a month's salary from her job at the insurance company. Nellis Air Force Base pilots airlifted the hay to the local landing strip.

According to Annie, money from the fund-raising events somehow found its way to the National Mustang Association for distribution.[8]

Annie prepared to fly out of Tonopah on March 9 to survey the rescue efforts, but the ongoing storm closed the airport. Snowbound at the terminal, she took the opportunity to learn more about the National Mustang Association from a former board member of the organization who happened to also be at the airstrip. In a short period of time, Annie learned enough not to trust Tom Holland and his organization.[9]

Once the storm subsided, Annie and Dr. Michael Pontrelli of the University of Nevada took turns being flown over the area to check on the horses.[10] On March 12, Pontrelli reported the horses were still trapped and fundraising efforts were still needed to help the isolated bands of horses that were unable to break through the snowdrifts. Annie called Bob Minarek, this time requesting that her four-hundred-dollar contribution be returned so she could redirect it for the purchase of hay in a way she could track the funds.[11]

"Minarek promised it," wrote Annie, "and I asked him to call me when the check had been put in the mail. In about an hour, I received a call from Tom Holland who refused to send the money, but would have a P-34 [military airplane] and a crew of eight" prepared to fly 120 bales of hay to the horses near Mount Grant with the proceeds from her check.[12] She later learned this idea was not realistic; the P-34 was not a cargo aircraft that could handle 120 bales of hay, and the drop zone was outside the range of other cargo planes that would fly out of Nellis.

The animosity between the National Mustang Association and Wild Horse Annie came to a head just before midnight on March 13, 1969. Frank McMahon of the Humane Society of the United States (HSUS) called Annie. According to her transcribed shorthand phone notes, "McMahon was sarcastic throughout—and I just couldn't realize it, for we have always had good working relations. I kept thinking he was just putting me on. When I said that Holland refused to send me any money, McMahon said there was no reason why he should. I explained that it was the only source I had for help for the horses at this time, and would have to work out something else."[13]

The discussion then became focused. According to Annie's shorthand notes, McMahon's accusations included, "Do you really want to save the horses or are you just talking? Tom Holland has done more to save the wild horses than you have ever done. Now do you want to do something for those horses up there or don't you? Annie, to be a real humanitarian, you have to care about all animals, not just mustangs. Why do you say you can get along with an officer in his organization [Bob Minarek] but you can't get along with the president [Tom Holland]?"

The conversation digressed to personality conflicts, and Annie pointed out that even Holland's own board of directors was in the midst of an organizational civil war over Holland's leadership and fund-raising techniques. When Annie inquired into the whereabouts of Holland, McMahon first said he had gone back to Washington or somewhere else around the country, and then later in the phone call confessed that Holland was sitting next to him. Annie asked him what the purpose was for his call and why he would lie about Tom's whereabouts. McMahon said he was just leading her on to hear what she would say and then hung up on her.

Annie then contacted Bob Minarek, who informed her Holland and McMahon had brought a couple bottles of alcohol to an association meeting in Las Vegas. References to Annie as an "Indian giver" and other like comments had punctuated the meeting. Annie wondered if Holland and McMahon had been working on a plan together in Washington. She also pondered their animosity toward her. "It is quite possible that McMahon resents my appointment to the Pryor Mountain Wild Horse Advisory Committee instead of him, and it is possible to be the case with Holland, also." Annie summarized her impressions on paper after the late-night phone confrontation with McMahon. "His attitude was at times belligerent. At others belittling. Almost like a prosecutor badgering or baiting a witness. He kept drumming at me that he just couldn't understand my attitude [about the Holland organization] and acted quite superior."

Early the next morning, Tom Holland called Annie, wanting to meet with her despite her fully scheduled day. Assertively, Holland procured directions to her office and arrived with his organization's new secretary-treasurer, Roger Owens. After exchanging social pleasantries, Holland proposed they work as a united force. Annie expressed concern that he had accused her of being uncooperative in the past and had demonstrated a lack of courtesy during her period of bereavement following Charlie's death. At that point, Annie noticed Owens had a camera in his hand. When he saw her glance at it, he casually covered it with his hat, commenting that he had taken some pictures of a nearby hotel fire just down the street.[14]

Holland blamed several unnamed members of the board of the National Mustang Association for the organization's reluctance to reimburse Annie's personal contribution for the hay lift. They too were allegedly snowbound and could not be reached for their approval.

Holland went on to explain that McMahon had been in Las Vegas for a week. The owner of the Tropicana had allegedly picked up his hotel bill and contributed two thousand dollars for the hay lift. Photographers had snapped posed pictures of Holland and McMahon loading hay onto a military plane and distributed the photos to the newspaper wire services. Holland commented on McMahon's ability to generate press coverage that would specifically generate income for the East Coast organization he represented. "The Humane Society of the United States would reap a-plenty from this, as McMahon was in on the whole thing."[15] Annie responded that it was a shame Holland and McMahon misrepresented themselves and their purposes in order to obtain money from an unsuspecting public.

Annie had known Frank McMahon for years and had worked well with him on several cases. She could not understand why he would telephone her in the presence of Holland and speak to her in such a disrespectful manner. Annie's notes continued, "Holland said [McMahon] was drunk and that had he known what McMahon was going to say to me, he would not have let him do it." Annie said (and Holland agreed) that the Humane Society of the United States should know how its field representative conducted himself. Annie not only knew McMahon, but was also on close speaking terms with his boss, Mel Morse, president of the HSUS.

When Holland asked if he could get a picture of the two of them together, Annie refused. She told him she was reviewing her file of their correspondence and telephone conversations, a revelation that surprised him. She pulled out a file of shorthand notes and held it up, but would not let him see the contents.[16]

At a social function on March 30 that raised seven thousand dollars for emergency hay lifts, Tom Holland worked the room, making himself conspicuous for press interviews. Annie noticed the television crews never paid any attention to him. She shared her feelings at the time about Tom Holland and the National Mustang Association in a letter to a friend. "It is sad when opportunists seize upon a worthy project, and the efforts of someone else, to gain financially. The president has caused me no end of heart-break and worry, and it makes me ill when I think of the money that an unsuspecting public has poured into his coffers. . . . You would think that IRS or the postal authorities would have something to say about it."[17]

Use of the funds by those involved with the hay lift became an issue for the Bureau of Land Management as well. The media, concerned about alleged mismanagement of the contributions, pulled their support from the operation. Because suspicions were cast upon every group involved with the hay lift, including Wild Horse Annie's International Society for the Protection of Mustangs and Burros, she began to collect evidence for a potential lawsuit to stop the National Mustang Association from raising further funds on behalf of the wild horses, though she did not want to tie up her time and limited resources by taking the case to court.

Congress did step in and questioned the ethical behavior of the National Mustang Association's fund-raising efforts during hearings of a related wild horse issue that was brought before Congress. Representative Sam Steiger (R–Arizona) recounted the story of the "orphaned colt" whose photograph had been used by the NMA to generate funds for the organization. "[Tom Holland] told me yesterday he raised $160,000 since July of last year based on this photograph." Steiger said there was some question as to the validity of the picture, though as he said, "The important thing is that [the mare] was destroyed by Mr. Holland. Whether that is valid or not I do not know. But the point is that he raised $160,000 with this, thirty percent of which went to the advertising agency and forty percent of which went to the lawyers who put this scheme together. This means that all of it obviously was painfully collected a dollar at a time from children who are concerned." As Steiger pointed out, "It doesn't leave very much for the mustangs by the time the advertising people and the lawyers get through with it. I think the mustangs are going to get very little of it." Steiger lamented those who would take advantage of people's emotions to raise money, saying they "do a tremendous disservice to the cause that they support or reportedly support." Steiger also noted that Holland was being sued by the board of the directors of the NMA, who believed he had allegedly stolen fifty thousand dollars from the organization.

Annie went to great lengths to contrast her work with the NMA's. "I have consistently sought and supported federal legislation for the protection and management of wild horses and burros on all the public lands in all of the Western states which they inhabit," wrote Annie to all inquiries about the differences between Holland's organization and hers. "I have not attempted to raise funds to establish a privately owned sanctuary, if it were possible under present federal regulations to do so."[18]

Tom Holland, original president of the National Mustang Association, feeds an "orphaned" colt. Representative Sam Steiger (R–Arizona) introduced this photograph into a federal hearing for alleged fund-raising improprieties. Courtesy of the National Mustang Association.

Annie had learned much through her recent experiences with the International Mustang Club, the Nevada Wild Horse Range, and the Pryor Mountains Wild Horse Area. She was operating a strictly all-volunteer grassroots organization. Annie's salary came from her daytime job with Gordon Harris, not from grants or endowments or corporate sponsorships. The International Society for the Protection of Mustangs and Burros barely had enough to pay administrative expenses. Annie's international organization operated out of the spare room in her house. Her efforts certainly would have benefited from a $160,000 marketing campaign that was supposed to help the wild horses.

THE NATIONAL MUSTANG ASSOCIATION maintained a 68,000-acre ranch composed of 800 acres of deeded lands and 67,200 acres of public land available on a permit-use basis from the Bureau of Land Management. The preserve was created with a down payment and the balance acquired from leasing the public land with the claim the organization was grazing livestock as a bona fide livestock operation. Annie disputed that claim. "[The NMA] cannot qualify as being a livestock operation, nor was it ever assured of being granted permits for wild horses, and it has been officially notified that the area of public domain is not available under the circumstances," Annie said in a letter to a friend.[19] Nonetheless, Holland began a nationwide fund-raising effort through an advertising and public-relations campaign to help subsidize the ranch.

Because of the attention Wild Horse Annie earned internationally, she received many inquiries into the legitimacy of the National Mustang Association's refuge. She was convinced that people sent money to the National Mustang Association, erroneously thinking the funds were actually going to Wild Horse Annie's efforts to save the wild horses and burros.

A limited number of horses might be protected in a private sanctuary on the National Mustang Association's ranch, but just as she noted while a member of Colonel Ed Phillips's International Mustang Club, the cost of acquisition and maintenance, in relation to the small number of horses being preserved, would be exorbitant. Second, if a private sanctuary became overstocked through the transfer of other horses, it could result in auxiliary feeding operations that would create a roadside-zoo type of operation with considerable maintenance costs. The overcrowding and human contact would break the normal behavioral pattern and destroy the concept of a wild, free-roaming animal. Third, the animals would be at the mercy of other special-interest groups who preferred exclusive use of the public lands through elimination of the wild horses and burros. Those groups falsely claimed wild horses ate twice the forage shared by domestic livestock and target animals.

Annie often cited the behavior of the Chincoteague–Assateague Island ponies located between Maryland and Virginia. The ponies, considered to be descendants of a shipwrecked Spanish galleon centuries ago, are gathered every Fourth of July weekend. The volunteer fire department conducts an East Coast version of a "wild horse" roundup by swimming the horses from the island to the mainland in a fund-raising effort for the firefighters. The constant handling of the ponies and familiarity with tourists have reduced the "wild ponies" to little more than untrained horses.

Annie was opposed to the establishment of private sanctuaries like the one operated by Holland and the National Mustang Association. She was an advocate of sanctuaries in the form of wild, open, natural habitat—the fenceless terrain indicative of the term *wild and free roaming* when applied to the character of the horses. If deemed advisable, wrote Annie, specific ranges could be designated as sanctuaries, but not to the exclusion of protection of the horses and burros in areas not designated as sanctuaries. "I strongly endorse the 'open' range stipulation for many reasons," Annie wrote, "among them the fact that partitioning off our vast rangelands would severely harm all wildlife, and the immense cost to enclose them would defeat us. Never have I advocated an elaborate tourist-attraction type of refuge." She did not discourage public access as long as the range and the horses went undisturbed, "for it is upon public support that we are depending for enactment of the legislation, and it will be public funds that will provide for the welfare of the animals and the enforcement of the law." As she said, "The prime concern should be the wild horses and burros, rather than the public."[20]

Instead of moving the horses into private sanctuaries out of the jurisdiction of federal caretakers, Annie believed the benefit of "wild free-roaming horses and burros" roaming the public lands, as they did for centuries, would be lost as the heritage of the American West:

> Since the wild horses and burros are a part of our national heritage, belonging to all the people of America, and inhabit the public domain that also belongs to all the people of America, I believe the only way to guarantee the survival of these animals that are a symbol of the freedom upon which our country was founded, is to continue to work for federal legislation toward that end, and to place them in the custody of the government of the United States, which represents the people of America, with their welfare to become the responsibility of a specific agency of our government.[21]

Years later Tom Holland's successor, Grant V. Messerly, reflected on missteps made during the founding years of the organization. "There have been a lot of mistakes made over the years by this association. I'll admit that readily. But the aim has always been one of service to the wild horses, and from the beginning to now, everything has been aimed in that direction." He commended Annie for her work and admitted she had "accomplished a great deal on behalf of the wild horse. However, at this point in time, I feel that she would be much better advised to start making a few of her own decisions on behalf of the horses, and to start looking around and seeing what is happening." Messerly strongly believed the BLM was an organization of and for the stockmen. He claimed that decisions about the wild horses on "435 million acres of public domain are made in the air-conditioned offices of Washington, and not from any underling in the field." Annie followed Messerly's advice and looked around to see what was happening. She had been doing that since 1950 and knew to keep her friends close, and her enemies closer.

The National Mustang Association continued to push its agenda to preserve only the wild horses that exhibited Spanish Barb and Andalusian breeding. When Kent Gregersen, executive secretary of the National Mustang Association, and U.S. Senator Frank E. Moss (D–Utah) submitted Senate Bill 2166 for consideration, Wild Horse Annie was dismayed. The Moss Bill (as it became known) restricted protection to Spanish Barb and Andalusian wild mustangs as an endangered species, threatened with extinction.

Some equestrians blur the similarities of the two breeds that originated in Spain. The Andalusian horse is 15–16.1 hands high at the withers (base of the neck). Horse handlers use the equation that one "hand" is the equivalent of four inches (the width of a man's hand). The Spanish Barb mustang is 13.2–15 hands high. Spanish Barb Mustang Registry founder Bob Brislawn noted the breed's short back was due to a genetically missing vertebra. Through the Moss Bill, horses exhibiting the specific characteristics of the two breeds would be preserved, protected, propagated, and placed in special refuges. The rest of the horses would be disposed of (in the public interest).

In mid-May 1969, Representative Baring's staff sent a copy of the bill to Wild Horse Annie. Louise Dollard, the congressman's assistant, informed Annie that no one was willing to cosponsor the bill. It was sent to members of the Senate Commerce Committee, which included the sponsor of the bill, Senator Moss. Baring's office was concerned that people would think the Moss Bill supplemented the Wild Horse Annie Act instead of directly conflicting with it. The Wild Horse Annie Act of 1959 was intended to preserve all wild, free-roaming horses and burros on the public land, not specific breeds.

As Annie prepared to fight to defeat the bill, individuals rallied around her to provide expertise in specific areas of legislative law, biology, range management, and more. Annie's resource for biological issues was Dr. Michael J. Pontrelli of the University of Nevada's Department of Biology in Reno. "I am of the opinion . . . that if passed in its present form," Dr. Pontrelli wrote in his four-page analysis to Annie, "the bill would only create problems for wild horses, rather than solve them. After considerable study, it is my sincere belief that it is potentially dangerous and not in keeping with the public image of wild horses nor with the scientific basis of the concern with an endangered species."

When Annie reviewed Dr. Pontrelli's report, she used his conclusions to formulate her "unalterable opposition" to the Moss Bill, which included the following four points:

1. The history of the horse on the North American continent is shrouded in conjecture, and it is most debatable that there is a continuous bloodline relationship from the early introductions.

2. The Indians and early Western settlers made no discrimination in bloodlines and it is of that era in the history of our country that the wild horse of today has come to be a symbol—rather than a specimen of early blooded horse stock.

3. Based on the foregoing, the elimination of all but the Spanish Barb and Andalusian would result in virtually wiping out the wild horses in our country, and this would not be tolerated either by those working closely on their preser-vation and protection or by the vast army of individuals who support such a program.

4. The public expects the wild horse to continue to be part of the Western scene, and because it is a horse, running free and untamed, the public is quite satisfied with its mixture of origins, since it does not contemplate going into the horse-breeding business.

Instead of conducting a drastic reduction of the horses as authored by the National Mustang Association through the Moss Bill, Annie suggested legislation with severe penalties for intentionally releasing domestic horses on the open range. "This would treat the disease," wrote Annie, "rather than the symptoms." Second, Annie said the wild horses should be removed from the "feral" classification and be given status with adequate protective, management, and control procedures.

Annie told Representative Baring, "I will recommend opposition to any method of reduction or control that allows any element of commercial exploitation whatever to enter, on the grounds that once that door is opened, we will be right back where we were in the 1940s and 1950s." She also told him the provisions of the Taylor Grazing Act already empowered commissioners on issues of federal grazing.

When Senator Moss received a copy of Annie's response to the bill, he expressed his sorrow that he had missed an opportunity to discuss the issue of the wild horses and burros with her when she was in Washington ten years previously. After reviewing her written analysis, Senator Moss acknowledged, "Perhaps the bill should be modified."

The Pryor Mountain Wild Horse Advisory Committee met in Washington, D.C., in June 1969. Chairman Wayne C. Cook temporarily excused Annie as a member of the committee and asked her to bring the rest of the group up to date on the Moss Bill. She was caught off guard, but fortunately had her written analysis with her. Before an audience that included the director of the Bureau of Land Management, Annie expressed the concerns she had already shared with Representative Baring and Senator Moss.

The National Mustang Association bristled over the organized opposition to the Moss Bill. The executive secretary of the NMA wrote to Dr. Pontrelli regarding the doctor's analysis for Wild Horse Annie:

> If the nit-picking continues there will be no bill to bargain with. I certainly cannot see the ISPMB point of view. Either you go to bat on this one with us or the stockmen will continue to sell the horses for pet food for their own gain. I don't think you learn these things getting a P.H.D. [sic] like we who see these stockmen operate. They have had a golden highway to ride and if the horse groups don't get together *now* it will all be lost. I'm sorry this bill could not include the burro, but to do so would be a contradiction and would help defeat the bill more than anything. ISPMB, *please wake up.*[22]

Between Gregersen and Wild Horse Annie, the vitriol was increasing. "Your group has wanted protection for all 'wild horses,'" Gregersen wrote. "This is impossible and a bit ridiculous. . . . You should know how hard it is to get a Senator to go out on a limb for us on this subject. Now you want to saw the limb off while he is on it. . . . I don't mind anyone criticizing, but for what they tear down, they should put something constructive back in its place." Gregersen said that if Annie could improve the material sent to Moss, he would greatly appreciate it. "However," he stated, "I believe all aspects were covered."

In a letter to author and television journalist Hope Ryden, Annie summarized her thoughts about Gregersen's vitriol: "I'm handling the NMA people with kid gloves these days, and taking a lot of crap from them in order to keep this thing from erupting to the disadvantage of the horses. If only one of them had had the good sense to contact some of the rest of us at the time their legislation introduction was being considered, it would have been much simpler."[23]

Annie took the introduction of S. 2166 as both a challenge and an opportunity to fine-tune the 1959 federal law. During conversations with western federal legislators, Annie knew the Moss Bill was dead from lack of support, but she also recognized that legislators were looking to her to recommend ways to strengthen the 1959 law.

In a letter to Senator Alan Bible (D–Nevada), Annie began to set her own agenda. She reminded him that when she testified before the House Judiciary Committee in 1959, she "recommended a management, protection and control program, because I have always felt that it was not enough simply to say 'leave them alone.' Now, ten years later, it has become apparent that such a program must be established, and many organizations, individuals, the land management agency, fish-and-game commissions, wildlife interests and domestic livestock operators have come to that way of thinking."

Kent Gregersen had chastised Annie for tearing down their bill without replacing it with something constructive. Annie was now busy developing those constructive replacements, and she was true to her word that replacement legislation would carry the ISPMB banner and the good reputation of Wild Horse Annie's name among legislators. Among her recommendations were six key points that would need to be included in future federal legislation:

1. Wild horses and burros must be under the jurisdiction of the federal government, specifically the Secretary of the Interior, and must be protected as a national heritage.

2. More areas must be set aside which have as their primary function the preservation of these representatives of our national heritage.

3. In other areas of the West where wild horses and burros now exist, they should be included as a component of the range and be managed along with other animals in a multiple-use concept. Wild horses and burros should not be removed from all other lands not specifically set aside for them.

4. That there be strict prohibitions against the release of domestic horses on public land for purposes of harvest. (The most common use is sale for dog food.)

5. That studies be carried out so that management practices can be implemented from a sound ecological base and insure humane procedures.

6. That a national advisory board be maintained to be responsible to the public, and to advise the Secretary of the Interior.[24]

Pearl "Billie" Twyne, Wild Horse Annie, and BLM wild horse specialist Ron Hall listen to a BLM presentation on the Pryor Mountain wild horses during a meeting of the National Wild Horse and Burro Advisory Board. Courtesy of the author.

Annie and the International Society for the Protection of Mustangs and Burros had been monitoring several other attempts to amend the 1959 federal law. Each amendment died in committee. Annie confided to Pearl "Billie" Twyne that, based on this experience, all future legislation must be uniform with Annie's objectives if it was going to bear the endorsement of the International Society for the Protection of Mustangs and Burros. "I'm so damned weary," Wild Horse Annie wrote Billie. "There have been so many holes in the dyke to plug."

The Pryor Mountain advisory board had taught Annie much about negotiating among representatives of livestock, fish-and-game, humane, conservation, wildlife, and range-management interests. Each component of public land use was represented in an environment of education and civil discourse. The "working staff" of the advisory board was a civilian advisory committee authorized to work with agentcies involved with implementing the terms of the legislated program.

BECAUSE WILD HORSE ANNIE'S renewed campaign to tighten the loopholes of the 1959 act was under fire by state and federal bills that attempted to fight her on all levels, it may be prudent to review the situation that Annie was trying to stabilize and to identify what steps she was successfully able to take on behalf of her "wild ones." When Annie testified before Congress in 1959, she included a point of view that was often forgotten by the myriad of other advocates of the wild horses and burros: "Because so few of the animals are left, it is now that we should not only pass legislation for their protection, but plan for their control as well, so that there will never again be an excuse for the mass extermination programs as heretofore." Her insight into the need to create a workable management plan for the horses' protection, management, and control was a well-intentioned but toothless appeal, however. Without increased funding for surveillance and investigation, the implementation of the law by the Bureau of Land Management was no more than a wink and a nod between those who violated the law and those who were supposed to enforce it.

In retrospect, Annie failed to secure a clear test case of the federal law, but she did begin building a foundation of legal benchmarks that could be used for future litigation. Some elected and public officials working within the system were also becoming frustrated with the control that was still being exhibited on a local level, keeping the younger generation of land managers from implementing more modern ways of becoming good stewards of the public lands. Young college-graduate recruits at all levels of the Bureau of Land Management and Forest Service privately opened a pipeline of information that kept Wild Horse Annie informed of the decision-making process in Washington. Meanwhile, more belligerent organizations chose to fight the BLM rather than appeal to the few administrators who shared some aspect of Wild Horse Annie's plan to develop an effective and efficient wild horse and burro program. Annie's "outfielders" now wore suits and worked in Washington, D.C., and other strategic places where wild horse and burro management decisions were made.

ANNIE RETURNS TO WASHINGTON, D.C.

The country was experiencing a reassessment of national perspectives and priorities in the 1960s and 1970s. Discourse (not always civil) about the Vietnam War, civil rights, women's rights, the environment, animal protection, conservation, and similar issues sparked lively public debates. Whereas most organizations that took on the cause of wild horses and burros reduced the issue to an "us-versus-them" level of simplicity, Wild Horse Annie recognized that an understanding of the complex gray areas was crucial to the success of the cause.

One of the easiest ways an organization can raise funds, political capital, or media attention is to exploit the situation on a purely emotional level. Every campaign needs a protagonist and a hero. Financial contributors do not have to muddle through complex issues that would dilute the effectiveness of an emotion-based campaign.

It would have been far easier to raise public interest and organizational funding by publishing a photograph of horses and burros on their way to a slaughterhouse or publish an "aw-gee" photograph of a sleek, beautiful horse or a cuddly burro along with a plea to send money so that an organization could "save the wild horses and burros." Tom Holland did that and was publicly castigated during a hearing in Washington. None of the organizations actually had any jurisdiction to "save the wild horses and burros"—that ability fell primarily on the shoulders of the Bureau of Land Management and not private individuals or nonprofit organizations.

Wild Horse Annie maintained mutual respect with the federal agencies that did have that ability to make or break the wild horse and burro program. They did not always agree, but Annie and the Washington office of the Bureau of Land Management, at least, were respectful toward each other.

Some people believed that protection, management, and control of the wild horses and burros should be determined on a state-by-state basis. Annie believed the wild horses and burros were part of the national heritage; they belonged to the people of America and inhabited the public lands that belonged to everyone (not just to special-interest groups or industries). Therefore, the welfare of the animals should theoretically become the responsibility of an agency underwritten by all the people of America.

Wild horses and burros, domestic livestock, and target animals inhabit states with wide expanses of federally administered open rangeland. "Being neither an edible nor a trophy animal," explained Annie, "the wild horses and burros are considered intruders by . . . powerful interests. Lacking a loud voice in their behalf, they are treated as the most expendable of the inhabitants of our public lands."

She went on to explain what was already apparent. State committees identified with public-land resources were composed of a majority of individuals whose interests and sympathies were already ensconced with the livestock and hunting interests. "Measures aimed toward benefiting the wild horses and burros," continued Annie, "are of secondary interest at best and have [a] slight chance of getting out of those committees in states where domestic and target animals abound, and where the wild horses and burros struggle against overwhelming odds in their efforts to survive."

The Wild Horse Annie Act of 1959 was her "foot in the door," as Representative Baring stated when it passed. Annie had more than a decade to gather additional reports from her outfielders. She also had opportunities to meet with ranchers, government officials, and land managers to understand the complexities of land-management issues and how the 1959 act needed to be strengthened. Annie's reputation for taking both sides of the land-management issue into consideration earned her respect from unlikely sources.

Clifford P. Hansen, a Republican senator from Wyoming, was from one of the most influential rancher strongholds among the western states. Shortly after the Moss Bill died, Senator Hansen introduced a bill in October 1969 apparently to test some of Annie's ideas for a stronger management plan. His bill proposed to "authorize the Secretary of Interior to protect, manage and control free-roaming horses and burros under the exclusive jurisdiction of the Secretary of the Interior for the purpose of management and protection"—words that seemed directly from Wild Horse Annie's own playbook.

The bill provided federal rangeland for protection and preservation of free-roaming horses and burros "as a national heritage." Excess horses could be removed, "except that they may not be disposed of knowingly for commercial products." The secretary would also appoint an advisory board of no more than seven nongovernment experts to advise on any matter pertaining to free-roaming horse and burro management and protection. Violations could incur maximum penalties of one thousand dollars, a year in jail, or both.

The new bill included all the "buzzwords" that appealed to Annie, but wisdom gained from her past experience told her that not all legislative offers to help the wild horses and burros had good motivations behind them. Annie began to look into the details before endorsing Senator Hansen's bill.

In a sixteen-page analysis of the three-page Senate bill, Annie hoped the livestock and hunting industries would recognize the public's interest in the animals roaming on public lands. She challenged the western concept that ranchers and hunters have eminent rights to public lands as their private domain. If they did not expand their perspective to include other vested-interest groups, Annie warned, "it will have to be left up to the people of America, who have already abundantly indicated their interest in—and support of—a protection, management and control program." Annie acknowledged that the public would be satisfied if the horses were classified as "a national heritage" instead of "wildlife" and if commercial exploitation was addressed, but she still did not believe the bill was strong enough.

Annie began to recognize that there was no reason wild horses (and burros) could not coexist with other animals on the public land if all animals (domestic and wild) were subject to independent land-management criteria. As a result, she amended her concept of wild horse (and burro) sanctuaries to include the concept of multiple use of the federal range—wild horses and burros did not need their own exclusive habitat. Commercial livestock use, recreational hunting use, and aesthetic and recreational observation of wild horses and burros could be accommodated fairly under the multiple-use concept.

She noted that the state and federal fish-and-game agencies had advocated the elimination of nontarget animals from public lands to ease damage to vegetation and water holes. The revenue to perpetuate those agencies, Annie explained, "is in direct proportion to the number of hunting licenses sold and the amount of ammunition expended." Annie warned that as public resources diminished, public concerns increased. The only equitable resolution was to fairly take all interests into consideration for the long-term benefit of current and future generations.

Following introduction of the bill, Wild Horse Annie was invited to meet with a specially appointed joint committee of the American National Cattlemen's Association and the National Woolgrowers' Association. Their purpose in meeting with her was to review the provisions of the Hansen Bill and, if possible, work out compromise recommendations for legislation acceptable to all special-interest users of the public land.

The livestock members disapproved of the clause in the Hansen Bill that would prevent commercial processing of any wild horse and burro herds that some unnamed individual could claim if they exceeded range capacity. Annie explained that the provision was designed to deter commercial exploitation of the wild horses and burros that could escalate into another government-subsidized mustanging operation. The public reaction was hostile to the commercial slaughter of wild horses and burros at taxpayers' expense for the benefit of relatively few private users of the public lands. Annie rhetorically questioned whether it was the Department of the Interior's responsibility to preserve, protect, and manage the public resources entrusted to the federal government agency—or was it to provide a tax-supported resource for private industry at the exclusion of the noncommercial public benefit?

Annie's most formidable opponent was not the individual rancher, but the philosophical dominance of the livestock industry using the public lands as their own exclusive property for private financial gain. Anything that did not contribute to their private enterprise was in direct opposition to Annie's goals. The state fish-and-game commissions likewise were charged with the responsibilities of keeping the public land stocked with target animals for hunters and the industries related to hunting. Along with being neither trophy animals nor culturally edible, wild horses and burros do not financially contribute to the revenue generated on public lands.

The livestock industry contended that curtailment of their use of public lands through increased grazing fees or decreased grazing allotments would deal the industry a severe financial blow and create serious economic hardships for the nation's meat consumers by causing a spike in prices. Ranchers further argued that the domestic livestock industry was the lifeblood of small communities in the West, since it provided a market for commodities sold by local retailers.

Boyd L. Rasmussen, director of the Bureau of Land Management, rebutted the livestock claims by stating public-domain lands nationally administered by the BLM provided only 1 percent of the feed for all cattle and 6 percent of the feed for all sheep; the balance of the nutrition came from midwestern feedlots prior to slaughter. He broke down the statistics by noting that of the 14,419 grazing permits issued at the time of the Hansen Bill, fewer than 700 of them were actually for grazing livestock on the federally managed public lands. The majority of the permits were for livestock operations on state and privately owned rangeland. In most cases, absentee operators who leased 52 percent of the land left little of their profits to the local economy. The 48 percent of available land that was not leased through grazing permits was left to wildlife and other uses.

Furthermore, if the livestock industry was concerned about bolstering the local economy, they would have avoided the use of airborne and mechanized gatherings that involved fewer local employees. It was the sole purpose of airborne and mechanical roundups to reduce labor costs and expedite the transfer of wild horses and burros from the western range to the slaughterhouse.

Additionally, livestock representatives were opposed to prohibiting the release of domestic horses to run on the public land with wild horses and burros. They contended that putting domestic horses in pastures and feedlots would raise the overhead of livestock operations. Ranchers related that "other" livestock operators with permits to graze twelve domestic horses on the public land, for example, were actually grazing forty. Others, with no permit, illegally ran several hundred horses on the public land, thus depriving all other livestock of forage. To some ranchers, exceeding the number of horses on a grazing permit was no more harmful than driving ten to fifteen miles per hour over a posted speed limit. There was no harm done, unless the violator was caught.

Annie challenged the BLM's lack of planning and their attempt to use the horses and burros as scapegoats to justify poor range conditions. She issued a formal statement of opposition to the points raised in the bill. Although she agreed that western rangelands were in a serious stage of depletion, she vehemently disagreed with the cause of the depletion by using a formula based on information by independent range scientists.

By combining domestic livestock AUMs (animal use months) with the total AUMs attributed to use by wild horses, and once the estimates of the number of privately owned trespassing horses were deducted, the percentage of range use clarified the controversial issue. In the 1970s, domestic livestock utilized 97.1 percent of the potential rangeland, and wild horses used only 2.9 percent. The figures did not include trespassing cattle or sheep. If every wild horse in the entire West was removed, the increased number of additional livestock that replaced the equines was so small that no appreciable difference would occur toward range restoration.

The Hansen Bill initially looked like it met Wild Horse Annie's agenda, but analysis of the details exposed the flaws in the bill. It was referred to the Senate Interior and Insular Affairs Committee, where it quietly died.

Undeterred, Wild Horse Annie continued to focus the national attention on the welfare of the wild horses and burros and the need for stronger federal legislation. In an unprecedented wave of congressional response to renewed public sentiment, members of both the Senate and the House introduced new bills to provide the necessary management, protection, and control programs for wild horses and burros on public lands. The majority of wild horse and burro proponents chose to support S. 1116, introduced by Senators Henry M. Jackson (D–Washington) and Mark Hatfield (D–Oregon), and H.R. 5375, introduced by Representative Walter Baring (R–Nevada). Both bills had numerous bipartisan cosponsors.

After another meeting with representatives of the domestic livestock industry, Annie proposed several new inclusions for S. 1116 and H.R. 5375 to make her key points clearer to the legislators. The first was the prohibition against the release of domestic horses. Although the cattle industry spokespersons agreed there were flagrant abuses in the release of domestic horses on the public land, they once again did not want it prohibited and promised to come up with an acceptable regulatory alternative provision.

Annie dug in her western boot heels a little deeper this time. The fact that she had to revisit the same issues that were raised more than a decade earlier was a clear indication to her that the range-management problems were not being addressed or resolved. Administrative paralysis was affecting range-management conservation. Annie pulled out her notes from previous legislative debates.

"No one has been forthcoming," Annie stated, "and they prefer to fall back on existing provisions which have proven inadequate. Therefore, we stand fast in our position that domestic release must be prohibited." It was a common practice among some ranchers to turn out branded domestic horses to provide a nucleus for a later airborne roundup. Annie reiterated that if the mustanger was apprehended, he merely claimed he was gathering his own horses and "could not help it if a hundred or so wild unbranded horses got mixed in with his own. After all, it is nearly impossible [from the air] to identify whether a horse was branded or not."

The second issue, again, was the transfer of excess animals. The public was opposed to the commercial use of wild horses. As Wild Horse Annie stated, "We believe that profits which would be derived from what might be considered surplus animals would tend to encourage over-zealous control measures, and by elimination of the potential for financial gain, a more realistic approach to control measures would be taken."

Annie expressed grave concern that the legislation did not delegate specific policing powers to the land-management agency. They were charged with managing the public land and protecting the wild horses, but were not given the legal authority to issue citations if they witnessed violations of the act or were informed of violations by reliable witnesses. She believed that the Bureau of Land Management needed employees who were legally authorized to issue citations when violations occurred. Without such authority, BLM personnel witnessing a wild horse roundup would often have to drive hundreds of miles to the nearest federal office and bring an officer to the scene of the roundup to corroborate the violation and issue the warrant.

The horses and burros were still described as "feral"—a once domestic species of animal that had gone wild. Not considered "wildlife" in the sense that deer, elk, and antelope are considered wildlife, the equines did not come within the scope of wildlife management agencies that had jurisdiction over all the animals on public land other than domestic ones. Annie preferred to circumvent the wild horse, feral horse, or domestic horse controversy by describing the animals as "mustangs" and later encouraged that the horses be described as a "national heritage." She explained that the proposed legislative terminology of defining the wild horses and burros as a "national heritage species and national aesthetic resource" would create a new category of wildlife that would not conflict with present wildlife regulations. Instead, it would provide an opportunity to preserve and regulate other species that have significant heritage attributes; the buffalo or bison and American eagle could then be placed into this new category.

The proposed legislation also provided that specific ranges be set aside for wild horses and burros, which would satisfy a public desire to have an opportunity to see these animals in their natural habitat. This was only partially acceptable to Wild Horse Annie. She held firmly to the conviction that if wild horses and burros had their own sanctuary off the public land, all federal laws to protect the animals could be dissolved and the remaining wild horses and burros on public land removed.

In her testimony submitted to the legislature in 1971, Annie clarified her perspective on the roles of wild horses, burros, and livestock on the public land. Despite how much she was misrepresented by livestock operators and some local representatives of the Bureau of Land Management, Annie was always adamant about preserving a multiple-use concept for the public lands. The rangeland should be shared by livestock, game animals, and wild horses and burros, within the availability of vegetation. Without the cooperation of shared resources, the wild horses and burros "would be at the mercy of everyone to whom their presence has been undesirable, or to whom their capture and sale would represent a fast dollar." Annie believed the equines would become the subject of "massive range-clearance programs" without independent scientific biological or range-management studies to justify the removal of the animals. Everyone was going to need to learn to play nicely together.

During Annie's 1971 testimony for Senate Bill 1116, she explained why she did not specifically include the wild burro in her plea on behalf of the "wild ones." Opponents argued that the burro was not native to North America, but Annie explained they were in the same administrative limbo as the wild horses—neither wildlife nor domestic livestock. Like the wild horses, their habitat was being sought for huntable wildlife and additional livestock allocations. And just as with the wild horses, the burros had a significant contribution to the historic development of the mining industry, road building, and other aspects of westward expansion. When those projects were finished or pickup trucks made the burro obsolete (except to the most reclusive miner), the burros were released onto the federal rangelands to fend for themselves.

Wild burros were not usually rounded up in the same manner as wild horses. Thundering herds of wild burros pursued by cowboys were not normally seen running throughout the West. When a rancher deemed the burros to be intrusive, the slower-moving animals, with an impressive ability to bray to reveal their locations, became rifle targets for a category of shooters Annie described as "a bunch of Nimrods."

She explained to the Washington legislators that representatives of the livestock industry objected to including them in the wild horse legislation.

The ranchers believed that different control and management would be necessary for the burros. The unspoken issue was that wild horses gathered by aircraft can be herded more easily than the bands of wild burros that had a tendency to scatter. The weight of the horses made their gatherings more economical than gathering the same number of burros.

She did interject that legislation that included wild horses and burros did not mean they must be managed in the same way. Nevertheless, it was apparent to Annie that the need for protection, management, and control must be accomplished for wild burros as well as wild horses.

WHILE THE LEGISLATORS WORKED THEIR MAGIC on the House and Senate bills, Annie was back in Reno with her grassroots, home-based organization. Letters asking "What can I do to help" continued to fill her mailbox.

Of all the academic lessons taught in American schools, civics languished among the least-interesting subjects. Annie acknowledged that the American youth, recovering from turbulent, post-Vietnam distrust of the political system, were finding the wild horse controversy a more relevant way of learning civics lessons about how laws work their way through the system. "Through whatever tool that miracle is accomplished, in this instance the future of the wild horses and burros, our country will be the better for it, because it is the young people who will be our lawmakers in so very short a time."

Wild Horse Annie was able to muster a small core of Reno-area people who answered the growing correspondence the ISPMB received every day. Dawn Lappin joined Helen and John Reilly in the 1970s, freeing Annie to address the more complex political issues. Even octogenarian Trudy Bronn was still spry enough to help stuff envelopes and prepare the newsletter bulk mailings.

While other organizations focused on fund-raising for themselves under the pretense of "saving the wild horses and burros" with slick four-color magazines and paid advertisements, the International Society for the Protection of Mustangs and Burros was publishing its newsletter on a home mimeograph stencil machine and later on inexpensive newsprint with cut-and-glue graphics. The subject matter included BLM press releases, analysis by Wild Horse Annie, and folksy stories and letters from Annie's supporters. It had all the charm of the *Territorial Enterprise* (the first newspaper that supported Annie), with a small fraction of the production values of that newspaper. Paramount to the newsletter's content were detailed evaluations of legislative activities, but written at a level understood by both schoolchildren as well as adults. Annie kept her supporters informed without the dire emotions that other organizations used to pump up their fund-raising.

One of Annie's strongest links to young people was schoolteacher Joan Bolsinger at the Eastwood Elementary School in Roseburg, Oregon. Joan was instrumental in creating Annie's Pencil War. Schoolchildren provided their services by spreading the word about Wild Horse Annie's campaign and writing many of the letters that found their way to newspaper desks and to the offices of elected officials. It was similar to Annie's school-age supporters in the 1950s, but teaching was now at a more sophisticated level. For her achievements in the classroom, Joan was presented a certificate of selection as an outstanding elementary teacher of America in 1972.[1]

Annie was proud to learn from teachers throughout the country that schoolchildren were developing new study skills, a larger vocabulary, and the ability to research and learn civic lessons. In an effort to provide a good impression, students improved in their spelling and grammar skills when they wrote to express their views in letters to their legislators. Geography and science classes used range topography, climate, and flora and fauna to explain range-habitat issues. Backgrounds and the legislative histories of the elected officials with whom they corresponded brought civic classes to life. Biology, western history, and culture all became part of the curriculum that captivated the attention of the energized students.

Through the eyes of the children, according to Annie, their parents also came to realize the extent of the exploitation of natural resources and "the lack of care and concern for all that is not commercially profitable to some individual." It did not surprise Annie that the children (and parents) had become so disillusioned with the "establishment," which had become a target of criticism and rebellion in the 1970s. For someone who began her campaign two decades earlier with patriotic stars in her eyes, the behavior of those in charge with the stewardship of the public land had tarnished Annie's perspective of the federal government.

Trudy Bronn reflected on her daughter's analytic abilities and the mercurial relationship of trust Annie had with the Bureau of Land Management. "I think it was her ability to listen, because I think you find out a whole lot more in this old world by listening than you do by talking. And she had that ability to listen, and to not be unfair. If someone had a problem, she was always willing to listen to see if it could be changed."

There were other people who came to Annie with offers of assistance. She learned to openly welcome them, but she astutely monitored them to assess their true motivation. As Trudy Bronn explained, "She was very aware of what other people did to help and also what they did to hurt."

Annie's report to the legislators reminded them of the heritage the wild horse (and burro) brought to western America and how stronger legislation would help make up for the mismanagement problems of the recent past. It would be a way to make up for "the destruction and waste of much of their heritage that can never be replaced. A gift to future generations of which our generation might well be proud."

Even though administrators within the Bureau of Land Management failed to grasp the enormity of the impact of Wild Horse Annie's campaign on behalf of the American people during the previous two decades, Annie did. Federal legislators told her that during the height of the Vietnam War, more letters were written to senators and congressmen about the wild horses and burros than the total number of letters written to the legislators concerning the war.

Annie and Charlie were staunch Goldwater Republicans, but the legislative battles were nonpartisan. An equal number of senators and congressmen from both parties rallied behind Wild Horse Annie. When Annie was greeted with so much support in the nation's capital, even her mother agreed the surprising level of international support was what made the long campaign "so worthwhile."

A record number of witnesses representing many special interests testified at the House hearings in Washington on April 19, 1971, and at the Senate hearings the following day. Although most of those presenting testimony supported the legislation, opposition by some of the lawmakers surfaced in subsequent committee meetings. S. 1116 contained nearly all of the recommendations set forth by a special congressional committee and unanimously passed the Senate on June 29, 1971. Similar to the Senate bill, the House version (H.R. 5375) was more bitterly contested and never would have emerged from committee if it was not for the dedication of its sponsor, Representative Baring. Amended and redrafted as H.R. 9890 with approximately two hundred bipartisan cosponsors, it passed the House unanimously on October 4, 1971.

When Annie testified before Congress in 1971, she recounted her earlier fight to save the welfare of the horses and burros against the domestic livestock and pet-food industries and against the Department of the Interior's Bureau of Land Management—the custodians of the public lands. She stated the BLM considered the commercial harvesting of wild horses an expedient means of clearing the range to provide more forage for the benefit of the vested-interest groups. Her battle now confronted most of the same issues still unresolved more than a decade after the passage of the 1959 law.

After differences in the two bills were resolved in conference committees, the consolidated measure passed both the Senate and House and was signed by President Richard M. Nixon on December 15, 1971, as Public Law 92-195, or the Wild Free-Roaming Horse and Burro Act of 1971.

The law officially defined all unbranded and unclaimed horses and burros on public lands of the United States as "wild free-roaming horses and burros" and made the secretaries of agriculture (U.S. Forest Service) and the interior (Bureau of Land Management) jointly responsible for the management and protection of the animals. They were classified as components of the public lands in a program designed to achieve natural ecological balance. The phrase "wild free-roaming" circumvented the issues of "wildlife" and "heritage."

Although the new law did not provide the panacea its proponents hoped to achieve, wild horses and burros of western America were ensured greater protection. In the *Congressional Record* on July 21, 1959, Annie's testimony before the Subcommittee of the House Judiciary Committee included her recommendation that population controls be developed while the numbers were low. The department failed to implement Annie's recommendation in 1959. With more than a decade between wild horse laws to prepare, Annie noted that the Bureau of Land Management should not have felt they were caught unprepared in 1971 for this cry for better range management.

Under the new federal law, indiscriminate reduction programs were prohibited, but humane destruction of old, sick, or lame animals could be ordered if an area was overpopulated. Excess animals could be captured and removed for private maintenance under humane conditions and care. The remains of deceased wild, free-roaming horses or burros were not to be sold for any consideration, directly or indirectly, nor could they be processed into commercial products. Only a federal marshal or agent of the secretary was authorized to remove or destroy a wild horse or burro that strayed onto private lands. Anyone who violated the terms of the act was subject to a fine of two thousand dollars, one year's imprisonment, or both.

Section 7 of the Wild Horse and Burro Act authorized and directed the secretaries of the interior and agriculture to appoint a joint advisory board of not more than nine members. The board would advise the secretaries on any matter relating to the management and protection of wild horses and burros.

Passage of the Wild Horse and Burro Act was a bittersweet victory for Wild Horse Annie. There was now a federal law that, as Annie described, "had some teeth to it," but some critics of the law went so far as to say the law was still unenforceable. The anecdotal increase in the population of the animals gave justification for the widespread slaughter of wild horses in the 1940s and 1950s. At that time, the newly formed Bureau of Land Management could have implemented management and control of the horses, but those components were not addressed until Annie insisted management and control be added in the form of the 1971 congressional mandate. A high-level Washington, D.C., administrator for the Bureau of Land Management once confessed to Annie that the agency had been pressured by private-interest groups for decades, and it was now difficult for them to think in positive terms when faced with the responsibility for the welfare of anything other than domestic livestock.

Annie placed responsibility for the new federal law squarely on the backs of western ranchers. "For decades they have released privately owned horses on public lands, have paid no grazing fees on them, and thereby had a sustained yield basis for added income—namely harvesting for commercial slaughter." With a little personal pride, she reminded the ranchers that beginning December 15, 1971, they would no longer be able to gather the wild horses without submitting proof of ownership. They would be able to gather their own horses, but that privilege came attached with a substantial trespassing fee. Without that profit-producing income, Annie noted the ranchers were quick to resume complaining that the wild horses (including the unbranded domestic horses released into the wild bands) were taking forage needed by the domestic livestock. "The ranchers aren't going to break their necks gathering their horses that they must now pay trespass on," Annie said with a modicum of satisfaction. "So instead of assuming the responsibility that is rightfully theirs, they have selected the wild horses for which the Act was designated to provide to help to be the scapegoats."

The 1971 act provided three methods of controlling wild horse and burro population increases. First, animals could be relocated to other areas where wild horses or burros roamed when the law was passed in 1971. They could not be relocated to areas where the wild horses did not historically maintain their habitat. Second, individuals, organizations, and government agencies could "adopt" a wild horse or burro, providing the animal remained the property of the United States. And finally, if the previous two measures failed or were impractical, the government had the right to destroy the equines in the most humane manner possible.

Supporters of the act sought civil and criminal sanctions, but the former were omitted from the final version of the bill. Furthermore, the statute did not adequately immunize the secretaries from the influence of state wildlife agencies and other local governmental bodies with whom they were authorized to establish cooperative agreements. Long-standing pressure groups in areas of strong domestic-livestock and target-animal interests prevailed and almost immediately diluted the legislative intent of the Wild Free-Roaming Horse and Burro Act of 1971.

The most serious gap in PL 92-195 was the lack of appropriate funds necessary to implement the provisions of the act. The obligations to protect, manage, and control wild, free-roaming horses and burros on deteriorating public lands throughout the eleven western states increased tremendously. The Bureau of Land Management now faced the impossible task of range management without a legitimate strategic plan and with a budget already overextended with other programs.

Before the ink on President Nixon's signature was dry, Representative John Melcher (D–Montana) ignorantly blasted the Wild Horse and Burro Act. He claimed the new wild horse and burro bill protected the animals so stringently that a rancher could not even take a sick horse into his corral for treatment as a humanitarian act. (There is no documentation of any rancher ever taking any sick wild horse or burro into his corral for such humanitarian purposes.) Melcher then continued his unsubstantiated tirade. "A computer operator tells me that with a normal rate of increase, without any molestation and assuming adequate food, our wild-horse herd may grow to around fifty billion head by the year 2020." While Melcher was strongly in favor of protecting wild horses with sensible management and on designated ranges, he thought the current law was too extreme because of the increased need for wild horse and burro pastures and expansion of the number of federal personnel that he claimed would be necessary to implement the law. "I hope that Congress will realize the error of such an extreme response to over-zealous friends of wild horses and correct this error in the near future."

It did not take long for the Bureau of Land Management to launch a campaign to "manage" the horses and burros, but without the same emphasis on "protection." In a *Los Angeles Times* article, "Law Backfires: Now Wild Horse Population Exploding," staff writer Mike Goodman's lead paragraph began, "An exploding wild horse and burro population caused by a law that back-fired is threatening the future of livestock, wild game and recreation lands across the West, government officials and ranchers said."

Even though the BLM, ranchers, and other special-interest groups portrayed the wild horses as emaciated and inbred animals, the health of the animals suddenly reversed with the passage of the law. Unnamed officials were credited with stating that "hardy, prolific herds of so-called 'mustangs'" were increasing at rates of 20 percent or more every year. The unnamed experts claimed there were at least twenty thousand horses "on the verge of overrunning some top rural grazing areas." Unnamed ranchers in the article claimed there would be fifty million wild horses and not enough room for a single cow.

The alleged "population explosion" among the wild horses, as Representative Melcher prophesied, was a tool that continues to be used against the welfare of the wild horses more than four decades later. Without any independent studies to even establish a benchmark for the rate of increase among herds of wild horses or burros, the BLM and livestock community could pull any figure out of the air and repeat it enough times with authority, and the statistic would become etched into the government "management" policy without reproach.

Annie was taken aback when she heard the fallacy of the population claims made by officials of the Bureau of Land Management and the misquotes of her own point of view made by the journalist in the *Los Angeles Times* article. When she confronted the reporter, he did apologize for the phrase "population explosion," but stuck to the rest of the story. Annie set forth on a quest to find the source of the "population explosion" of wild horses breeding at an annual rate of 20–25 percent.

Wild Horse Annie traced the overpopulation claim to its source—Kay Wilkes of the Bureau of Land Management in Washington, D.C., who readily admitted to giving the reporter that information. Wilkes later withdrew his press statement and went on to explain the information on the wild horse and burro population explosion was a computer percentage derived by the use of the following premise recorded by Annie's shorthand notes: "Start with equally sexed animals. You compute an optimum population potential. Totally even age structure. Assume they start breeding at two, and produce the first foal at three. Stop producing at seventeen. Live three more years after that. No other problems. No death loss from predator, disease or starvation. Every foal that is born lives. You will come up with forty-one percent. We know that isn't right. Divide forty-one percent by two and you come up with twenty percent. Assume, too, that every adult horse lives out its full span."[2] Even the most carefully functioning breeding farms could not support Wilkes's statistical premise, but his theory of reproduction is still used by the Bureau of Land Management more than forty years after its faulty creation.

The Bureau of Land Management's task force on the "effects of livestock grazing on wildlife, watershed, recreation, and other resource values in Nevada" released its report in April 1974. Although the report specifically dealt with the situation in Nevada, Bureau of Land Management director Curt Berklund indicated that information from similar evaluation reports from other western states indicated that the findings in the Nevada report were not unique to that state. The charges made by the bureau's own task force included:

1. The objectives of the Bureau of Land Management were dominated by, and oriented toward, satisfying the interests of the livestock operations;

2. That severe overgrazing and other aspects of poor range management on public lands have led to loss of wildlife habitat, destruction of cultural sites, and damaging erosion; and

3. That stream riparian habitat where livestock grazing is occurring has been grazed out of existence or is in a severely deteriorated condition.

Attention was called to the density of wild horse use in some specific areas that was causing a problem. However, for every dense area of horses, there were more than a few dense areas of domestic livestock concentration where damage was also taking place. In areas where wild horse density occurred, reduction of wild horses was under way in an effort to cull the herds.

Instead of mustangers thinning the herds for commercial exploitation, the tax-supported Bureau of Land Management and U.S. Forest Service were subsidizing and implementing the program. In some areas, wild horses were blamed for depleting the fragile vegetation. In the name of range restoration, the wild horses and burros were completely removed and replaced with huntable herbivores like bighorn sheep and deer.

UNFINISHED WORK

The first two decades of her campaign were primarily conducted through the facade of "Wild Horse Annie," but as the opposition became more organized, her fragile "Velma Johnston" interior began to weaken from the unceasing workload. The news media helped create her persona, but reporters were not in the libraries while Annie spent long hours trying to document her responses to her critics. Cameramen were not there to record the road trips she made to bring her message to audiences around the country. Despite having the International Society for the Protection of Mustangs and Burros as an organizational shield, it was still a one-woman campaign, and her body was beginning to protest the strain. "I already had the hard knocks," Annie confided to a friend, "the shivering fears that accompany standing alone and being counted . . . sickened and revolted at man's destruction of the habitat of wild creatures and the inroads he was making into his own." Her stamina and determination compensated for the physical toll the campaign was taking on her. In a letter to Marguerite Henry, she passed off the writer's concern for Annie's welfare by admitting, "I've had nothing but problems all my life, and I guess the courage it took for me just to grow up has conditioned me to meet whatever has to be met the only way I know how—head on! I just don't like to hurt anyone else in the doing of it is all."

Wild Horse Annie's campaign was not just to advocate for the animals, but also to safeguard the welfare of the next generation that was drawn to her. Nearly four decades after the passage of the Taylor Grazing Act, Annie saw an influx of young men and women pursuing new careers in biology, land management, public administration, and other fields relevant to professional range management and public policy. A few of the college students wrote to Annie and explained that their range-management careers began with their grade school letters written to Wild Horse Annie. She hoped her responses had contributed to "alerting an apathetic populace" to the problems associated with range management in the West. "I like to think," Annie wrote in a letter to a friend, "that in a way, the fate of the wild horses and burros has provided the symbol of these frightening things. If that be the case, then all the tears, fears, barbs, jibes, work, worry, strain and heartache was a small price to pay. If, on the other hand, that not be the case, and instead only projects a heightened ego, I have paid too high a price to walk tall during the remaining years."[1]

The fight to save the memory of horses and burros roaming free and wild on the public land taxed Annie's health. While packing for a Wild Horse and Burro Advisory Board meeting in 1974, Annie tripped over her suitcase in her darkened bedroom. Momentarily knocked out and breathless, Annie lay sprawled on the floor. When she awoke, her cocker spaniel thought Annie was playing a new game. The more she pushed him away, the more vigorously he came romping back, licking her face and wagging his tail. The ruckus attracted Annie's mother, who rescued her daughter from the well-intentioned family pet.[2]

If she went to the doctor's office, Annie would have missed her plane. Feeling "battered, bruised and somewhat woozy," Annie headed to the airport. After battling high blood pressure and phlebitis in her left leg,[3] Annie welcomed the hospital bed that greeted her return from Washington, D.C. She attributed her four-pound weight gain to the bandages that covered her entire left leg, torso, and right wrist. Her hospital stay was the first rest with "wonderful sleep" that Annie had enjoyed in years.

As a result of the fall, she also had a traumatized tooth that needed root canal work. Her own dentist, catching her down in spirits, tried to rekindle the relationship of good humor he always had with his patient by making a pseudoconfession that he was a member of the vigilante committee that dogged her during wild horse investigations.[4] His assignment, he joked, was to torture her to death in the dental chair.

Because of the polio-caused deformity of her lower jaw and the impact from the fall, her dentist sent her to a specialist in Las Vegas whose star-studded clientele claimed he could work miracles. After visiting with him for a consultation, the relationship was apparently so demeaning to Annie that she wrote an extremely long and bitterly sarcastic letter to the specialist. She made frequent references to the comfortable life of his wealthy clientele, as well as the posh accoutrements in his office waiting area. She also described the demeaning attitude she had received from his office staff.

Annie then shared a lengthy description of her humble beginnings and the nonmaterial wealth she had acquired from her experiences as Wild Horse Annie, daring him to match her relationship as a role model to thousands of schoolchildren against his material wealth. It was the only example I ever saw of Annie venting any anger directly toward a stranger. While two copies of the long letter were in her files (one with the doctor's name and the other intentionally without), the original copy was not in the files. No response from the dental specialist was in the file, either.

HOLDING DOWN FULL-TIME EMPLOYMENT as Velma B. Johnston and maintaining the reputation of Wild Horse Annie at the same time caused her to consider retiring from one profession or the other. Finally, on May 15, 1974, Velma Johnston left the only full-time, paid job she had ever held. "From a financial and an emotional standpoint," Annie wrote in a letter to a friend when she got home with her box of personal belongings from the office,

> the decision was a difficult one, and Mr. Harris didn't make it any easier for me, as he took it personally that I chose the Wild Ones over him. I am going to try hard to keep the wound to his vanity from festering, and will seize every opportunity I can to pop in on him at his office for a visit. He hadn't even intended to tell me goodbye when I left, and he has not wished me good fortune. But I wouldn't let him get away with the "goodbye," and I am hopeful the time will come when he is proud that he gave me up to be where I've longed to be these past many years— working for that in which I believe.[5]

On her last day at work, Annie described the only elements that were missing—a casket, some flickering candles, a few funeral wreaths with "Rest in Peace," and the musical accompaniment of a church organ. The previous week was tearful for Annie—not because of leaving, but because she felt she was taking away a part of Gordon Harris. Annie found consolation from a friend, who corrected her perspective. "It would be you who would be destroyed if you stayed, dividing your reserve of mental and physical stamina between two rough commitments." Annie had earned the right to take her last few years to "run my own show."[6]

It did not take long for Gordon Harris to "forgive" his secretary for leaving him. Annie finally received a letter from him. He kept his own health problems from Annie. With accolades about his faithful former employee, Harris wrote, "The world is made up of three kinds of people. First and least—those who make things happen; second—those who watch things happen; last and most—those who don't know what's happening. Go girl, go!"[7] Also enclosed was a check for one hundred dollars for his lifetime membership on behalf of his former secretary's cause. He wrote the check from a hospital bed and did not want Velma to visit until he returned home. She learned the condition of his health meant life membership would not last long, but she still found time to visit her old employer.

Annie reflected on this new chapter of her life. Free to be her own boss and spend all her time on the fight instead of balancing two full-time responsibilities, she was finally able to sit back at the end of the day and listen to the silence.

Under Gordon Harris's employ, Annie had learned how to use a manual typewriter with frustrating results. Now that she was on her own, she was forced to face a modernized version of her nemesis. Her typed letters on her new IBM Selectric were attempted before the addition of correction ribbon. Her letters were punctuated with X-ed-out typed phrases and even more uncensored laments of her frustration with the new electric typewriter. Through the decades she served as a professional executive secretary, her "hard-hitting finger tips" were accustomed to manually pounding on the "word machine."[8]

In a typed letter to a friend, Annie wrote of her love-hate relationship with the typewriter:

Did I ever tell you that I think through my fingers when they are on typewriter keys? Kind of goofy, I guess, but so many, many times when I am at a loss as to what to write or what I should say, I can just let my thought and fingers go; and believe it or not, I usually come up with just what I was seeking in my mind. If—that great big if—I ever get the time to write that book I've been longing to, it will be my fingers that write it! I'm not even very successful on tape, which would be much easier because I could just loll comfortably on a sofa and talk away, whereas there's not much lolling at a typewriter![9]

The fight on behalf of the wild horses and burros began in 1950 by Annie and Charlie on a "do it yourself—pay for it yourself" basis.[10] When she became president of the International Society for the Protection of Mustangs and Burros in 1964, she received some reimbursement for campaign expenses, but never received a salary.

Annie sold the rights to her story to Marguerite Henry for one dollar and intentionally never received a penny in royalties by agreement with the author of *Mustang: Wild Spirit of the West*.[11] Late in 1970, author Louise Harrison (granddaughter of Adolf Coors, founder of the brewery in Golden, Colorado) was willing to modestly underwrite a foundation if Annie would serve as executive director and chairman of the board. WHOA! (Wild Horse Organized Assistance) served as a companion organization to the more politically based International Society for the Protection of Mustangs and Burros.

When Annie was asked the reason for having two organizations doing similar jobs, she explained that nonprofit organizations are supposed to do only a limited amount of lobbying. The ISPMB was becoming almost entirely focused on the 1971 federal legislation and subsequent revisions. She feared the Bureau of Land Management would contact the Internal Revenue Service and pull the organization's 501(c)3 nonprofit status. In case that happened, WHOA! was established as a safety net to ensure that Annie would continue to have a nonprofit organizational forum.

The work of running two national volunteer organizations at the same time was an administrative nightmare. Leaving her full-time paying job freed her schedule, but Annie had her living and travel expenses to consider. One of her organizational trustees agreed to underwrite most of the office expenses. To help compensate for the loss of her weekly paycheck from Gordon Harris, Annie was put on the organization's payroll at a modest salary of $500 a month, comparable to what she was earning under Harris's employment. Her "chief operating officer," Helen Reilly, received a lesser salary; their two on-call office workers received $2.25 an hour, but only when their services were needed.[12]

Newspaper advertisements in the early 1970s were able to boost the membership rosters of both her organizations. The infusion of new memberships enabled Annie to ever so slightly even the playing field "that is so unevenly matched between the commercial exploiters of our public land and those who would preserve it and the animals on it for future generations to enjoy as we have enjoyed them."[13]

The responses to the advertisements provided an opportunity to send more information to people still unaware of Annie's ongoing fight on behalf of the wild horses and burros. Approximately 10 percent of the organization's income went to administrative costs. Ninety percent was used for surveillance, maintenance for wild horses they rescued, printing and mailing of educational material for students and others throughout the country, investigations of reported violations, attendance at critical meetings affecting the welfare of wild horses and burros, and providing someone to be in attendance at places where roundups were conducted during the reduction programs carried out under the Wild Free-Roaming Horse and Burro Act of 1971 to ensure that humane and selective reductions took place.[14]

During a rare, quiet evening at home when the telephones finally stopped ringing and the typewriters were silent, Annie sat at her electric typewriter to share some personal thoughts:

> For I have had my hour, the last 2 1/2 months, doing what I want to do for the Wild Ones to whom I am committed. Oh sure, I work like a mule; demands are incredible; danger very real; and uncertainty of the future always there. But—I have had, and am having, my hour. You see, I used to feel that way when I was a wife—for I reveled in the role of Charlie's wife, loved my home, was happiest concocting goodies in the kitchen or grubbing in the garden, or racing the wind, he and I, together on our spirited mounts. That, too, was my hour. Then Mom came to share the home, the work, the expenses—and it was "our" challenge. I worked for Mr. Harris and it was "his" hour. But here, it is "mine" once again, my hour to work for that in which I believe.[15]

The "free time" provided opportunities to renew friendships with people who joined Annie behind the scenes. In early June 1974, she traveled to Southern California as the houseguest of author Marguerite Henry. There, she met a movie producer who took a one-year option on Henry's book about Wild Horse Annie as a potential *TV Movie of the Week*. "It seemed strange to sit there listening to them discuss whom they would like to have play my part, Charlie's, my Mom, Grandma, Dad," wrote Annie to a friend. "Almost like I had died and my spirit was hovering around eaves-dropping."[16] The program, with Betty White playing the role of Wild Horse Annie, was filmed but never aired.

A week later Annie and Helen Reilly flew to Washington to participate in a symposium on threatened and endangered species and their habitats, hosted by television's *Wild Kingdom* spokesman, Marlin Perkins, from the Wolf Sanctuary in St. Louis. Mr. and Mrs. Perkins invited fellow conservationists to form a coalition of all the leading organizations to unite against the destruction of wildlife and their habitat.

Annie's health at the time of the trip was frail. She would not use a wheelchair to travel down the long concourse at the airport because she did not want to be conspicuous—a flashback to her days when her tormented torso was freed from the body cast. Helen, aware of Annie's fragile heart condition, insisted her friend "have a seat in that chair and I'm going to wheel ya!"

After collecting their suitcases, they were greeted by Congressman Morris Udall (D–Arizona), who took Annie's hand and guided her to his car. "She was beaming after that," Helen related to me while we were reminiscing about our mentor, "getting all that attention from a gentleman; she liked that very much. She ate good, and had her highball. She was having a good time; I'm so happy that she had gone [on the trip]."

As part of the dinner party at the home of Marlin Perkins, Annie was singled out for special recognition. She received a standing ovation from the guests, while her hosts presented her with a bouquet of roses. Annie even had an opportunity to pose for a picture with another guest, actor Jimmy Stewart.

Her return home on the fifteenth gave her only a couple of days to refill her suitcase before she left for Greeley, Colorado, where Annie was invited to be the keynote speaker at the Colorado Cattlemen's Association annual convention. She was met by an unnamed "cattle baron" (as she described him in a letter to a friend) in Denver who "regaled me with lamentations the entire hour or so during our drive to Greeley. The wild horses were eating all the grass and depriving his cattle; the coyotes were eating up his calves; and nobody, but nobody was buying his beef. He did, at one point during the tiresome tirade, inform me jubilantly that he had just bought himself a new airplane the day before, and had the weather been less threatening he would have flown me to our destination. I can't afford an airplane, can you? I can't afford even to buy his damned beef!"[17]

That evening a steak barbecue was prepared for several hundred people, and her host was determined that Annie meet everyone. "Apparently the cattle barons hadn't expected Wild Horse Annie to dress or act like a lady," she continued, "and in this instance we approached a group of about five men. Before my host had an opportunity to introduce me, one of them said, 'Well, old buddy, I hear you got stuck with hosting old Wild Horse Annie!' Where-upon I said in a soft voice, 'I'm Wild Horse Annie—Mrs. Johnston, and how very nice it is to meet you!' He tossed off the rest of his libation in one gulp, stammered a bit, then excused himself to rush off to another group." Her host apparently learned his lesson. For the rest of the evening, when he and Annie got within five feet of another group to meet, he would loudly announce, "Well fellows, here she is at last! Mrs. Johnston—Wild Horse Annie." It was the only lighthearted memory Annie had of what she called "the whole beastly affair." The audience had politely applauded and Annie had not allowed time for questions and answers, but "it wasn't very pleasant, and I wondered afterward why they had asked me, since they practically have a bounty on my head."[18]

Happy to leave the cattlemen "to their own grumblings and their steaks and their airplanes," she traveled to Colorado's Western Slope in early June 1974 for a bone-jarring drive into the Little Bookcliffs Mountains to see the wild horse area that was in the midst of a controversial management plan. She took the opportunity to personally file an official complaint with the Bureau of Land Management before bringing the case to the public with interviews at two local television stations, a radio studio, and the local news-paper. That evening, she brought the information to an audience that gath-ered in an auditorium at Mesa College in Grand Junction.[19]

Returning home on the twenty-first, she transferred her luggage to her Ford Mustang and drove 240 miles for her niece's wedding the next day. It was back to Reno on the twenty-third, only to fly to Washington the next day to confer with members of Congress and then attend an oversight hearing.

On June 26, 1974, the Honorable Henry M. Jackson (D–Washington), chairman of the Committee on Interior and Insular Affairs, brought the congressional oversight hearing to order. Senator Jackson was scheduled to question the Bureau of Land Management and Forest Service as to why the agencies were not enforcing the Wild Free-Roaming Horse and Burro Act of 1971. Three years previously, Congress granted responsibility to the Bureau of Land Management and the Forest Service to manage the physical welfare of wild horses and burros on the public land. With increases in the number of examples of blatant disregard of the law, Congress recognized that their mandate was not being implemented as intended.

As Senator Jackson voiced during his opening statement, "The intent of the Congress in adopting this act is clear—these animals are to be protected—

not managed to extinction. Concern has been expressed that the administration is, in fact, using the act to confine these horses and burros or to rid the range of them altogether; that they would fence-off these animals in zoo-like refuges—over managed to the point where the concept of wildness this legislation sought to preserve is destroyed." Jackson cited "justifiable concern that congressional intent to preserve these animals as part of our western heritage is not being fully followed by those charged with administration of the law."[20] During the discussion of the legislative history, the committee confirmed that the basic intent of the federal law was "that wild horses and burros should be considered as components of the public lands coequal with wildlife and domestic livestock."

Having been caught unprepared and unequipped to deal with the 1959 and 1971 legislative efforts to protect, manage, and control the wild horses and burros, the BLM officials and a select party of senators were prepared to bring their management objectives to the 1974 committee hearing. Senator James McClure (R–Idaho) reported his concern that "any herd of animals will overpopulate its range until nature thins the population unless man interferes with that condition." He also refuted Annie's claim that horses were a natural part of the North American environment. Rather, McClure believed they were introduced within the last part of the previous century.

During the twelve years between the federal laws and the additional three years until the oversight hearings, the Bureau of Land Management had adequate time to develop a methodology to survey the wild horses and burros and develop a method of consistent inventory control. Likewise, the agency had an opportunity to review livestock permits to determine the extent of overgrazing by the current permittees.

Assistant secretary Jack O. Horton, assistant director of the Bureau of Land Management George L. Turcott, and Jim Coda of the Solicitor General's Office acknowledged there were few efforts to determine the extent of the wild horse and burro population. Field estimates derived from indirect sources provided the agency with an anecdotal benchmark of the wild horse and burro populations in 1971, but there was no identification of how many of those horses were claimed by private parties. Despite the questionable 1971 benchmark data, the BLM noted the 1974 field reports indicated that "since the passage of the act, wild horse populations have substantially increased," according to Horton.[21] However, no consistent scientific census counts were made between 1971 and 1974, either.

Undersecretary of the interior J. Phil Campbell told the committee there were approximately ten thousand unauthorized horses and burros on the public land in 1974. Ranchers turned out the unlicensed and illegally grazing animals on the public lands, according to the undersecretary.

Expanding beyond Kay Wilkes's infamous claim that wild horses were breeding at a rate of 20 percent, Horton increased the rate of reproduction when he told the committee, "Let us restate that problem of wild horses and burros. Their populations are growing at a rate between 18–30 percent or 8,000–10,000 new animals per year. The isolated herds are scattered over 50–60 million acres of BLM land and 10 million acres of Forest Service land." After painting a dire scenario about the growing horse herds, Horton softened the rhetoric by expressing his department's commitment to the wild horses as "a special population to be protected and preserved, as an expression of the spirit of the Old West, and as a continuing symbol of the heritage and generosity of our western lands."[22]

The Bureau of Land Management still claims the often-quoted source of the statement that "two million" wild horses once roamed the American West was J. Frank Dobie's book *The Mustangs*. Additional information of similar wild horse numbers was based on nineteenth-century literary and newspaper anecdotes. Both the BLM and Dobie agreed on the value of those early census counts. "All guessed numbers are mournful to history. My own guess," wrote Dobie, "is that at no time were there more than a million mustangs in Texas and no more than a million others scattered over the remainder of the west."

Nearly forty years after the oversight hearing, the 2010 BLM official website stated that Dobie's "guess" has now become a source of "fact." However, the BLM prefers to conveniently address the "historical wild-horse population" with its own "substantiated and more relevant figure," which was the number found roaming in 1971, "when the BLM was given legal authority to protect and manage wild horses and burros. That number was 17,300 mustangs (plus 8,045 burros)."

Wild Horse Annie continued to remind her readers the official government count that indicated seventeen thousand wild horses roamed the public lands in 1971 was as much of a guess at that time as Dobie's one to two million "guestimation." She tried to explain that the "population explosion" as claimed by the Bureau of Land Management was also an arbitrary concept generated by the imagination of one government official. She also reminded people the use of airplanes to keep the population of horses under control was made illegal in 1959.

She believed that two issues were emerging: the federal law was consistently violated, resulting in fewer wild horses in 1971 than in 1959 when the first law was enacted, and the population increase since 1971 was highly exaggerated by the Bureau of Land Management in an attempt to justify two amendments introduced at the Senate oversight hearings. She said it would open the door to commercial slaughter of excess animals in order to simplify the BLM's management, protection, and control responsibilities.

The proposal presented by the U.S. Department of the Interior included the amendments Annie predicted. First, "The Secretary is authorized to sell or donate excess animals to individuals or organizations on written assurance that such animals will receive humane treatment. . . . Upon sale or donations . . . or destruction . . . animals shall lose their status as wild free-roaming horses and burros and shall no longer be considered as falling within the purview of this Act." Second, "In administering this Act the Secretary may use aircraft or motor vehicles and may authorize such use by other persons under his supervision."

Pursuit by aircraft for capture provided a certain ease of operation, but Annie believed it was not humane. Although "humane procedures" would be called for, personal supervision by land-management personnel was physically and fiscally impossible. The extent of damage caused to an animal could not be determined from the air. At the conclusion of a gathering, it would be too late to avert injury or even death.

The Wild Horse Annie Act of 1959 prohibited the use of aircraft and mechanized vehicles for the purpose of capturing and killing wild horses. It did not prohibit the use of mechanized vehicles in management and control operations, such as inventorying or spotting. Opinions obtained from the solicitor's office of the Department of the Interior and from the Office of the General Counsel of the U.S. Department of Agriculture (USDA) confirmed this point. As Annie alleged, state livestock inspectors were sympathetic to the livestock industry. After all, most of them were ranchers or members of ranching families and generally favored removal of wild horses and burros from public lands.

Annie explained that the abuses incurred when aircraft roundups were conducted were abundantly documented. Even with the promise that an employee of the federal land administration would be riding in the airplanes, there was no guarantee that controlled management would supersede the economic need to expediently gather the horses. "Why then," Annie continued, "all the pressure to restore the use of aircraft through Congressional amendment unless it would be for the purpose of capturing and killing? And once that got underway again, who is to say at what point it would be stopped? With ground operations, manually carried out, there is at least an opportunity for public surveillance. In the air there is not."

Secretary Horton explained that efforts to gather private animals has been unsuccessful due to the rough terrain, the enormous expanse of the rangeland, and the restriction to gather the horses only at water traps or from the backs of saddle horses. The ranchers were reluctant to gather horses they claimed were running on the public land because of the trespass fees that would be levied against them by the BLM. Horton said other efforts to gather domestic horses were abandoned because "the claimants do not have the capability to remove their horses without the aid of motorized vehicles," even though roping wild horses was a long-standing tradition in the West, as demonstrated throughout the year at local rodeos.[23]

He stated that the BLM investigated "hundreds of rumors and reports of possible violations of the Act." The agency investigated approximately twenty-five actual cases, but only three of them were submitted to the Department of Justice. In the first three years of the new law, there had been no prosecutions. Limited personnel for enforcement and inaccessible terrain made herd surveillance and investigation of violations difficult.

In subsequent dialogue during the hearings, the ulterior motive behind the Bureau of Land Management's hidden agenda became apparent. When Secretary Horton tried to explain that the purpose of the two proposed amendments was to help manage the wild horses and burros and "when necessary, to thin the herds when overpopulation exists," Senator Alan Bible was quick to challenge the assistant secretary. "Wait a minute," interrupted Senator Bible, "do not go too fast. Thin the herd. I imagine that strikes terror in the hearts of all the horse lovers because I suppose that means to dispose of them humanely."[24]

Secretary Horton and BLM official George Turcott tried to mitigate their image as wild horse adversaries by describing the horses as starving and not of a confirmation or disposition desirable to most horse lovers. The BLM proposed that the excess horses that were not adopted by private backyard stables could then be transferred for any other purpose.

Senator Bible refused to move off the government's proposal to transfer wild horses out of the responsibility of the federal government. He asked Secretary Horton, "What if I got a mustang transferred to me fee simple, I guess that is the correct legal term, and then sent it in to the dog-meat factory, could I do that? Once I had the title, I could do anything I wanted to do with it, could I not?" When Secretary Horton responded, "As long as you did it in a humane way," the Washington, D.C., public gallery began to laugh derisively. "I do not think our young friends in the audience think you could transfer an animal to a dog-meat factory humanely," Senator Bible responded. "I hope we have suggestions as to how to work out this problem. I am convinced there must be some answer to this."[25]

When the Bureau of Land Management explained that their statistical data for the "population explosion" claim were based on only two vegetative seasons of information, Senator Mark Hatfield remarked that the BLM was pushing for legislative change without sufficient statistical data. "It seems to me, first of all, your statistical data is, at best, on a very unsure foundation and your solution is based on the derivation of that statistical base."[26]

With regard to the 1971 population counts used by the Bureau of Land Management, the BLM added a supplementary report to the oversight hearing. Senator Hatfield responded, "These figures (17,000 wild horses and 10,000 wild burros) were the best available at that time. They were used as a benchmark or starting point and not for management decisions until such time as the planning for all multiple uses can be completed for any particular geographic area. Are these increases due to increased foaling or refined statistical gathering techniques, which?" Secretary Horton replied, "I would think neither of those."[27]

George Lea, deputy director of the Bureau of Land Management, expressed some of the problems his department had in managing the equine census. Without knowing how many animals were on the open range, any management plan would be ineffective. He swore that "all population estimates of wild animals are estimates." When the BLM said there were thirty-six thousand wild horses in Nevada, Lea said, "That is our estimate of those numbers."

A heated exchange between Senator James Abourezk (D–South Dakota) and Secretary Horton ensued about the Bureau of Land Management's priority to thin the herds of wild horses for the benefit of "dog-food manufacturing" instead of protecting the wild equines on behalf of the voters who stood

MRS. VEI MA IQHNSTON   GEORGE TURC

Wild Horse Annie was able to express her incredulity during a session of the National Wild Horse and Burro Advisory Board in Washington, D.C. BLM associate director George Turcott sits to her left. Courtesy of the author.

behind Wild Horse Annie. George Turcott reiterated their "first preference is individual acquisition and second, sale for disposal as the buyer sees fit."[28]

After failing to get Horton and Turcott to clarify the BLM's second preference, Senator Abourezk grew exasperated. "It seems under this amendment, Mr. Secretary, that the Department of the Interior really intends to wash its hands of wild horses and the care of the horses. . . . Actually, what you are saying, if I might be allowed to interpret, you are not really washing your hands of the problem, you are just justifying washing your hands of the problem by saying that you cannot handle it bureaucratically."[29]

"Can't you just see 'killer buyers' and/or their agents lining up to receive excess wild horses and burros?"[30] Annie wrote to a friend. She contrasted the Bureau of Land Management's motivation with her own. She noted the BLM was the custodian of the public lands, but appeared to respond to only the most vocal of the special-interest groups. Annie's support, on the other hand, came from a more diverse cross-section of the country. Based upon the thousands of letters she received from supporters, Annie was assured that "without exception, the wild horse or mustang, more than any creature alive, symbolizes to them the freedom upon which our country was founded. The response to the plea in their behalf comes from every part of our nation; from every level of our society, from every age group."[31]

While legislators and government officials argued over population explosions and management techniques, Annie's request for an independent advisory board composed of experts in the various disciplines that influenced the myriad of range-management issues was granted. The newly formed National Wild Horse and Burro Advisory Board was composed of many of the members from the Pryor Mountains Wild Horse Advisory Board.

Annie received the news of her appointment to the board while she was on a field tour of the Pryor Mountain Wild Horse Area. The two-way radio in the four-wheel-drive government vehicle crackled with a request for her to call Washington, D.C., when she returned from the mountainous region. She got back too late to phone the Washington office of the BLM, so the official news arrived the next morning. Aside from Annie, the initial board included C. Wayne Cook, head of the Range Science Department at Colorado State University; veterinarian Floyd W. Frank, head of the Veterinary Science Department at the University of Idaho; Ben Glading, retired chief of the Game Management Branch of the California Department of Fish and Game; Ed Pierson, retired state director of Wyoming's Bureau of Land Management; Dean Prosser Jr., past president of the national Livestock Brand Conference and member of the Wyoming State legislature; Pearl Twyne, executive director of the Virginia Federation of Humane Societies, president of the American Horse Protection Association, and past president of Defenders of Wildlife; and Roy Young, a rancher, past president of Nevada Cattlemen's Association, and member of the Nevada legislature.

Annie knew the public exposure of serving as one of two board members representing humane issues and particularly her role as the sole representative of the wild horses and burros would put a target on her back throughout the eleven-state western region where the wild horse faction and the livestock industry had conflicts. Annie wrote that one of her outfielders had gotten into a fight in Idaho a couple of weeks previously "with a man who tried to get my address so he could personally shoot me." Annie knew that serving on the board "is going to be no picnic." She had had other threats in recent years—all of which she kept from her aging mother.

It took more than a year for the government agencies to draft a set of regulations that were eventually submitted to the federal National Wild Horse and Burro Advisory Board. Nearly three years after the passage of the federal law, local offices of the government agencies began to receive policy protocols from Washington on wild horse and burro issues. The reluctance to implement federal procedures on the local level was so evident that during the early 1970s, there seemed to be a deliberate attempt to subvert the intent of the law.

The resolution presented to the board provided the one element that was the bane of Annie's campaign—the reintroduction of aircraft to gather wild horses to resolve a myriad of range conservation issues. Despite the vast impact of recreational interests, mineral-use lessees, and the long-standing domestic livestock interests also competing for access to the public lands, it was wild horses and burros alone that shouldered the administrative blame. Annie believed that if overgrazing livestock, foraging by game animals, energy development, and other potential abusers of the public land were addressed, "I will support the reduction and designation of specific areas *if* that part of the resolution is presented separately from the recommendation for restoration of use of aircraft."[32]

Given the opportunity, Annie once again challenged the BLM's claim that the aircraft were needed because of the alleged rapid proliferation of wild horses and burros since 1971. Throughout the record of the meeting of the National Wild Horse and Burro Advisory Board, she argued, "It would have been impossible for the free-roaming horses to have done the damage to the range in two-and-a-half years since the signing of the 'Wild Horse and Burro Act of 1971.'"

Ignoring Annie's opinion, fellow board member Dr. Floyd Frank provided his own version of the population status of the wild horses:

According to another piece of testimony, there will be an increase of population in two years. It took twenty years to get the 1971 Act through. Based on Nevada figures of 20,000 animals, if it takes two years to get a modification of the Act through, there would be 30,000 animals in Nevada alone; by 1984, 150,000; in twenty years, 1,280,000 in that ball park. If you are going to get the animals in Nevada down to the 1972 levels, it would be reasonable that you are going to have to take off 7,000 animals. Does the BLM have the capability of doing that in two years? No. Do you think Annie is going to let you take 7,000 off? Hell no.[33]

Using those figures, Dr. Frank prognosticated that there would be thirty thousand wild horses in two years, more than half of which would need to be removed from the public land. More desirable would be to use Annie's preference of water trapping the horses. Corral traps would be constructed around water holes; a trip wire would snap the entrance gate closed as the horses leisurely entered the watering hole. The process was the most humane, but would also be the slowest means to gather that many horses.

Drawing inferences from the darkest years of wild horse management, Dr. Frank believed the only way to expedite the removal of the horses was through the use of aircraft. "Why put these land managers in a situation like putting their feet in a sack and making them run a quarter-mile race?" Dr. Frank rhetorically asked the board. "I am all for preservation of the wild horse and wild burro. But I am not in favor of preserving every damned one of them to the extent they get less rare as a symbol of national heritage. To make them valuable, remove them from this general management and put them in special places. What Congress intended was that they be assigned to refuges. It is an impossible management problem. Assign them to definite areas; not with BLM efforts." He also raised the old issue of "the world is starving while we argue about saving wild horses."[34]

Wild Horse Annie requested and was granted equal time. She acknowledged the land described by another board member, Ben Glading, was in bad condition because of a severe drought and overgrazing by the livestock operator. But she took umbrage with Dr. Frank's reference that wild horses should be blamed for an international food shortage. The irony of replacing the wild horses with more meat-producing livestock to help alleviate world hunger was not lost on Annie. As she pointed out, the people in the countries that were most susceptible to hunger caused by the droughts of the 1970s were culturally vegetarian.

She noted that Dr. Frank tried to make the link that the threat of a worldwide food shortage and human starvation could somehow be attributed to wild horses and burros depleting western rangeland. He never mentioned the overuse by domestic livestock, but proposed the only way to preserve the range was to use aircraft to remove the wild equines. It was becoming an oft-repeated claim, but Annie believed the root of the problem was the BLM's failure to control the release of domestic horses into the wild bands and the failure to keep domestic livestock use within the number allowed in the annual livestock permits.

Most of the board meetings included a field trip into a nearby wild horse and burro area. Government field representatives provided board members with an opportunity to see range conditions and occasionally meet their four-legged wards. The advisory board members flew more than 250 miles of wild horse country during one such two-hour flight over the Pryor Mountain

Wild Horse Area and saw more than eight hundred horses. Advisory board member Ben Glading noted the animals were in good condition, with an average of one foal for every five animals (20 percent). But he also noted the range was in bad condition.

As Annie gazed out the window of the plane, she saw the harsh condition of the range, but also focused on the bands of horses. Whereas some board members saw the horses as a detriment, Annie saw them as her inspiration. Later, the tour continued on the ground. Annie observed, "I got the thrill of a lifetime by getting within fifty feet of a wild band before they caught wind of me, and the stallion nipped his harem into hasty flight." It was a rugged experience, "more befitting a graduate of army survival school than this little old lady." She and the other female board member, Pearl Twyne, managed to keep up with their male counterparts quite well, although, as Annie said, "about all that was holding me together at the end of the six days were my girdle and my hair spray."[35]

Annie reiterated her stance with a tad more vitriol when the advisory board meeting resumed after the field trip. She no longer recognized any potential for effective collaboration with the Bureau of Land Management for a meaningful management plan. She dug her heels in for a long, hard battle. Since the passage of the 1959 law and again after the 1971 law, the land-management agencies had the opportunity to use their administrative mandates to conduct range-use studies on the public lands. Instead, anecdotal reports indicated that domestic horses were still being released into herds of wild horses, allegedly to improve confirmation and increase herd numbers. Furthermore, no *comprehensive* long-range management plan for the public lands had ever surfaced.

Addressing the allegations of depleted grazing habitat, Wild Horse Annie made it clear she would not condone misrepresentations, unjustifiable reductions, or negative attitudes whereby wild horses and burros became the scapegoats. She claimed livestock overgrazed long before any wild horse and burro legislation passed. Annie also said there was "a tendency to favor interests oriented toward consumptive uses of the public land which return short-term economic benefits to the relatively few, while short-changing the many whose interests are not of an economic nature."

The agencies, according to Annie, failed their management directives to confine domestic use within the limitations of forage production. Because Dr. Frank's resolution combined human starvation with the BLM's interest in returning airborne roundups to the western rangeland, Annie was forced to vote against it. She lamented that it put her "in the position of caring less about human survival than about the animals."

Wild Horse Annie was a steady advocate of "control" of the wild horse population in tandem with their "protection." She was willing to make appropriate compromises except in the area of returning to the use of aircraft in wild horse roundups. She had fought for twenty-four years to eliminate airborne roundups, and "I would stand adamant on opposition to restoring that expedient means of removal."

The motion was carried with seven yeas and Annie's solitary nay. Annie knew she was being cornered to cast a vote that could put her in jeopardy with her support base. She made her decision with a clear conscience, however. She was up against the top echelon of the BLM management, sheep and cattle livestock representatives, and fish-and-game personnel who were united in their stand against Wild Horse Annie on this issue. She also received daily reports that conservationists from other fields were having second thoughts about the survival of native wildlife habitat and withdrawing their support from Annie. "Public support for a cause will go only so far," Annie explained, "and as has been dramatically demonstrated throughout man's existence, his primary concern is for his own survival, with the destruction of any or all of the other creatures that share this planet a matter of least concern to him if it will improve his own chances of survival—little realizing that it will be only temporary at best."

Wild Horse Annie, in disagreement with most of the philosophical origins of the other advisory board members, submitted a minority report with regard to the amendment that would allow wild horses and burros to be gathered with the assistance of aircraft. Annie challenged a board resolution mandating the removal of wild horses and burros from public lands in order to make more forage available for food production and in order to reduce and control the number of animals via the use of aircraft. She knew that her vote would unfairly cast her in a role of not caring about world hunger, but she also wanted to see the damage to the western U.S. rangeland repaired.

THE LITTLE BOOKCLIFFS
WILD HORSE AREA

It was an area replete with western clichés. A cattle rancher moved his stock the old-fashioned way— on horseback. A Basque sheep rancher, situated far enough away from the cattle, called out to his flock. A coyote prowled the region, waiting for a young calf, ewe, or young mule deer that may have strayed from the rest. Swits, mountain bluebirds, sandhill cranes, turkey vultures, and eagles flew overhead. Below the cliffs, the lights of Grand Junction, Colorado, are sandwiched by the red sandstone of the Colorado National Monument on the opposite side of the Grand Valley, nearly on the central Colorado-Utah border.

Wild Horse Annie loved the Little Bookcliffs.[1] The range above the cliffs contained one of the most picturesque herds of wild horses roaming what was once forty-six thousand rugged acres. Today, following periodic political management plans, a small herd now roams on twenty-six thousand acres.

The Little Bookcliffs Wild Horse Area was a special case for Annie. It was the only example of forest-dwelling wild horses in the United States. It was also one of the rare situations where a rancher bought an allotment for his cattle operation because he enjoyed seeing wild horses purely for their historical and aesthetic reasons. It was an area that was ideal to study Annie's interest in multiple uses of the public land. And it was a situation that yielded a series of administrative errors that reduced the range area by half while keeping the same herd size.

The history of the Little Bookcliffs herd can be traced to the 1680s when Ute Indians avoided the desert conditions in the valley below and set up residence above the mountain cliffs. In the vicinity of Red Rock Canyon, archaeologists were able to discern a Ute Indian burial mound and found tepee poles stored in the underbrush. The last wolf in Colorado was also caught in the immediate area. The name Bookcliffs describes the cliff range of mountains that begin in Grand Junction and extend west into Green River, Utah. An early visitor to the area thought the area looked like the rough pages of a stack of books haphazardly placed on a shelf.

In 1888 western settlers began to move into the Grand Valley as the Utes were forced onto reservations. A few years previously, several Indian sub-chieftains vented their frustrations against the local federal agent, Nathaniel Meeker, resulting in the "Meeker Massacres" north of the area in 1879. As part of the Utes' punishment, many of the Indian ponies they owned had to be left behind. Early Grand Junction homesteaders remembered seeing two to three hundred wild horses roaming the highlands of the Little Bookcliffs. One early homesteader, known to history as "Old Man Lane," built a cabin in a secluded gulch in the middle of the Little Bookcliffs. Several former residents of the area claimed Lane worked with forty to fifty "broom tails" in the same area. There is no explanation as to who Lane was, what he did with the horses, or when he left the area. The remains of his cabin are still located in what is appropriately described as "Lane Canyon," immediately northwest of the Round Mountain Ridge.

Robert "Bob" Brislawn and his brother, Ferdinand, were once mapmakers for the United States Geologic Survey and were familiar with the Bookcliffs Mountain Range. While charting the Utah section of the range in the early 1900s (approximately twenty to twenty-five miles west of the Little Book-cliffs Wild Horse Area), they discovered that wild horses with strong Spanish Barb confirmation were still roaming the area. When the Brislawns established the Spanish Mustang Registry in Oshoto, Wyoming, they returned to the Little Bookcliffs to capture representatives of what would become the foundation stock for their registry. Bob Brislawn once told me that he believed the Little Bookcliffs wild horses included some of the progeny of those horses with strong Spanish Barb characteristics.

At approximately the same time, rancher Dave Knight set up camp in the Little Bookcliffs across the canyon from where Old Man Lane lived. Knight brought 30 horses he purchased from Ira Boyce in Peaceance Creek in north-western Colorado. Ironically, those 30 horses were originally captured out of the Little Bookcliffs herd. Knight brought the horses to the town of DeBeque, where he established two formal cattle operations in the Little Bookcliffs area.

According to a property survey conducted in the mid-1940s, Dave Knight made an application to the Bureau of Land Management on June 27, 1936, for 100 cattle to graze the area year-round and 50 cattle to graze for only six months. Because Knight was experiencing unspecified problems on his Little Bookcliffs grazing allotment, he was issued a temporary license for only 60 cattle in 1937. In 1939 he again applied for a permit for 100 cattle. All but 41 were rejected. The Bureau of Land Management records show he did not apply for a grazing permit for any of the horses seen in the area. By July 3, 1945, Knight was permitted to graze 250 cattle and 30 domestic horses.

The wild horse population was never mentioned in any of the government records. The permit holders feared that by claiming the wild horses as domestic livestock, it could lower the quantity of their cattle permits. Local residents and ranchers took sport in culling the herd and taking home a fine young horse. Few horses remained in the Little Bookcliffs due to the mustanging and legal government roundups in the 1930s and 1940s.

Wild burros, progeny of the coal-train burros used in the mines that honeycomb the face of the Bookcliffs, were let loose in the mountains when the mines closed. In 1942 T. Joseph Snyder, district grazer of the Department of the Interior Division of Grazing, issued a letter to Dave Knight, instructing him "to remove, from the Federal range north of Cameo, wild burros. . . . [T]here are quite a number of wild horses running in the same area as are the burrows [sic] and that after the trap is built it will be comparatively easy matter to remove these horses from the Federal range. . . . Any horses on this range are now in trespass and unless removed, action by the Grazing Service will be necessary." The wild burros were successfully gathered, using a figure-eight corral trap in Winter Flats. The horses remained a part of the ecosystem.

When Dave Knight died in late 1945, DeBeque resident John Baker was hired by the estate of Dave Knight and the new tenant, W. Russell Latham of Grand Junction, to gather more than 468 head of cattle included in the two Knight operations. This was approximately twice the number of cattle Knight was permitted to graze in the Little Bookcliffs. Other contractors removed more cattle. Recognizing the cattle were overgrazing the area, the Bureau of Land Management placed grazing restrictions on the Latham operation. In 1951 he was allowed 375 cattle, but only for a two-month period of time. Range conditions continued to deteriorate, and Latham's permit was reduced to 323 cattle the following year and 300 head in 1955.

Latham's cattle allotments continued to be reduced and then suddenly were increased, even though there was no evidence any range repairs were made in the area. Calculated in animal unit months (the number of cattle multiplied by the number of months the livestock are permitted to graze), Latham's permit indicated an unusual pattern: 1951, 844 AUMs; 1952, 740 AUMs; 1953, 694 AUMs; 1954, 694 AUMs; 1955, 1,178 AUMs, temporarily; and 1956, 1,268 AUMs, with 2,518 AUMs available to him. In 1956 his cattle operation was not large enough to maximize the grazing availability the BLM was willing to provide to him.

On February 20, 1969, the state director of the Bureau of Land Management reported the wild horse herd status to the Colorado Game, Fish, and Parks Commission. BLM Colorado state director E. I. Rowland stated the herd population the year before was estimated to be approximately 100 head of horses. In 1969 the population was estimated to be fewer than 35; he could offer no explanation for the reduction in the size of the herd. Rowland ordered a comprehensive survey of the wild horse area the same year. The results indicated that "the area is very subject to erosion due to shallow soil, steep terrain, and high intensity summer thunderstorms which occur." No previous studies were conducted in the wild horse area, so no range-trend studies could be calculated.

In 1966 and 1967, two attempts at range restoration were made to deal with the problems being experienced by Latham. "Chaining" was an experimental process whereby heavy tractor chains were dragged across marginal-use vegetation, uprooting sagebrush and other low-nutrition forage. The objective was to replant the cleared area with more viable range grasses. On Round Mountain, 1,457 acres were chained, as were 2,006 acres in Pine Gulch.

Two years later, the BLM internal report noted the chaining process failed to appreciably improve the vegetation in the Little Bookcliffs resource area. The report noted that the juniper trees were satisfactorily removed and a few ponds and springs were minimally improved in the grazing area. Of a more critical nature, the report noted that the land managers failed to reseed the disturbed topsoil in the chained grazing area. What little topsoil and naturally available range grasses survived the churning process failed to enable the rangeland to recover. Instead of admitting to the range mismanagement, the BLM blamed the wild horses for the range deterioration. During an airplane surveillance of the area during the winter of 1968–69, approximately 42 horses were spotted. During the fall of 1969, only 25 horses were seen.

OFTEN THERE ARE INDIVIDUALS in a community who take wildlife issues to heart and with much zeal. Such was the case with Howard Caudle. From his Grand Junction home, he adopted the Little Bookcliffs wild horses as his own, yet he never personally visited the wild horse area. Whenever a rumor of wild horse abuse was heard, Caudle made sure the press heard about it through his letters to the editor. For a while, he served on the board of directors of Wild Horse Annie's International Society for the Protection of Mustangs and Burros.

In Grand Junction, Caudle's vigilance probably prevented the herd from being totally harvested. In the early 1960s, some youngsters caught four unbranded horses out of the Bookcliffs herd and brought them to the stockyard. Instead of being reimbursed for their efforts, the brand inspector confiscated the horses. With the attention instigated by Caudle and a growing interest in the Bookcliffs by the U.S. Congress for the development of a possible wild horse refuge, Bureau of Land Management officials pondered what to do about the herd. Their first problem was to determine who actually owned the horses.

In 1968 district manager Keith Miller wrote about the wild horses in a memo to the Colorado state director: "We could either have them sold or establish a refuge. We would need to arrive at desirable numbers and control techniques to maintain them at this level." He continued, "Some of the individuals around the country have let it be known that they have [domestic] horses [among the wild horses] and would like some time to gather their own, and I have informed them that we haven't set any timetables nor have we formulated any plans for these horses at this time, but I have indicated they (ranchers) had better get theirs out of the area (because the horses are in trespass)."[2]

Caudle immediately seized on the idea of a wild horse refuge and generated a large number of support letters that he forwarded to the Grand Junction district office. While word spread of a potential refuge, reports of wild horse abuse also circulated. The district manager described one account of wild horse abuse in the Little Bookcliffs. Two young boys were trying to get themselves a horse. They were surprised by other people coming into the area and ran away. As they did, a mare got caught in the snare they had set, wound herself around a tree, and was strangled during the struggle to free herself.[3] Several young men caught a wild horse and attempted to lead it down an extremely narrow trail on the steep face of the Bookcliffs. The horse spooked and fell to its death, according to employees of the local BLM.

District manager Miller wrote again to the state director to express his concern: "I have noticed that some people are, perhaps, stretching the truth on wild horses. One of the items that bothers me the greatest is the comment that horses are coming through the winter with nothing but skin and bones. This just isn't the case, and if it were, it would be an indication of excessive use of the forage in the area in which they were roaming. I realize that many may be overstating the facts due to pending legislation; however, it is a reflection on our management of the public lands as well as being not true."[4] The establishment of a refuge, Miller continued, would not guarantee protection for the wild horses. At that time, there were no laws that would prevent additional wild horses from being shot, roped, or harassed.

Wild Horse Annie also wrestled with the idea of a wild horse refuge in the Little Bookcliffs. Using data reported by Howard Caudle, she considered proposing a "wild horse multiple-use range" rather than a "refuge," which would have excluded use by other wildlife and livestock. Annie told Caudle that it would be important to keep the public interested in the horses because it was becoming apparent that "it is only [through] public pressure that any response is granted" from the Bureau of Land Management. She did not believe the livestock should be eliminated, since the relationship between the horses and livestock had been favorable for many years. "A 'refuge,'" explained Annie, "would eliminate the cattle, and I believe opposition from the domestic interests would be intense, delay action on the part of the Secretary of the Interior, and expose the horses to possible elimination by some trigger-happy individual who would oppose exclusive wild horse use." She did not favor disturbing the wilderness aspects of the Bookcliffs or establishing a "zoo-type" exhibition of the wild horses. "It is my feeling that the people who really want to see them should be willing to go into the area in other than luxurious comfort of transportation, on roads that would not encourage a freeway-type of driving. . . . I truly believe that the public would be happy just to know that there are areas, such as the Bookcliffs, where wild horses are protected, and would be content not to have to see them there."[5]

Under normal conditions, the Grand Junction area can be described (at best) as a borderline desert. In 1972 the Grand Valley surrounding Grand Junction was struck by one of the worst droughts in recorded local history. Despite the atypical growing season, the Grand Junction district office of the BLM dispersed a team of five men into the wild horse area to conduct vegetative studies on July 11–20, 1972. Even by driving over the dirt roads in the government vehicles to raise enough dust to rid the area of biting gnats, the "flying teeth" continued to attack the men. One BLM official wrote in his report that the area was not fit for man or beast. After two days with the gnats and heat of the Little Bookcliffs, one research team left; the next day, a second team left. Within eight days, the gnats had the Little Bookcliffs to themselves. The original plan was to survey the area for two weeks.

The published report declared that in the estimation of the Bureau of Land Management, the Little Bookcliffs Wild Horse Area could not support more than 450 AUMs. The government also inflated the wild horse herd census to 45–64 from the previously reported 25 horses. Since the wild horses would be consuming 540–768 AUMs (45–64 horses times twelve months), there was not enough vegetation for even the wild horses, according to the bureau.

John Hill, the rancher who purchased the Latham cattle permits for the Little Bookcliffs management area, did not like the implications of the drought-survey results. Hill had purchased the grazing permits with the understanding that the existence of a wild horse herd would not be a detriment to his cattle operation. "They assured me that there was a workable agreement on a multiple-use concept," explained Hill, "and that the horses would be maintained at 35–50 head of horses. I've got a 1,244 AUM permit. I figured that between my acreage and the horses—they wouldn't hurt me in any way, shape or form. So I went ahead and purchased the ranch."

The following winter, deep snows fell in the Little Bookcliffs. Despite the adverse weather that kept the vegetation covered, the horses survived in excellent condition. Hill was scheduled to turn his cattle out on the range by April 5. On March 20 he took the district grazer for the Bureau of Land Management into the permit area to show him snowdrifts up to three feet deep and asked for a delay of a few days. According to Hill, the BLM officials refused to allow the delay, even though the available forage was covered by snow. The BLM state director overrode the local-district decision.

Animosity between the BLM and the livestock operators continued. On July 23, 1973, almost a year after the vegetative study was conducted during the drought, letters were sent to those ranchers who had permits to graze within the wild horse area. Hill was told his total grazing privileges were being held for indefinite suspension because the known 64 wild horses needed 768 AUMs of range—more than the current forage that was available. His grazing privileges would be held in suspended nonuse until the final determination was made on what would happen with the Bookcliffs wild horse herd.

It became clear that once again, the wild horses were being used as scapegoats to antagonize the ranchers against the wild horses. Here was a rancher who actually acquired his cattle permits in the Little Bookcliffs because of the wild horses. He admired the horses and found no historical reason that horses and cattle could not share the same habitat. Annie was caught in a dilemma. She had never come forward to address any particular battle between a rancher and the BLM when it came to wild horse issues. However, the Little Bookcliffs wild horses represented a perfect example of how her multiple-use concept of horses and livestock sharing the same rangeland was possible.

Hill took his case before the executive committee of the National American Cattlemen's Association. The BLM spokesman was Kay Wilkes of the Washington office of the Bureau of Land Management, the author of the claim that the wild horses were breeding at 20–25 percent each year. Following Hill's presentation to the cattlemen's association, Wilkes stepped forward to rebut his allegations. "I don't know what you expect me to say! I'm not familiar with all the details of the case," Wilkes continued. "I think it would be remiss if I didn't say there will be adjustments in livestock use."

Wilkes then cloaked a warning to the livestock operators who were grazing fewer cattle than their permits allowed. He "suggested" the ranchers pump up their livestock operations and start grazing the maximum number of livestock their individual permits allowed. If they did not, the unused permits would go away. "You might ask how we have been getting along through the years and how some of these situations have come to life. A lot of it has been because of the non-use you fellows have been carrying in your grazing privileges. When the non-use is absorbed, then you're going to see some direct competition—you're going to see changes in your range areas. As far as Mr. Hill's situation, I can't remember ever being involved in a range survey that wasn't made in a dry year." Ranchers like John Hill were wise stewards of the public land and released fewer livestock onto the public land during drought years. Land managers like Kay Wilkes wanted the ranchers to maximize the allotted number of livestock despite what the range surveys indicated.

On September 15, 1973, Wild Horse Annie wrote to George L. Turcott, associate director of the Bureau of Land Management in Washington, D.C. She sensed great danger to the wild horses, not only in the Bookcliffs but also on other federal public lands. The horses were being used as scapegoats, and the Wild Free-Roaming Horse and Burro Act of 1971 was being blamed. Earlier that year, Annie learned that a BLM district manager took it upon himself to tell ranchers that forthcoming cuts in grazing allotments were specifically due to "wild horse occupancy" in their area.

Annie was adamant that the livestock and wild horse chasm was growing and bitterness increasing. She predicted that severe reprisals against the wild horses by livestock operators were festering among the ranchers. As Annie reported to George Turcott, "I have not heretofore entered into any livestock operator versus BLM situation involving public-land use, but I cannot, in good conscience, sit back and allow this particular instance in the Bookcliffs to become an issue that will provide domestic livestock operators with still another excuse to carry on their vendetta against wild horses and burros."

The battle continued while Hill awaited word as to the "temporary" duration of the grazing closure. As far as Hill knew, he would be out of business when it was time to release his stock onto the public land the following spring. Hill later explained that he had no intention of actually taking ownership of the horses, but simply wanted to force a decision from the BLM. His rationale was that the grazing permits changed hands several times, and on occasion, a domestic horse could have escaped and been lost into the wilds.

According to the legal brief filed on Hill's behalf, "Although said horses were not physically rounded up and transferred each time that ranchers transferred their fee and BLM permits, it was the intention of said ranchers to actually transfer said horses and the right of the transferee to roundup any of the said horses if he so desired." It was a clear indication that this method of claiming wild horses under domestic livestock ownership had been done before by the livestock industry and with the knowledge of the Bureau of Land Management.

Bureau of Land Management officials speculated that the perceived battle between wild horse and livestock interests could not be resolved without some sort of firm policy decision by the government. It was decided that in order to resolve the problem, the Little Bookcliffs Wild Horse Area would be divided in half, with the livestock utilizing the northern range (Dave Knight's second cattle operation area) and the horses the southern range (Knight's first cattle area). It did not seem to matter that, according to the Bureau of Land Management's range studies, the horses were getting the area with less rainfall, less vegetation, and topsoil in fragile condition. In order to preserve the value of the range, the BLM proposed to reduce the wild horses' grazing range by half, maintain the same herd size, and then compare the grazing impact with livestock grazing on slightly better terrain for only two months out of the year. The fate of the Bookcliffs wild horses was an example of pre-conceived destiny.

Annie described the proposed wild horse management as being "like a pair of shoes so small that you whack off part of your foot. It's reducing the occupancy of horses to fit the territory."[6] The district Bureau of Land Management office justified the separation by explaining, "Evaluation is the key reason for the division." No explanation as to how the evaluation would be made was ever established.

Dr. C. Wayne Cook, former head of the Range Science Department of Colorado State University and past chairperson of the National Wild Horse and Burro Advisory Board, warned of superficial comparisons as proposed by the Bureau of Land Management. Cook explained there was no set ratio of exchange for various species of herbivores on rangelands. The exchange ratio depended upon the weight of the species, the physiological functions being performed, the topographical features, and vegetation composition.[7]

Despite the learned advice from the National Wild Horse and Burro Advisory Board, the management plan for a divided wild horse area was implemented. One of the problems was how to logistically move the northern horses down to the southern wild horse designated area. Initially, the plan was to drive the horses into the new area.

At one point, the road from the northern area through Main Canyon to Round Mountain banks high on the right, with a radical drop-off on the left. Horses, realizing there was no escape route when being driven, could easily panic. Halfway down the Main Canyon road was a blind U-turn. The horses would have gone over the fifty-foot cliff. While the district office in Grand Junction officially denied the horses would have been driven down the Main Canyon road, five staff members of the BLM privately confirmed this intended route as accurate.

The Grand Junction district office received 973 letters, telegrams, and petitions expressing concern for the welfare of the horses after several magazine articles about the Bookcliffs wild horses were published.[8] During the planning period, an additional 2,000 people wrote to request the establishment of a wild horse refuge, including the entire multiple-use range in the Little Bookcliffs. When the Bureau of Land Management scheduled public hearings, the response was clear. According to the environmental assessment report for the Little Bookcliffs horse movement, the majority of the public input opposed the movement of the horses and did not want the size of the wild horse area reduced. They expressed their opinion that confining the wild horses to a smaller area would result in a smaller herd. The report also stated the public did not want to have the horses run and be captured because of the potential harm to the wild horses in an area riddled with pinion pine and juniper trees that blocked the views of deep washes and arroyos.

In a settlement between the Bureau of Land Management and John Hill, he disclaimed ownership of all the horses, branded or unbranded, in the Little Bookcliffs Wild Horse Area. He signed a new grazing permit for the 1974 season; four hundred cattle were allowed on the public land between April and May (a reduction of only twenty-two head of cattle from the previous year).[9]

The Bureau of Land Management prohibited the issue from being thrown open to the public for vote or appeal. The National Advisory Board for Wild Horses and Burros also had no authority to change or augment the decision. Annie discussed the board's seeming lack of interest in specific management cases. "It is my hope that the Board will address [the Little Bookcliffs]," Annie explained, "but you have seen already, through your attendance at the other meetings, there seems to be a reluctant attitude insofar as management issues in specific instances are concerned."

Annie sanctioned four miles of fencing to keep the horses and cattle from straying on each other's allotments. In conversations with Mrs. Harrison, Annie's Colorado-based benefactor, Annie learned she had been wrongly informed by the Colorado state office of the Bureau of Land Management. She was told the separation would be only for the two months of the cattle allotment and that the area would be accessible to the wild horses for their summer range.

The resulting separation of wild horses and burros into separate ranges against the desire of Wild Horse Annie and more than three thousand private citizens cost approximately $250,000. Several miles of pole fencing were helicoptered into the horse area and assembled with the assistance of the Junior Conservation Corps. Between 1974 and 1975, fourteen springs were developed and three catchments and six reservoirs built; 12 miles of pipeline, 3.3 miles of pole fencing, 9.2 miles of wire fencing, seven cattle guards, two corrals, and 10 miles of trails were budgeted within the combined horse and cattle ranges.

Once the fence was erected, several informal attempts to drift the horses into the new area via a succession of open and closed gates during the horses' normal migration failed. By the fall of 1975, approximately 50 wild horses remained outside the newly designated wild horse area; 40 were already in the new area. The 50 horses were rounded up and trucked into the new "Little Bookcliffs Wild Horse Area," as it became officially known.[10] The choice of *Area* instead of *Refuge* was intentional on the part of the BLM to assure their constituents that they were not acquiescing to the desires of "the wild horse faction."

By 1977 the population rose to approximately 110–20 horses, according to BLM surveillance. In November 1977, the BLM conducted a roundup of 50 horses; 40 were removed, and 10 were returned to the range. Two of the horses returned to the range were marked with surveillance collars to aid in studies of wild horse movements, reproduction, and behavior. The studies, if ever conducted, were never used in any subsequent management plans for the wild horse area.

THE RELATIONSHIP between the Bureau of Land Management and Wild Horse Annie had both a sense of professional respect and a growing sense of distrust. Annie's recommendations were soundly based as a logical business model, but the federal government agency policies remained based on a nineteenth-century concept of range management. As more BLM offices hired a new generation of college-educated range-management staff, conflicts began to develop within the federal agencies. Quietly, Annie fielded calls from BLM administrators and field managers who agreed (off the record) with Annie's multiple-use concept of range management on the public lands.

Annie recognized that the BLM management plan "was never designed to help the horses" and lashed out at the agency in a *Grand Junction Daily Sentinel* editorial. She wrote, "With Western range lands in the depleted condition they are—man's encroachment, diversion of water, fencing—everyone has pushed the panic button and, except for the handful of us who are their champions, the Wild Ones have been made the scapegoats. We are feeling the pressures of the livestock operators every way we turn out here, and a few of them have been mighty bold in their comments about me. They are not about to be thwarted in their dominant use of your land and mine."

Other than possibly the Pryor Mountain wild horse herd, no other wild horse area in the country received as much publicity, at that time, as the Bookcliffs. At the center of interest in the Little Bookcliffs wild horses was

Wild Horse Annie. She made several visits to the area and maintained constant contact with her volunteer outfielders as well as through official communication with the Bureau of Land Management.

On unseasonably warm November 7, 1980, the Little Bookcliffs Wild Horse Area was dedicated to Mrs. Velma B. "Wild Horse Annie" Johnston. This was only the second wild horse area designated as such and accessible to the public. The Bureau of Land Management and the Lovell Chamber of Commerce dedicated the Pryor Mountain Wild Horse Refuge (now Range) on the central Montana-Wyoming border in 1968. The refuge at Nellis Air Force Base continues to be closed to the public.

Among those speaking at the dedication that was conducted at the base of the Little Bookcliffs was Helen Reilly, Annie's successor as president of the International Society for the Protection of Mustangs and Burros. The plaque dedicating the Little Bookcliffs Wild Horse Area to Velma B. "Wild Horse Annie" Johnston was later moved to a permanent monument within the wild horse area.

Since then, Annie's wish to see natural refuges of wild horses expanded for a while as the Bureau of Land Management established several other wild horse and burro areas that incorporated the animals' natural habitat. But future administrations of the U.S. Department of the Interior would reverse the concept of a natural wild horse habitat. Instead of following Wild Horse Annie's belief in multiple-use habitat for the horses and cattle, philosophical divisions continued to broaden to the detriment of public land-management conservation.

10

THE "HOWE, IDAHO, MASSACRE"

Four o'clock is a time when people start anticipating leaving work and spending a relaxing night at home. Four o'clock at neighborhood bars is the beginning of "happy hours" at the end of a workday. For Annie, four o'clock was neither. It was four o'clock, and Wild Horse Annie's home phone was ringing. When she picked up the receiver, she immediately knew it was going to be a very long night at the house on the hill above the lights of Reno.

Annie was used to getting phone calls from ranchers; after all, her phone number was in the book. Occasionally, a rancher would rant in opposition to her work or turn in another rancher who was violating some sense of decorum among the livestock men like junkyard dogs marking their territory. At four o'clock on February 26, 1973, a nervous Idaho rancher began telling Annie a story after eliciting a promise from her to keep his identity to herself.

With stenography pad in hand, Annie's shorthand squiggles were interrupted by the names of Little Lost River ranchers, dates, times, and graphic descriptions that caused Annie to grip her pencil just a little tighter than usual. Annie's caller reported that the Idaho Bureau of Land Management was encouraging local ranchers to gather wild horses near Howe, Idaho, 'seventy-eight miles northwest of Idaho Falls.[1] The Wild Free-Roaming Horse and Burro Act of 1971 was in effect, even though the advisory board was still working on defining the regulations. Annie's notepad rapidly filled with her pencil notes: two branded horses got loose and ran off with the wild horses; several unbranded horses had been shot; seven others fell or were driven over a cliff and killed; the status of surviving wild horses was unknown.

The wild horses had been grazing in the Little Lost River area for at least thirty years. Ranchers Frank Hartmann and Bill Robison were new to the area and were just learning to fit into the politics of local ranching. Local BLM officials told them that by eliminating approximately sixty free-roaming horses from the public land adjacent to their leased land, it would enable them to increase the forage potential for their sheep and cattle operations. The neophyte ranchers found the proposition appealing.[2]

After concluding her conversation with her informant, Annie's next call was to George Lea, deputy director of the Washington, D.C., Bureau of Land Management. Their friendship and mutual respect enabled Annie to have access to his home phone number for emergencies like this. The gravity of the information prompted him to ask Annie to call BLM associate director George Turcott at his home. They agreed that if this type of illegal roundup was occurring in the Idaho Falls district, it was probably indicative of many other BLM districts.

Sifting through the information her network of informants and Bureau of Land Management insiders provided, Annie began to quickly sort out and verify each piece of information. Her skills as an executive secretary were never so acutely alert as they were that night as she began transcribing her shorthand interview notes.

The story actually began a year earlier when Idaho BLM state director William Mathews sent an instructional memo to all district managers, on February 16, 1972. Any rancher, the memo explained, who wanted to reclaim any domestic horse that strayed into a herd of wild horses could file a claim of ownership at the local BLM office. That was in accord with PL 92-195 that allowed domestic horses to be extracted from the herds of wild horses after a trespass fee was paid.[3]

A follow-up internal memo was sent to the western state offices. District managers were instructed to "be reasonably sure that the claim is valid. Protection of wild horses and burros should be [the] primary concern."[4] Before the roundup could commence, the claimant had to provide evidence of a valid state-approved livestock inspection certificate to the district manager for each claimed animal in the wild horse herd. The memo technically expired on December 31, 1972, but a published federal directive extended it for another six months.[5]

Annie was incensed when she learned the Little Lost River horse roundup was authorized by what she described as a renegade district manager of the Bureau of Land Management under the command of the Idaho state director. During her conversation with George Turcott, her frustration with the western BLM administrators was apparent. "Before we have any other problems, Idaho State Director Bill Mathews must be jerked up short."

The following morning, Mathews called Annie upon instruction from his boss. With great regret, he confirmed the rancher's story as accurate. A wild horse roundup was conducted near Howe, Idaho, and several unbranded horses were dead at the bottom of a cliff. He could not determine whether they were wild horses or not.

A month before the 1972 memorandum was to expire, the Idaho Falls Bureau of Land Management Advisory Board met to discuss what should be done with the wild horses roaming on the public land before the regulations took effect. Rancher Robert Amy recollected that after the meeting, BLM district manager Walter "Ed" Jones of Idaho Falls told Bill Yearsley, a Blackfoot, Idaho, real estate agent, to do "something" about the range-horse situation on the Badger Creek Bar section of the Little Lost River near the village of Howe. A meeting in Howe was scheduled, and word spread throughout the valley that "something" could be planned to rid the area of the wild horses.[6]

Following the meeting, Bill Robison met with Bill Yearsley at the Rexburg, Idaho, livestock auction to discuss the possibility of gathering the sixty-four wild horses that roamed the Badger Creek Bar. Yearsley never saw a wild, free-roaming horse and was intrigued by the prospects of a real wild horse roundup. To satisfy the memo, Ed Jones instructed Robison to be sure the horses were privately owned. Jones was a longtime Idaho rancher and mustanger, so he knew how to circumvent the federal wild horse law by "domesticating" wild horses or burros on paper prior to a roundup.

In a federal report, government investigators asked sheep rancher George Woodie how much knowledge the residents of the area had about PL 92-195. "I don't think anybody, including myself, was knowledgeable of the Wild Horse Act," Woodie responded. It was "a small pamphlet with fine print. I have never read it all the way through myself."[7]

According to PL 92-195's rules and regulations, wild, free-roaming horses and burros

> means all unbranded and unclaimed horses and burros and their progeny that have used public lands on or after December 15, 1971, or that do use these lands as all or part of their habitat, including those animals given an identifying mark upon capture for live disposal by the authorized officer. Unbranded, claimed horses and burros where the claim is found to be erroneous are also considered

as wild and free roaming if they meet the criteria above. However, this definition shall not include any horse or burro which entered or was introduced onto public lands after December 15, 1971, by accident, negligence, or willful disregard of ownership.[8]

The sworn, tape-recorded depositions from the federal investigative report clearly indicated the confusion among the Idaho residents. Even Ed Jones, the district manager responsible for seeing that the animals were protected under the new law, was ignorant of the legislative proceedings. When questioned, Jones told investigators he knew the Wild Free-Roaming Horse and Burro Act of 1971 was passed by Congress, but he had his own interpretation of the interim instructions until the formal regulations were developed. Since the BLM district manager did not believe there were wild horses in his grazing district, all the horses were unbranded claimed horses belonging to local ranchers. "I told the people when they said they owned the horses," Jones testified on the tape recording, "if they are yours, then you move them off of there. They took that for permission to say yes, to gather the horses."

Jones attempted to downplay the events by claiming the horses were approachable and gentle. He said the horses could be spooked with airplanes or chased on horseback for good-natured fun by valley children just to see them run. Contradicting himself, Jones also told investigators that the same horses he described as "gentle" would be more difficult to capture because of the frequent recreational hazing conducted by the valley residents.[9]

The BLM district manager reflected on his own mustanging experience before becoming a government official in charge of protecting the wild horses and burros. "Unless you can identify a brand on an animal," Jones testified, "or somebody admits that he belongs to him, how can you tell a wild horse from any other range horse—that runs on the range. They all look pretty much the same. I've chased a lot of wild horses in my time and you can tell an area where wild horses will generally get—and they generally go back in the higher country where it is hard to get them out, so they just kind of leave them."[10]

Management of wild horses was not a responsibility Ed Jones cared to consider. He grew up among ranchers who frequently released unbranded animals in trespass on the public land, often without paying a grazing fee for the privilege. Horses were gathered or released indiscriminately by ranchers.

Legally, since no one formally claimed the animals, no one had to pay grazing fees to the government. Bills of sale for the animals were written only for the state brand inspectors who required proof of ownership to satisfy interstate transportation criteria. The sale bills were rarely checked to authenticate whether the seller actually owned the horses. The lack of legal documentation was a normal aspect of range management, but it was a major issue that angered Wild Horse Annie. "As for the state brand inspector's clearance," she wrote, "I wouldn't trust one of them as far as I could throw a bull by the tail."[11]

Robison trusted Jones for advice on how to legally gather the horses despite the federal law. Jones erroneously informed Robison that the law had not gone into effect, but nonetheless encouraged Robison to seek legal counsel. Rexburg attorney Harold Fourbush was contacted and advised Robison to leave the roundup idea alone. Robison opted to ignore legal advice and proceeded with his plan to use an airplane to gather the wild horses.

Robison and Frank Hartmann Jr. began to gather impromptu written bills of sale from resident ranchers L. R. "Slim" Hawley, Leo D. Amy, and Jay Little for horses allegedly released in the 1940s and 1950s. Amy's claim was based on a stallion and a mare that he lost in the area in 1951 while he was moving horses. Little's unsubstantiated claim was based on a possibility that some of his horses may have escaped from his ranch prior to selling it to Robison in 1970.[12]

On December 19, 1972, the Bureau of Land Management Advisory Board meeting in Idaho Falls was attended by ranchers Leo Amy and George B. Woodie and BLM personnel Jens Jensen and Walter "Ed" Walker. The status of PL 92-195 and the proposed regulations implementing the law were among the topics of the meeting. Amy, Woodie, and Jones each left the meeting with the understanding that if the herd of horses in the Badger Creek area was not removed from public land within ninety days, the animals would be declared wild, free-roaming horses under the protection of the federal law.

Following the meeting, Ed Jones, Dave Lindberg, and Ralph Sharp of the Idaho Falls Bureau of Land Management exchanged phone calls. Repeatedly, Jones told the ranchers that if the horses were their property, the ranchers had to gather them or be fined a trespass fee or lose them to the federal wild horse and burro act. The emphasis of Jones's request was on the potential expense that would be assessed to the ranchers if the wild horse law claimed the animals. Robert Amy commented, "They agreed right then at that meeting that they couldn't live with the law, that they didn't want a wild horse deal."[13]

Hartmann, Robison, Jones, and another local rancher reconvened on December 28, 1972, at the district offices of the Bureau of Land Management to further discuss the ramifications of the wild horse and burro act. Frank Hartmann Jr. verified Robison's statement. "[Jones] says we did not need written permission. He says these are deeded horses, these are private horses, and the law has no major effect on wild horses at this time. You boys have ninety days before this law goes into effect, to take these horses off."[14]

Each day, Robison told the local group that the Idaho Falls Bureau of Land Management was pressuring him to capture the horses and to shoot any he could not capture. However, Jones stated under oath that other than the December 28 meeting, he did not tell Robison to remove the horses from public lands.

Without the BLM officials present, a meeting was held on December 29 at the Howe schoolhouse. Once again, Robison led the discussion about the need to remove the horses. Leo Amy, Hartmann, and Robison agreed to gather the horses.[15] Additional bills of sale were transferred; Hartmann transferred ownership of the Badger Creek Bar horses to Yearsley. His claim was based on his possession of the ranch previously owned by Andy Little. On his grazing permit, Little never claimed any horses were roaming on the Badger Creek Bar.

On approximately January 5, 1973, Ed Jones notified forest supervisor Richard Benjamin of the Challis National Forest that Howe ranchers were going to gather "domestic" horses in the Badger Creek Bar area. The next day, the roundup began when Bill Yearsley commissioned a helicopter piloted by Sam Buckley of Mountain States Helicopter Service in Rigby, Idaho. The first attempt was extremely unsuccessful, with only one white horse captured when it jumped a fence into a corral of domestic horses. The horse of the day was kept by one of Hartmann's ranch hands.[16] Dave Lindberg, assistant area manager of the Idaho Falls Bureau of Land Management office, explained that the helicopter ran out of gas and the pilot set the craft down as the horses scattered and ran back toward the hills.[17]

Because of the weather conditions, the group waited two more weeks before using the chopper again. In the meantime, Yearsley regrouped the amateur mustangers and requested the assistance of Max Palmer of Sugar

City, Idaho. For his help on January 6–20, Palmer agreed to receive half the horses captured. He stated to federal officials that "he never intended to do anything else with the horses than to sell them for slaughter."[18]

A second helicopter flight was made on approximately January 20, but was unsuccessful in gathering any horses. Yearsley flew as a passenger with either Hogan or Max Palmer to "tell [the pilot] exactly how to have these horses."[19] The team began to bicker among themselves on the best way to gather the horses.[20] Finally, Buckley set the helicopter down and told his passengers they were grounded. He proceeded to haze approximately fifteen horses by himself, but the animals continued to dodge the aircraft.

An airplane was brought onto the scene and used sometime between January 20 and February 10, according to Yearsley, but this attempt to gather horses was also futile.[21] An eyewitness said the copilot crippled two or three horses with his shotgun. Snowmobiles were dispatched, and the crippled horses were put down with rifle fire. Bill Robison explained the aircraft was "not [intended] to run [the horses] to death, but just to haze them down onto the flats and eventually into the corral; that was the idea. . . . It didn't work. It just plain didn't work. The horses didn't even seem to be scared of it. They would go around it and went back."[22]

With the failure of the helicopter, the mustangers realized they needed more help. Apparently, no one knew how to effectively gather horses with motorized vehicles and aircraft, but old-timers like Slim Hawley, Andy Little, Jay Little, and "Scrub" Hawley were familiar with the old-fashioned horseback method.

Yearsley again reminded the men that Robison was in daily contact with the BLM and the government was pressuring him to get the horses off the federal land. If they could not accomplish this feat, Yearsley, Robison, and Palmer understood they were to shoot the horses dead. Jones denied telling the ranchers to shoot the horses they could not capture.[23]

They went back onto the Badger Creek Bar and continued to pursue the horses on horseback almost every day between February 5 and February 25, 1973. Yearsley stated he personally observed several mares in the band with signs of blood around their tails, indicating they aborted foals during the roundup.[24] During approximately forty-five days of hazing, the horses were unable to settle down to graze properly and began to show signs of malnutrition. According to Annie's chief informant, the horses were lathered in sweat during the daylight harassment and then left alone when the night temperatures dropped as low as minus thirty-four degrees in Idaho's harsh winter environment.

On February 15, the BLM office in Idaho Falls and the U.S. Forest Service office in Ogden, Utah, received inquiries from U.S. Senator Frank Church (D–Idaho) concerning the roundup. News of the investigation reached the men staying at the Robison ranch, who discussed Senator Church's inquiry on the evening of February 16. They decided to ignore the outside curiosity and continue their attempt to gather the horses.[25]

Since Lynn Munn had achieved success in chasing the horses up to the mountain corral, the men decided to change their roundup technique and chase the horses into the Lemhi Mountains. On February 17, Yearsley, Palmer, and others chased approximately twenty-one horses to a holding corral that was approximately seventy-five hundred square feet, positioned on a cliff edge in a high rimrock area.

During the roundup, Palmer shot three of the animals because their legs were broken during the chase when the animals attempted to escape. Two other horses were found dead of "unknown causes." The horses that reached the holding corral were left unattended at the site of their capture until the morning of February 19. A young suckling colt was found outside the trap and was taken home in the cab of a pickup truck by Lynn Munn. The colt subsequently died.[26]

Leo Amy explained that on Friday, "some of these horses went up in the timber [to a corral area]. . . . [I]t was dark, so the [ranchers] drug a bunch of dead trees and stuff up there, and they left the horses right there on a Saturday evening. Bill Yearsley and Max Palmer wanted to go to church so they didn't come back on Sunday. We waited until Monday morning."[27] The men did not realize the clearing where they herded the horses was not a gentle pasture. The snow lightly covered the extremely craggy rock surface.

When they reached the corral Monday morning, Amy and Lynn Munn found a palomino stallion and three colts had fallen over the cliff. A white mare was spared the fall, but had a hoof wedged between rocks at the edge of the precipice. According to Amy, Munn claimed "he could smell a cougar around the outfit." Concerned for their own safety, the men left a sorrel horse that had fallen over the cliff but was still alive.[28] When they returned the next day to retrieve the sorrel horse, the animal was gone. "But a few days later," Amy continued with his testimony, "I was out there riding and I rode past him. He died."

The ranchers were concerned that once the horses had a chance to rest, they might try to escape the makeshift trap. With the consultation of a veterinarian in Rexburg, Idaho, they decided to use an outdated technique of restricting the horses' nostrils with "hog rings" so the animals could not get the necessary air if they attempted to run.[29] The men considered loosely wrapping the horses' legs with chains, but a local veterinarian told Max Hogan that stapling the horses' nostrils was more humane.[30] The chains would inflict pain if the horse attempted to run away. Their legs "would just be hamburger," Bill Robison testified.

Leo Amy continued with his sworn deposition:

> We put these rings in the white mare's nose and then decided we better get her foot out of the rocks. . . . [T]he first one we roped was a sorrel mare and we laid her down right there and put these rings in her nose and while she was getting up, she was flying around there, she got her feet caught in the rocks. The next one was a black horse and we broke his leg. When we turned him up, he floundered out and fell over the cliff. . . . We thought we got to get rid of the horses down there, we have got to rope these horses . . . lay them down, and get these rings in their noses. So that is what we did. We disposed of them and cut their legs off, I mean it was gruesome, it was pretty tough. We sawed that one sorrel mare's leg off with a chain saw—and now that's the truth.[31]

Between February 19 and February 25, approximately twenty additional horses were gathered and shipped to Palmer's ranch in Sugar City. Lynn Munn used his snowmobile to haze the horses into a mountain corral.[32] Yearsley stated that Munn bulldogged a horse from his snowmobile while another man reportedly roped one of the horses from his snowmobile.

The surviving horses were trailed down the canyon to the Badger Creek Ranch, where they were fed for the first time. On February 24, Bill Robison called assistant area manager Dave Lindberg at home and reported they had completed the horse roundup and almost all the horses were captured.[33]

A third roundup was carried out a week later to gather the rest of the horses. Palmer received a total of thirty-nine horses; five were disposed of by Palmer, one was claimed by Robert Hall of Howe, a young colt was sold to Gary Griffith of Rexburg for thirty dollars, a third horse was sold to Ronnie Moss of Rexburg for ten dollars, and Palmer consigned the remaining thirty-one to "Bish" Jenkins of Idaho Falls, who shipped them to the Central Nebraska Packing Plant in North Platte,[34] where Crown Prince Dog Food was canned.

After the February 26 phone call to Wild Horse Annie, she commissioned photographer Hal Perry to fly to the site of the roundup. Just ninety days after open-heart surgery, Perry jumped out of a helicopter to photograph the dead horses on behalf of WHOA!, the companion organization to Wild Horse Annie's International Society for the Protection of Mustangs and Burros. The $1,120 transportation bill was paid by WHOA!

Because Perry also worked with the Salt Lake City regional office of the Humane Society of the United States, he was obligated to inform HSUS Rocky Mountain director Franz Dantzler of the location of the horses. Using WHOA!'s rented helicopter, Dantzler made his own trip to the roundup site at WHOA!'s expense and brought a Salt Lake City television crew into the Lemhi Mountains. Dantzler and his organization made the network news and took full media credit for "discovering" the Howe, Idaho, Massacre. Wild Horse Annie was never mentioned.

The Humane Society of the United States and the American Horse Protection Association frequently worked together. AHPA vice president Joan Blue joined Dantzler in a press barrage against the Howe, Idaho, roundup "they" had discovered. By the first of March, the two eastern organizations and WHOA! began pressuring government officials for an investigation into the roundup. Facing public pressure, Palmer called Yearsley and proposed that they dispose of the captured horses, but neither of them had a workable plan.

On March 1 state brand inspector Boyd Summers inspected the thirty-one horses and found them to be unbranded. Since Palmer did not have bills of sale transferring the ownership of the horses to him, he requested Hartmann, Robison, and Leo Amy sign the brand inspection certificate as owners.[35]

At the Jenkins stockyard, one horse was removed from the truck because it was believed to be too weak to make the trip. When federal investigators interviewed Jenkins on March 3, the horse was found dead. Seven additional horses were then added to the shipment to North Platte. According to the investigative report, many of the mares in the herd were pregnant, but most lost their foals either during the roundups or at the packing plant in Nebraska.[36]

When I called Dwayne Struther of Central Nebraska Packing, he acknowledged receiving a call from a government investigator assigned to the case at Wild Horse Annie's request. Struther described the horses as being "in a very emaciated, weak, rundown, very unthrifty condition. The horses, in my opinion, are about half sick."[37] When asked about the condition of the first shipment of thirteen horses that arrived from the Howe, Idaho, roundup site, Struther said they were in fine shape and were slaughtered immediately.

Ed Jones told the ranchers to contact Sheriff Dick Lords of the Butte County Sheriff's Department prior to the roundup. After the roundup, Lords defended his neighbors. "After these ranchers, working three hours to [free the horses' legs from the crevices] they had to kill the animals right there. It was the only humane thing to do. But at no time were these animals mistreated. They were doing the only humane thing possible to get the animals out of there because they were hungry." When the sheriff was asked if the horses were branded, he clearly stated, "None of them were branded."[38] Several of the original participants in the roundup were heard boasting about the "success" of the roundup and began to plan for the next wild horse roundup.

Requests to keep the identity of Wild Horse Annie's informant secret were not honored by Senator Church's office or by the Idaho Falls BLM. Once his name was released, he began to get anonymous threats against his family, and his haystacks were set on fire.

In the meantime, Joan Blue and the American Horse Protection Association conducted their own investigation. Blue followed every possible lead in order to obtain depositions from anyone who knew any information about the horses or about the roundup. The AHPA planned to sue the BLM for forcing the participants to round up the horses. In a phone conversation, Blue told Annie they intended to "get the jobs" of Mathews and Jones for allowing the roundup to take place. Blue proposed actual damages of one hundred thousand dollars and punitive damages of five hundred thousand against each of the seventeen defendants, ranging from Secretaries Morton and Butz to field officers in both departments for failing to enforce the Wild Free-Roaming Horse and Burro Act of 1971. If her organization could link Washington's George Turcott to the case, Blue planned to get his job, too.

The difference in style between Velma B. "Wild Horse Annie" Johnston's

Joan Blue, vice president of the American Horse Protection Association, listens to a federal hearing on wild horses and burros in Washington, D.C. Courtesy of the author.

two organizations (WHOA! and ISPMB) and Joan Blue of the American Horse Protection Association became apparent. Annie and Joan cautiously conferred with each other, offering tidbits of irrelevant information to appease each other. Blue's comments were laced with strong adjectives and adverbs when she talked about the BLM: "We've *bombarded* them from every side. . . . This *nasty* U.S. Attorney here whom we have been *forced* to deal with . . . Why not *force* them to do that . . . ?"[39] Annie's approach was softer and more diplomatic. Among western residents, that approach continued to earn respect and cooperation, and eventually she was able to persuade people to change their way of thinking about the wild horses. On the other hand, vindictiveness, hatred, and name-calling, especially from other horse groups who claimed to share Annie's dedication to the preservation and protection of the wild horses and burros, created a stone wall of frustration and noncommunication and a lack of productivity among the growing number of groups.

The ranchers were also growing defensive. *Horse and Rider* was the first publication to focus national attention on the atrocities surrounding the Howe roundup. Peer and family pressure spurred the participants beyond practical reason during the roundup. The same motivating factors unified the Howe, Idaho, families while they received hate mail from around the world.

In one paragraph, an anonymous letter writer quoted biblical scriptures on behalf of the horses. The same letter closed with a desire for the families of the ranchers to be unmercifully butchered and thrown over the same cliffs to eventually die with the decaying wild horses.

The Howe, Idaho, roundup began with blind faith in the Idaho Falls BLM district manager. It turned into a horrible emotional nightmare fanned from the East by overly emotional appeals to punish the government and the ranchers. Bill Robison defended the ranchers in his testimony to the federal investigators by describing his neighbors as animal lovers in the business of working with animals. He explained that the negative international attention placed on the small-town ranchers was sickening to the families. "Now my boy went to bed last night and asked if we were all going to jail," Robison explained. "Bill Yearsley's little kid goes to school and they are called killers. Their dad's a killer. Well, you know [where] they got all this, and this is bad. It's not accurate. It's not right. None of it's right."[40]

Reading through the typed depositions, the hurt felt by the Howe, Idaho, ranchers was more legitimate than the hubris expressed by mustangers during other roundups conducted elsewhere. They wanted nothing more than to be left alone to return to their small-town lives without feeling the wrath of national reporters and angry wild horse advocates after a roundup that was wrongly encouraged by BLM officials and woefully executed by ill-equipped and untrained ranchers.

The federal investigation was completed and submitted to the U.S. Forest Service and Bureau of Land Management on March 19, 1973, before their report was transmitted to the Justice Department for appropriate action. The report was then turned over to U.S. attorney Sid Smith, who subsequently reported back to the Justice Department.

Accounts of the "wildness" of the horses impounded at North Platte contradicted each other. A wire service story published in the Idaho Falls Post-Register stated, "Although most were thought to be wild, a Nebraska veterinarian said several were shod and others showed signs of domesticity."[41] However, six months before the story was published, the attending veterinarian in North Platte informed e that none of the thirty-one wild horses was branded or had any evidence of ever having being shod.

ANNIE BRINGS THE WORLD
TO HOWE, IDAHO

On October 1, Annie informed George L. Turcott, associate director of the Bureau of Land Management, that she was going to launch a public appeal to help return the survivors of the Idaho roundup to their former habitat. She also sought to declare the area a national wild horse range. In a letter to Turcott, she requested the refuge be "a lasting memorial to the wild horses that were run to death here by those engaged in rounding them up during February 1973; and to the surviving remnant of those once proud bands that roamed this land."[1]

She reminded the associate director that the BLM was responsible for carrying out the provisions of the law as a means of serving the public in the management of the land. Annie requested the grazing rights of those involved in the roundup be revoked and that Walter "Ed" Jones be transferred to some other assignment. Her letter was routed from Turcott to Mathews and eventually to Jones. Privately, Annie thought Jones would make a good elevator operator for the Bureau of Land Management office building in Washington, D.C. She believed the longer he remained a lightning rod, the longer hostility toward the remaining horses would incur. Annie and Turcott both knew the press was becoming critical of the entire BLM department based on the actions of a single district manager, and she wanted to preserve the fragile relationship she had with some of the top BLM administrators who were privately negotiating ways of resolving communication and management issues.

Incensed by Annie's request that he be put out to pasture, Jones called a meeting of the Little Lost River residents. He stretched Annie's request to establish a refuge in the existing wild horse habitat into a mandate to take over the entire Little Lost River area (including private land) and establish it as a wild horse refuge. In a phone conversation, Annie informed BLM state director Bill Mathews of the blatant misinformation that his employee was circulating. A proposal like that would injure the economy of the entire community and further alienate her fragile support in that area. "Now I feel that there is about as much chance as getting that designated [as a wild horse area] as a snowball in hell," Annie explained in a rare moment of candor with the state director. "I wanted to clarify that . . . there is no desire on my part at any time to deprive people of their livelihood. . . . I think I try to play it all above board. I know that you would want to clarify that misunderstanding at the first opportunity to the people up there."[2]

On October 11, 1973, the Department of the Interior's Bureau of Land Management issued a news release and announced the department would drop prosecution of the Howe, Idaho, roundup participants "because the availability of evidence is considered to be insufficient to successfully prosecute." However, "if further evidence should develop indicating criminal activity by any person involved in the roundup, the declination of prosecution would be reconsidered."[3]

The federal government impounded the second shipment of wild horses, and they were held in a holding pen at the North Platte, Nebraska, slaughterhouse. The pitiful-looking horses were in horrible condition when I arrived, sloshing through a muddy outdoor pen. One horse refused to get up when the yard foreman approached; the rest huddled on the far side of the pen. My photographs and personal observation showed the penned horses were not shod, in contradiction to the government claims that the "wild" horses were actually shod domestic horses.

To avoid the chance of being confused with the Animal Horse Protection Association's civil suit against the BLM and Forest Service, and Joan Blue's poor public relations in Idaho, Annie maintained a cautious campaign away from the clamor of the press. With the accompaniment of former Nevada governor Paul Laxalt's bodyguard, Jean Armand, Annie agreed to meet assistant attorney general Paul Westberg in Idaho. Armed with several one-inch-thick volumes of depositions from the residents of the Little Lost River area, copies of the Hal Perry photographs, and information obtained from her outfielders, Wild Horse Annie wanted to know the answer to one particular question: "What do you lack in information to have decided not to prosecute those involved with the Howe Idaho roundup?" Mr. Westberg declined to answer. Annie then asked, "Did you [the U.S. Justice Department] make an investigation?" He replied no. Once again Annie asked, "How then can you say there wasn't sufficient evidence upon which to prosecute if you haven't looked for it?" Westberg explained the FBI and not his office was the investigative branch of the Justice Department.[4] "Why then has the FBI not done it?" questioned Annie. "We're not requesting it," came the reply from Westberg.

The ranchers had until November 15 to file government forms to claim any privately owned horses that might have been loose with the wild, free-roaming horses. On the form, the claimants were required to describe each horse and indicate any identifying markings on the animals. Joan Blue intended to "try like crazy" to keep the horses in North Platte until after the claiming deadline.[5] She believed the ranchers would not be financially able to travel to Nebraska to identify markings required on the claiming forms if the horses remained there.

Annie had already received written confirmation from the Bureau of Land Management that the horses would be returned to Idaho Falls as soon as a secure holding corral could be located. Few people wanted to take the risk of reprisals for harboring the controversial herd.

Wild Horse Annie's greatest concern was the determination of ownership. Her most vindictive adversary was the Idaho Falls district manager and his stonewalling behavior. She told a friend, "I don't expect an agency that is working on behalf of MY land, paid by MY money, to go out and tell deliberate lies to incite people. And I think there is plenty of grounds for a change of—well, do you think Australia could use him?"[6]

The government planned to handle the claiming process in a special manner to ensure that all interested parties had an opportunity to submit any evidence they may have gathered. One of the department's administrative-law judges would hear the case, and witnesses would be cross-examined. Combined with promises from Westberg and Mathews to allow the power of subpoena to protect the witnesses from their hostile neighbors, Annie believed the Howe, Idaho, case would receive a fair hearing. If it was a civil suit, Annie could have had her own attorney attend, but since it was a criminal matter, she had to depend on government prosecutors.

Wild Horse Annie asked for Mathews's cooperation in resolving the Howe, Idaho, case. She believed there were enough misunderstandings and personal animosity that the investigation would never be completely and satisfactorily settled unless everyone adhered strictly to the facts. Annie tried to soften any past animosity between the two when she concluded her conversation with Mathews. "And I would like to tell you this—I am deeply appreciative of your own personal courtesy to me. . . . I am a gentle woman. I was not reared to fight a rough-and-tough western shoot-em-out-at-the-OK-corral type of thing."[7]

In a recorded phone conversation with one of her informants, Annie sincerely expressed how much she was depending upon people in Howe to provide her with information. As she told one of her insiders, "I have nothing to lose other than my life. At this point, I'd gladly give it up if it will help. . . . I'm out on a limb on this. I've given everything I have. I don't mean money— I mean time, honor—my promises."

Annie knew she was hitting at the core of the problem. More hate mail, postmarked Idaho Falls, began arriving. In one letter, the writer claimed a bounty hunter allegedly said that in his own time, he would "do away" with the people involved in the roundup. The letter, forwarded to her via an Idaho resident, contained a comment from the original recipient: "Does that give you some kind of thrill to know that you have given some mixed-up person what he thinks is a good reason to kill? Maybe you are paying him to do it!"[8]

In a letter to George Turcott explaining what was occurring behind the scenes, Annie confided, "It isn't pleasant, knowing that someone believes I would or could do that . . . but I guess that's the price for standing up and being counted. I'll not back down on paying the price, but occasionally that thought crosses my mind that the 'bounty hunter idea' could work both ways."[9]

The two federal departments also announced plans that involved the impounded horses in North Platte. Because the declination to prosecute did not constitute a determination of ownership, the horses still had to be returned to Idaho as wards of the government until the ownership of the animals was substantiated under state law. If no valid claims could be made, the horses would be held until spring and then released to the Little Lost River Valley where the roundup originally took place.

The National Wild Horse and Burro Advisory Board continued to work on implementing the regulations for PL 92-195. In her capacity as a member of the board, Wild Horse Annie issued a searing commentary at the fourth board meeting on November 7, 1973. "At none of the previous meetings has there been any significant amount of time spent or action taken in regard to the protection factor of the Act," she said. Yet, she pointed out, within six weeks of the board's first meeting, "a roundup of free-roaming horses took place in the Little Lost River area in Idaho. Its brutality is well documented. . . . I, as a member of this board, and as an individual, feel very strongly that the roundup matter has been, and is being, handled in a highly unusual manner. The Bureau of Land Management has acknowledged that removal of certain horses from public rangeland was encouraged by a Bureau official (in violation of the Bureau's own directives, I might add)."[10]

Asked if the board would discuss the Howe, Idaho, situation, C. Wayne Cook, chairman of the board, expressed his opinion that the function of the board was not to be involved in every controversial issue that came along. Annie disagreed, stating that the board had good reason to intercede. Annie strongly believed the board would be derelict in its duties to the secretaries of the interior and agriculture, Congress, and the public if it did not become involved with the Howe, Idaho, case.

Annie continued her advocacy at the next board meeting. She proposed that the board recommend that Secretary of the Interior Rogers C. B. Morton and Secretary of the Agriculture Earl Butz request the Department of Justice reconsider their declination of criminal prosecution and conduct an intensive investigation into the roundup.

Once again, a death threat was issued against Wild Horse Annie and others who helped her. A reproduction of a Revolutionary War flag was sent like a burning cross to Annie—a gift from "a vigilante committee of 10,000." Joining the nameless roster of the clan of Idaho, Utah, Nevada, and Wyoming residents were several anonymous Idaho legislators, according to Idaho farmer Del Ray Holm, the only identified member. Holm said the group's enemies were environmentalists, state fish-and-game people, hunters, rustlers, vandals, and other state officers "who forget who owns private land." Although the members did not plan to shoot people, the vigilantes threatened to shoot any vehicles that belonged to people who did not seek the landowner's permission before crossing private land. Members were screened to keep "radicals" out of the organization.

The rally flag was a sketch of a coiled rattlesnake, with *morte* printed below; the Revolutionary War expression "Don't Tread on Me" was included. Along the outside edges were rally slogans, "Down with intervening layers of lawmaking bureaucracy! We will, unitedly, maintain our basic God-given rights!" Annie's "flag" was sent to her from Idaho Falls, addressed with childlike handwriting but written by an adult. The "vigilante committee of 10,000," which allegedly had 3,500 members, considered Wild Horse Annie to be an environ-mental troublemaker. I also received a similar present in the mail.

Annie was surprised she was losing the political support she had devel-oped prior to the Howe, Idaho, case. She recognized that she was caught between the repulsion most people felt after reading the details of the botched Idaho roundup and the fierce antigovernment sense of indepen-dence from members of the ranching community. It was beyond Annie's comprehension how she had lost on all levels of the Idaho case. Her motiva-tion for federal legislation was due to the submissiveness of western govern-ment officials whose jobs were maintained by special-interest groups. Their intentions had been to clear the range of wild horses so livestock and hunt-ing interests could flourish. "The original legislation," Annie lamented, "was drafted to exclude this type of state-level decisions, but as happens so often, a provision was added in committee to allow the decision of ownership to be rendered by a state official. And so, each victory is only a tiny plateau of rest before tackling another steep climb toward the Utopia we wish for the Wild Ones." She knew they would likely never reach their goal, "but we keep on reaching, and praying that we don't stumble and fall into utter defeat. What a saga this has been. What a challenge. What a heartache."[11]

Eight months after arriving in North Platte, Nebraska, the survivors of the Howe, Idaho, roundup returned to the stockyards in Idaho Falls. The ranchers had the local media ready. One of Max Palmer's children was mounted bareback on one of the horses and rode him gently around the pen with only a rope halter. The local press reported the alleged wild horses were gentle enough for a child to ride, but eyewitnesses who were familiar with Bish Jenkins's domestic horses knew that some of those horses were mixed in with the wild ones. The animal selected by young Palmer to ride was one of the domestic horses. The wild ones were huddled in a corner of the corral.

On June 18, 1974, the state branding committee called a hearing for the purpose of establishing ownership of the Little Lost River horses. Several members of the hearing board were friends of the roundup participants. Realizing there was a blatant lack of impartiality on the board, Annie opted not to participate in the hearing, especially since none of the witnesses for the prosecution was subpoenaed. The hearing was stacked in favor of the livestock people. Annie's personal attorney had no jurisdiction in Idaho and attended strictly as a spectator.

The American Horse Protection Association and the Humane Society of the United States had attorney Robert McCandless as their legal representative. Because he neglected to obtain the proper Idaho registration, he could not actively participate in the hearing, either. McCandless's request to have a television crew film the proceedings was denied by the judge to prevent showboating the emotional issue. Instead of opting for a more subdued part in the proceedings, McCandless dramatically stormed out of the hearing room, followed by Franz Dantzler. The sudden display caught everyone by surprise. No camera crew was available to record the parade out of the courtroom.

State brand hearing chairman J. Burns Beal continued the hearing following the walkout. "I don't understand either the reason for Mr. McCandless leaving but I do think it should be made clear for the record that it was not under any coercion or pressure from the Department of Brands nor from the counsel. Time has been offered either from the first week in July or the week of the 15th and we feel like this should be made part of the record."

Ten photographs, many of them taken by the ranchers' wives, were used to identify the horses. None of the ranchers was asked to actually prove ownership. Contrary to witnesses who personally examined the same horses, several horses in the pictures "developed" saddle marks, brands, and shoes, and several even became geldings. Some of those "geldings" sired mares while in captivity. The state brand inspector did not question the existence of immaculately conceived foals in the horse pens.

The attorneys led their clients through the hearing and asked irrelevant questions like "Are you a good judge of horse-flesh? What do you think is a wild horse?" The legal description of a wild, free-roaming horse was already established by federal law, but ignored by the state brand board. Even though the actual horses were within a commutable distance, the board chose to use the snapshots to identify brands, recent or old gelding marks, shoes, and the degree of domesticity in the horses.

Throughout the entire investigation, there were many contradictions. Ownership of the horses, lack of brand certification for transporting the horses out of state, lack of determination whether the horses were geldings or stallions, and knowledge of the federal laws were topics debated among the roundup participants, government officials, and humane societies. Even Sheriff Lords falsely claimed Wild Horse Annie was at the roundup—which was of course totally inaccurate. His support of the mustangers being "humanitarians who wouldn't do anything to harm the horses" was retracted when the evidence became overwhelming against the Little Lost River mustangers.

On September 3, 1974, Judge J. Burns Beal reached his decision. The surviving horses of the roundup in January and February 1973 were "domesticated" horses and not "wild." Beal also determined that, based on the evidence presented, the horses were the property of claimant Max Palmer, rancher and livestock auction-yard operator. Beal's conclusion was formulated after examining the pictures that allegedly showed branded, halter-marked, and shod horses and from the photo captions that described the male horses as being gelded. Quoting from Beal's report, "Unless gelding was done after capture and there is no indication of recent gelding, nor remarks in the record about recent gelding of any of the horses, the fact that horses were gelded leads to the conclusion that the horses have been domesticated."

Tempers stayed hot after the hearing. The residents, not used to people looking in on their business, were becoming increasingly angry. Don Cammack, editor and owner of the *Arco Advertiser*, printed an editorial a year after the actual roundup. Cammack acknowledged, "Honest difference of opinion and occurrences over which no one had any control formed the basis of stories and actions which brought outsiders into the area to meddle in things of which they had little understanding at best. To be sure, the outsiders wish to do only good. But do-gooders have a habit of jumping in and stirring things with a dirty stick with the result that communities of good honest hard-working neighbors are agitated, pushed around, scandalized and kept from doing the jobs they are best able to do." But now that the "do-gooders" brought the case to an international audience and the surviving horses in question had been returned to Idaho, Cammack had a simple question for the "do-gooders": "Why don't they go home and mind their own business?"[12]

Annie had additional trouble on the home front. Joan Blue was preparing a lawsuit and contacted Steve Pellegrini with a proposition to send him to Idaho Falls and identify the Idaho Falls horses as wild. Pellegrini, a wild horse research biologist, described the tenor of the request during a phone conversation with Annie. "What irritated me the most was that she didn't ask me to go up there, to form an opinion. She told me to go up there and prove that those are wild horses. Well, I couldn't do that even if I wanted to."[13]

Blue demanded an affidavit from Annie describing her meeting with Paul

Westberg and his lack of action to conduct a federal investigation. When Annie diplomatically wrote that "to his knowledge, there had been no investigation," the split between the two organizations became irreparable.

More behind-the-scenes dealings surfaced in December 1974. According to Max Palmer and various wire service stories, American Horse Protection Association attorney Robert McCandless phoned Palmer and discussed the horse status for more than an hour. In what Palmer interpreted as a threat or a bribe, "[McCandless] told me if I let him have the horses, that [the AHPA] would drop all charges and they would go ahead and try to mend the laws—that they would drop all charges and have a news release—that I would deal with them and be a good guy and give them the horses—and they said we'd both be heroes!"[14]

Palmer gained respect for Wild Horse Annie's integrity and style. A velvet glove often earns more reconciliation from the opposition than does a vindictive nature. When McCandless called Palmer the next day, Palmer said he would not sell the horses to the American Horse Protection Association because he was already cooperating with Annie.

In desperation, McCandless asked what Palmer would take for the horses if the American Horse Protection Association made a bid that day. Palmer reiterated that the horses were not for sale. In an attempt to stop McCandless from badgering him any longer, Palmer, who operated the Rexburg, Idaho, livestock auction, said he would take fourteen thousand dollars for the fourteen surviving horses. McCandless laughed and countered with an offer of five hundred for the whole lot—a figure well below the rate paid even at the slaughterhouse. The American Horse Protection Association misinterpreted the information, and a press release hit the media, quoting Palmer as saying he wanted fourteen thousand dollars or he was going to kill the horses. "So the government really got real upset and got after me this morning," Max Palmer confided to Annie. "All I done was try to be right."[15]

Once again, McCandless called Palmer. A counteroffer of two thousand dollars was made and declined. Max reiterated he was trying to cooperate with Annie in the hope the horses could be brought to auction, where everyone would have an equal opportunity to obtain them. According to Palmer, McCandless allegedly told him, "Well, there isn't going to be any auction. If you won't sell them to us, you won't get them for yourself."[16]

Palmer respected Wild Horse Annie as an ethical western woman who was aware of western livestock problems and understood the ramifications of the federal wild horse laws she had helped draft. Palmer admitted, "If you and I could have sat down together, that thing (the roundup and subsequent ownership squabble) could have worked out without this mess."[17]

The transfer of ownership of the horses to the American Horse Protection Association and the Humane Society of the United States without the benefit of written agreements would have been media suicide for the principals involved with the roundup. The credibility of both organizations in this particular matter was rapidly deteriorating following their orchestrated walkout at the state brand hearing. The ranchers knew Joan Blue would not turn the ranchers into "good guys," nor could she get the government to drop any charges, nor could she change the federal law to accommodate the ranchers' cooperation.

Wild Horse Annie welcomed calls from the people she opposed. It gave her an opportunity to explain her purpose in fighting for the preservation of the horses without alienating her opponents. When Frank Hartmann Jr. called, Annie explained her perspective: "My main objective was to halt this trespass—this free-loading on our public land resources by the commercial dealers—the traffickers in horse flesh." She pointed out that the commercial interests were getting hundreds of horses for which they would pay no grazing fee. She hoped that "when it's all finally over and the dust has settled, we're going to have a lot better situation on our ranges than we ever had before. That's why 'management' is in the terms of the [Wild Horse] Act. But I've always said that it must be selectively and humanely done. That's what my fight has been all about."[18]

The ranchers were surprised to learn there was a difference between Wild Horse Annie and Joan Blue. Annie explained the difference to Hartmann. "You should be becoming aware by now—sometimes there are people that you just cannot work with. And if you knew the two of us, personally, there is as much difference as daylight and dark. Mine is the velvet glove maybe on an iron hand. I am a lady, a respected lady, and I have worked all my life among great men." She asserted she had been "so shabbily treated and so unfairly judged [by the American Horse Protection Association] because I have never waived in my intent that I began in 1950 . . . to get a niche carved for these animals in balance with Mother Nature."[19]

The case against the government was stubbornly fought at the physical expense of the horses. Normally, the hooves of the wild horses are kept trimmed by running across rough, rocky terrain. In the holding corral, the hooves grew out and split, requiring the horses to walk on painful "elf shoes." It was not easy to keep a wild horse's feet trimmed. The longer the people kept the battle in the courts, the more harm occurred to the horses.

In May 1975, Wild Horse Annie received two communications from the Idaho state director of the Bureau of Land Management. During normal hoof maintenance on the horses still held in protective custody in Idaho Falls, one horse died. "While immobilizing a black mare to give the tranquilizer, she fought the rope, breaking a leg. The veterinarian saw no alternative but to destroy her with a hypodermic injection." Two weeks later, on May 14, a palomino stallion died from a heart attack. "Dr. Dale Kinghorn performed an autopsy and found the stallion's heart to be about one quarter larger than normal, scar tissue and nodules from previous attacks, and one ventricle completely closed off."[20]

The BLM wrote there were now thirteen horses in protective custody—five stallions, five mares, a two-year-old-filly, and two yearling colts. Annie called acting state director Clair M. Whitlock. As recorded in her shorthand transcript, Whitlock referred to stallions. The moral ethics of the U.S. Department of the Interior and the livestock industry remained questionable to Annie. The horses, after all, had been rounded up with district manager Jones's approval—during a time when such roundups were prohibited. The horses were then shipped as stallions to a packing plant. Eighteen months later the Idaho state brand inspector looked at photographs and made the legally binding determination that the horses were domestic geldings. Back in Idaho, the same horses once again became stallions.

The September 1974 State of Idaho decree was overturned by an appeals court in the District of Columbia in February 1977, and the case remanded back to the district court. At that time, the district judge asked the parties involved to seek a solution that would be satisfactory to all. The final agreement was established on two major points: local ranchers would relinquish all claims to the animals to the United States, and the Bureau of Land Management would place the animals in the custody of individuals seeking to adopt excess horses under the adoption program sponsored by the agencies (in accordance with the Wild Horse and Burro Act). No government officials or participants in the roundup were prosecuted or reprimanded. Ed Jones quietly retired.

Four years of court battles and flip-flopping decisions made the wild horses the losers. Only eleven of the original sixty-four horses survived.

Instead of keeping the battle tied up in the courts any longer, Wild Horse Annie withdrew from the fight because of her health, and Joan Blue graciously agreed to an agreement with the Bureau of Land Management.

The American Horse Protection Association had long been an opponent of the adopt-a-horse program, but in this case, Blue agreed to adopt the horses despite the two stipulations dictated by the BLM. The government was well aware of the organization's flamboyant use of the media and constant use of the court system. The AHPA could have the horses if it dropped the suit against the BLM and signed the following agreement: "These animals shall not be used for purpose of publicity by the assignee or by the individuals having custody, or made available to any other person or organization for such purpose, including photographs, articles, exhibition, newspapers, newsletters, congressional hearings, posters, or any other printed material or similar uses for fund raising, membership drives, etc. except that there will be one story which may be published, to which story BLM agrees."[21] The American Horse Protection Association was furious with the stipulations, but accepted the horses. The eleven survivors of the Howe, Idaho, roundup were transferred to private farms in the Maryland and Virginia area. The Howe, Idaho, case was a stalemate. No one, especially the horses, won.

While she weathered the Howe, Idaho, case, Annie found that correspondence with her friends and supporters helped her regain her spirit. "In obedience to doctor's orders, I have slowed up, and that is why I get less done and more and more piles up to be done."[22] However, she had enough strength to release pent-up frustration in a letter to one of her supporters:

> I'm damned if I can overlook how WHOA! has been cut out of everything to do with the news media. There is no intention of recognizing that anybody did anything but HSUS and AHPA, but we'll see about that. Isn't it awful why all of us, supposedly working toward the same goal, can't deal fairly with each other? I've had several telephone calls . . . asking what WHOA! has been doing! And here, by God, had it not been for WHOA! the "heroes" would have nothing to be heroic about, and those damned ranchers would have gotten away with it. I'm bitter. YUP.[23]

The battle over the Howe, Idaho, massacre created as much internal fission among the wild horse opponents as it did between the advocates and the critics. Former president of the American Horse Protection Association Pearl Twyne left the organization and its vice president, Joan Blue, and joined directly with Wild Horse Annie. The dispute over Blue's aggressive and vindictive tactics and Annie's more diplomatic style escalated after the passage of PL 92-195.

In a confidential memo to Representative Baring's assistant, Annie wrote in reference to the American Horse Protective Association and the U.S. Humane Association, "I am sure you know I'm not naïve, or dumb, and can recognize the 'take-over' that is being enacted. For instance, the letter that clearly identified only the two Eastern organizations . . . with no mention of the group I head up, or me." She was determined not to let personalities or internal conflict "rock the boat, for the least indication of friction could scuttle the whole movement. . . . But all that is beside the point of what I started to write in this note—that whoever gets the credit is not as important as winning the fight."

The Howe, Idaho, decision finally was made, and Annie faded from the long-standing battle with Joan Blue. Congress was tired of the emotional pleas from eastern horse groups trying to compete with Wild Horse Annie. The same newspapers that supported the fight to save the horses saw there was no progress in the fight and moved on to other stories. The government did not know who to listen to, as a myriad of organizations attempted to out-shout the others as the self-appointed future successors to Wild Horse Annie.

12

FEDERAL OR STATE LAW?

When the Wild Free-Roaming Horse and Burro Act of 1971 was passed, the advisory board failed to develop a strategic long-range plan for the management, protection, and control of the animals. Likewise, the responsible agencies—the U.S. Department of the Interior and the U.S. Department of Agriculture—failed to prepare for the predictable confrontations that would immediately escalate over cultural differences.

The culture of the modern West began when the first settlers combined the animal management techniques of the Native American Indians and the vaqueros of Spain and Mexico with the settlers' own adaptations. The independence of the American cowboy became an international cultural icon. But in real life, the American cowboy was very self-assured and more comfortable in isolation than being scrutinized by urban media and Washington bureaucrats.

The ranchers and their former-ranching government overseers bristled as the nonranching "do-gooders" began passing county, state, and federal laws to challenge the long-established American cowboy style of range management. When the second federal legislation was passed in 1971, it became the tipping point that prompted retaliation by the livestock community.

Some people simplified the wild horse and burro issues on humanitarian grounds. The real source of contention was actually the confluence of cultural issues and historical heritage complicated by the cowboy sense of self-reliance and independence and the governmental world of regulations and bureaucratic standards. Wild Horse Annie's campaign challenged the livestock culture for its lack of respect for the equine heritage and myopic view of the causes of range deterioration while employing a grassroots campaign that was foreign to the bureaucratic administrative template of the federal agencies.

Without the development of a long-range strategic land-management plan that took these cultural differences into consideration, wild horse and burro decisions were arbitrarily made. The academic-style wild horse and burro advisory board was a new cultural entity to the debate and was still developing the guidelines on how the federal law would be implemented, several years after the passage of the law. A preexisting administrative attitude of "remove the horses" to manage the rangeland for livestock was already in place. The federal law to stop what was already being done had little effect. A committee was established to study the issue that was already under way in order to create federal regulations to govern it. This literally was a matter of putting the bureaucratic cart before the horse. Once the 1971 law was passed, ranchers began to try to execute as many roundups of wild horses and burros as possible before the guidelines were ready for use to prosecute violators of the law.

In the simpler years of Annie's campaign, the battle lines were drawn on a local level between the "save the horses" faction and the livestock industry. After 1971 Annie had to contend with the same two components of the debate plus the competitive federal agencies that were administered by the Bureau of Land Management, the Forest Service, and military and Indian agencies. Each agency contributed its own cultural style of administering the wild horses and burros. The advent of new and competing "save the horses" factions had now morphed into a directionless wave of well-intentioned advocates who often appealed to emotion. Later, some of the organizations combined legal research and media relations in ways that were unfamiliar to either the livestock industry or the federal agencies.

Wild Horse Annie's interchangeable missions between the International Society for the Protection of Mustangs and Burros and the Wild Horse Organized Assistance organizations served as a "voice of reason" for the time being. However, being led by the charismatic founder and chief executive officer left little opportunity for Annie's administrative silent partners (Helen Reilly and Dawn Lappin) to step in should Annie no longer be able to continue the fight. The effectiveness of ISPMB and WHOA! was dependent upon the continuation of Annie's charismatic leadership. Annie's health was weakening, as was her ability to arbitrate lasting solutions among the cultures that were involved with the complicated western cultural land-management issues.

Several efforts were initiated throughout the West to get the federal law repealed and revert control of the public lands to the individual states. Cliff Young, state senator and Nevada native, questioned the wisdom of the return to state control in a letter to the *Reno Evening Gazette*. He wondered how a country that was generous in helping foreign countries could do "so little to rehabilitate and increase productivity of our Western rangelands." He noted that 70 percent of the western public lands was under the control of the Bureau of Land Management. But he also noted that any attempt to curb abuses to the federal land or institute reforms raised the voices of politically strong organizations throughout the country, a loggerhead that accomplished nothing but delay meaningful reforms. He quoted President Theodore Roosevelt from a half century earlier: "To waste, to destroy our natural resources, to skin and exhaust the land instead of using it so as to increase its usefulness, will result in undermining in the days of our children the very prosperity which we ought by right to hand down to them amplified and developed."

Senator Young had optimistic expectations of the 1971 law as "a progressive, long-range, hard-nosed policy to correct deteriorating conditions of Nevada rangelands for the benefit of wildlife, livestock, wild horses, and other users." He recognized the acceptance of the law would be "a hard and positive step forward against predictable opposition." He realized some members of the livestock industry and persons in high political office would condemn the measure. Without pointing fingers, Senator Young said past range-management policies had been neglectful in preserving what they set out to preserve.

His letter to the editor continued with his observation that most people would not want to expend government funding on something that might be a low priority to most Americans, but Young explained there is never an opportune time to begin a proper management program that is satisfactory to all vested interests. With the current state of the range condition, he could justify no reason to delay.

Other states, however, did not share Young's interest in moving ahead with the wild horse and burro program. New Mexico cattlemen moved to challenge the legality of the federal law. In 1974 Kelley Stephensen, a New Mexico rancher, found several unbranded and unclaimed burros trespassing on his private property and the public land for which he had a cattle-grazing permit. The burros, Stephensen claimed, were "molesting" his cattle and eating their livestock feed supplements. Stephensen requested, to no avail, that the Bureau of Land Management remove the burros from his land. Out of frustration, Stephensen contacted the New Mexico Livestock Board, which took it upon themselves to gather the nineteen burros in question and sell them at auction, pursuant to the provisions under the New Mexico estray laws. The ranchers' lawyers were convinced Congress failed to prove that the wild burros were innocent of range damage on the public lands. The case was brought before a three-judge federal panel in Albuquerque on February 28, 1975. The panel ruled the Wild Free-Roaming Horse and Burro Act of 1971 was unconstitutional and permanently enjoined and restrained the federal government from enforcing it.

The next day, a board of county commissioners in Nevada began issuing wild horse hunting permits.[1] The reaction from Wild Horse Annie was swift and definite. "We expect the commercial mustangers to be out in full force. If something isn't done, there won't be a wild horse left on the range in 50–60 days." She noted that horse meat was now selling for sixteen to twenty-four cents a pound; if wild horses conservatively weigh five hundred pounds, each horse was minimally worth one hundred dollars on the hoof. A gathering of just one hundred horses would bring in at least ten thousand dollars for just a few days' work. "Wild horses and burros are unprotected at this time against any kind of capture or slaughter," Annie told the *Deseret News* of Salt Lake City. "I imagine they are piling up already."

Dean Rhoads, public lands chairman of the Nevada Cattleman's Association, took offense at Wild Horse Annie's statement as "an emotional appeal to the unknowledgeable public for further support to promote unreasonable legislation. This is the same emotional appeal that involved use in the destructive, unmanaged situation that existed under the Wild Horse Act."

Thomas Ballow, director of the Nevada State Agriculture Department, maintained the loss of the federal law was "a step forward as far as state's rights is concerned. . . . I'm satisfied myself that the county commissioners and ranchers will act in a responsible manner so they don't stir up any sympathies and antagonisms." E. I. Rowland, Nevada state director of the Bureau of Land Management (formerly the Colorado state director), supported Ballow's opinion that Annie's prediction of wild horse and burro slaughter was unjustified.

Lee Garner, executive director of the New Mexico State Livestock Board, likewise seemed surprised at the outcry his organization's challenge to the federal law created among the general public. "Don't get me wrong, I don't dislike wild horses. I just don't want to see some old wild plug grazing on land that a good horse or some cattle could use better. They're good for nothing, now that we can't round them up and sell them for pet food."

Wild Horse Annie, in a *Nevada State Journal* article, explained, "This is beyond the fate of a flesh-and-blood animal now. This boils down to restricting the dominant commercial use of our public lands in favor of conservation and preservation of our streams, forests, and even horses; so there's something left for future generations. It's been a long fight—twenty-five years for me. We might have to begin it all over again. But there are a lot of young people coming along now."

While the Supreme Court argued the merits of the claim, WHOA! was offered an unusual proposition by the counsel general of the United States to become a participating amicus curiae (a friend of the court) in the appeal. Because the docket for the U.S. Supreme Court was filled, the hearing would not be held until the following year. On March 14, 1975, the Washington Bureau of Land Management issued a memorandum from the associate director to all state BLM offices: "Until otherwise notified, take no further action under the Act [PL 92-195]."

The federal law confused both mustangers and BLM officials. James Gabettas, acting district manager of the Boise District Bureau of Land Management office in Idaho, recollected that Lyle Buhler called his office to explain he just shot two horses on public lands. Gabettas's manager informed him that if the horses were wild, his action was still in violation of the wild horse protection act. Buhler responded that he did not think he was in violation of the act.

The Washington office disregarded Wild Horse Annie's premonition and maintained there would not be a slaughter of wild horses by vindictive livestock owners, but Annie was quietly collecting sworn and signed affidavits of planned wild horse roundups. She learned that a central Nevada rancher had already obtained permission from the county commissioners and posted a two-thousand-dollar bond.

Jimmy Williams, a noted mustanger himself, came to Annie's defense when he provided an affidavit that one of the Fallini ranching family members posted bond for a gathering permit with the district attorney in Tonopah, Nevada. Fallini planned to "annihilate" a herd of approximately eight hundred wild horses while "this thing on wild horses is up in the air." Williams told the BLM district manager that he was concerned that if everyone started chasing or shooting wild horses again, people like himself would not be able to gather wild horses for sale.

On the basis of the affidavits Annie collected, a "stay of judgment" was passed in federal court, bringing the federal law temporarily back into effect. In commenting on the situation, Jack Horton, assistant secretary for land and water resources for the BLM, stated, "At this time, we cannot predict how long this stay order will be in effect. However, unless or until it is revoked, the Department will continue to fully enforce provisions of the 1971 Act."

Despite the stay of judgment, the Bureau of Land Management continued to receive reports about individuals killing or capturing wild equines grazing on public lands. The Justice Department contrarily advised the Bureau of Land Management to enforce the law, but they should stop short of making arrests of any persons who may be caught violating the Wild Free-Roaming Horse and Burro Act. In typical bureaucratic language, the BLM was instructed to document all situations involving alleged improprieties and explain to the violators the wild horse and burro regulations were still in effect. If they refused to stop their alleged illegal actions, the government employee was supposed to leave the scene and contact the nearest U.S. attorney.

While New Mexico's challenge to the constitutionality of the Wild Free-Roaming Horse and Burro Act was being argued, Wild Horse Annie scheduled another field trip to a wild horse area prior to a meeting of the National Wild Horse and Burro Advisory Board. In Stone Cabin Valley, north of Las Vegas, Nevada, a rancher acknowledged 800 horses were grazing in the adjacent Reveille Valley, where his cattle competed for 25,000 AUMs. His 2,120 head of cattle grazed there all year (using 25,440 AUMs) without an opportunity for range rehabilitation. His permit allowed him to graze 25 horses, but he claimed that of the 800 wild horses, 75 were actually his.

The BLM *Management Framework Plan* written in 1966 indicated "severe grazing by horses" was recorded in the area. "This same area is identified in the MFP as critical deer summer range," according to the report. In 1957, the BLM district manager reported 50 wild horses were in the area. A joint BLM-district advisory board determined 125–50 roamed the area in 1966. The following year, the BLM recorded 139 horses; in March 1969, an airplane count identified 288 horses. A helicopter inventory in January 1973 spotted 748. The July 1974 census reported 917 horses. The BLM report justified the erratic census numbers by explaining the counts were made at different times of the year. Seasonally, the horses from the Nellis Air Force Base Bombing and Gunnery Range were known to drift across U.S. Highway 6 and into the Reveille Valley.

Horses were gathered in the Stone Cabin Valley area prior to the passage of the Wild Horse Annie Act in 1959, according to the BLM *Management Framework Plan*. Until the late 1940s, local ranchers allegedly introduced "high quality pure bred horses into the wild horse herds and actively culled the bands to improve the quality of these horses." Anecdotal information from local residents reported that "several thousand horses were harvested from this area during the 1940s," continued the report.

In the spring of 1975, Annie explained there would be a "gathering" (as she euphemistically mocked the working of the BLM announcement of the wild horse roundup) of approximately half of the 800–950 claimed free-roaming domestic and wild horses in the Battle Mountain District of the Bureau of Land Management, commencing the first of May. The Clifford brothers, ranchers in Stone Cabin Valley, filed for a permit to gather the horses, claiming them as privately owned. "This is the 'blighted' area (caused by horses, naturally, ha! ha!) south of Tonopah, and in my opinion ALL use should be terminated—permanently." Annie continued to describe the range as being in very bad condition following the worst drought in thirty years. In her opinion, there were too many livestock on that range, some left there on the public land year-round. "Lots of politics involved," Annie warned.

She explained that this was the same area toured by the National Wild Horse and Burro Advisory Board five months earlier and again with another committee of which she was also a member.[2] "On that first field trip," Annie related, "the ranchers had gathered and were hostile—damned hostile. Trouble could have exploded like a Fourth of July fireworks display. Guess you know who was right in the middle of it. That was when, I learned later, a mountain-lion bounty hunter planned to kill me, but there were too many people around."

Annie was fighting two battles—a public battle on behalf of the wild horses and burros and a private one against her own physical gremlins, as she described her health. She was a little more frail looking, but she was successful in masking her health problems from even her closest friends—at least until her fingers reached the typewriter keys. "I've been ill," she uncharacteristically

Wild Horse Annie at the site of the Stone Cabin Valley roundup near Tonopah, Nevada, as a member of the National Wild Horse and Burro Advisory Board as well as the president of two advocacy organizations. Courtesy of the author.

wrote. "Three levels of discs deteriorated and progressing; oral surgery; headaches blinding—you name it. Am at the office today for a few minutes before I keep my appoint[ment] at the MD."

Annie's doctor lectured her in vain to relax. "All that crap about my back and the deteriorating discs and the agonizing arthritis has been only a prelude to the latest developments, and I'm having to learn to live a whole new life." At one time the fourteen pounds of fluid buildup gave her a feeling of having a nice new figure, but the blood work, EKG, and X-rays at the doctor's office provided the diagnosis—heart failure. "All my health problems finally culminated in heart failure (literally) and I am on slow, slow schedule." Annie wrote. "No stress, no physical activity. Digitalis to regulate my heartbeat. Lots of rest. And the medical man says IF I adhere strictly [to his instructions] in a month or so he can start building me up again. I've been one mighty ill Annie. But so many of my friends wonder how I've been able to go like a bat out of hell all these years anyway. Guess I've been pushing too hard. The New Mexico decision seemed to have put the frosting on the cake."

Annie succinctly related her doctor's summary: "You've worn [your heart] out and there's no going back, Annie. No more stress, either mentally or physically. No more pushing physically, either. You may continue to live IF you control your activities to a point where your heart can keep up with your body, but it is enlarged and very, very tired. You used it all up on your wild ones."[3]

Somehow, Annie held things together. Whether her doctor was aware of her trip from Reno to Tonopah (with Helen Reilly accompanying her) or not, she accepted the invitation of the BLM to meet the Cliffords prior to the proposed "gathering." She was hard-pressed to find any forage on the bone-dry wasteland void of anything but rare patches of grass, shaded by scrub oak and other brush. For several hours, Annie and her entourage listened to the ranchers describe the damage allegedly done to the rangeland during just the past two years. It was disingenuous to place the blame upon the withers of the wild horses. Annie could not believe that any rancher could maintain a living there with a livestock operation amid the sagebrush and rocks in the barren land in Stone Cabin Valley where the Clifford family had its own colorful history.

Brothers Ed and James Clifford discovered a vein of silver in the Stone Cabin Valley in December 1905 and sold the claim for $250,000. Prominent silver miners (including Charles Schwab and "Diamonfield Jack" Davis) flocked to the area. The growth in the town of Clifford peaked in 1908 before the town began to die. There was a brief revival in 1925 when the Clifford Gold Mines Company purchased the claims before the town died again in 1929. The last two buildings in the town of Clifford burned in 1946, according to ghost-town writer David A. Wright. Guy Rocha, former Nevada state archivist, wrote that the Clifford family ranch, in addition to the silver legacy, might also be "the oldest, continuously operating family-owned ranch in Nye County."

The poor range conditions warranted an emergency reduction of livestock and wild horses. Annie accepted the decision to reduce the overall wild horse herd down to 400 horses—half the estimated population of wild horses in the area. Annie and WHOA!'s wild horse adoption coordinator, Dawn Lappin, were quickly able to find and screen 192 applicants to "adopt" some of the horses for domestic purposes. By July 1975, the Battle Mountain BLM District Office reported receiving 1,600 requests to adopt the horses from forty-eight states, Canada, and Puerto Rico.

The 120-day roundup contract was issued to Thomas Warr of Las Vegas to gather 400 horses at a cost of $26.50 per horse. The thirty-one-year-old was employed as an engineer for the City of Las Vegas Fire Department, part-time rodeo rider, and horseshoer by trade. His horse "running" experience began in northern Utah in 1958 as a teenager. "I started running horses for the sheer challenge of it," he explained in a BLM press release. In the early 1960s, he moved on to Ely, Nevada, and began successfully water-trapping wild horses. "I just chased them and caught them because it was fun to do.

It was just the challenge. The ones we'd manage to catch we'd either keep or give them away for ranch stock. But I never did use any aircraft or any mechanical means. I never did sell any horses to any dog-food outfit or for any other inhumane purpose."

The BLM planned to experiment with Wild Horse Annie's idea to conduct the roundup as gently as possible. Corrals were built around existing water holes and left unattended while the horses got used to the wooden structures surrounding their normal sources of water. A spring-loaded gate was kept open until the horses approached the water hole. "The traps are the manual kind and someone will be behind a blind to close the gates on the horses," Warr explained. The horses then could be directed through a narrow passage and loaded onto stock trucks. If that approach failed, horsemen would be dispatched to haze the horses toward the corral trap using nineteenth-century technology.

The roundup commenced on July 23. Unlike other humane organizations that tried to stop the roundup in court, WHOA! did not oppose the roundup. It was in compliance with the National Advisory Board, under full supervision by four representative of WHOA! and a representative from the Animal Protection Institute of America.

Within five days, the Federal Bureau of Investigation abruptly stopped the roundup. The Bureau of Land Management contractors gathered the first 70–75 horses, but the Nevada state agricultural director, Thomas Ballow, impounded the animals. Ballow claimed his agency was responsible for livestock-related issues in Nevada, and horses were the property of the State of Nevada under state statutes covering unbranded, unclaimed animals running at large. By state law, the ranchers would be provided with an opportunity to file a claim of ownership—a requirement that was conveniently easy to do with a wink and a nod before the federal laws were passed to remove the cozy relationship between state administrators and the livestock industry. "We've got a dispute over ownership," Tom Ballow told the *Prescott (Ariz.) Courier,* and by law when we have such a case, the state agriculture department has the responsibility for determining the rightful owner. You've got the federal government on one hand saying they own the horses and they're rounding them up, but you've got the ranchers on the other hand saying they own them."

A spokesperson for Nevada governor Mike O'Callaghan said the governor "was surprised" by Ballow's decision and suggested the state agricultural director meet with the deputy attorney general to "check out the legal aspects" of what Ballow had done by stopping a federal roundup. People around the country who came to Nevada to collect their adopted wild horses also filed complaints with the governor's office.

The Clifford brothers took claim on the horses, but rescinded their decision when they realized that claim to ownership also included a substantial penalty for grazing unlicensed horses on the public land without paying the grazing fees. Annie noted the brothers dropped the claim that the domestic or wild horses were their private stock—"too much trespass fee," she sarcastically commented in a letter. "They've been helping themselves to [the wild horses] up until December 15, 1971 [the date the Wild Free-Roaming Horse and Burro Act was signed into law], and selling them for commercial processing."

Carl Gidlund, a public relations BLM spokesperson, was concerned the 75 horses would die because they could fight among themselves in the crowded holding pens. The BLM flack raised Annie's ire when he told reporters, "It's too bad we're at loggerheads because both the federal government and the state want the same result—fewer wild horses on rangelands," according to an interview published in the *Kingman (Ariz.) Daily Miner*.

The bureaucratic stalemate between the state and federal agencies that claimed jurisdictional governance over the wild horses remained unresolved. Neither agency was willing to pay the bill to house the animals while testosterone between the agencies flared. Since the BLM authorized the roundup, assistant interior secretary Jack Horton and BLM national director Curt Berklund instructed Ed Rowland, BLM director for Nevada, to release the horses for humanitarian reasons. When the *Los Angeles Times* tried to contact Ballow for comment, the state agricultural director was unavailable.

Annie hailed the decision because she claimed the ranchers and Ballow's state agency were not acting in good faith during the process to resolve the land-management problem. "We feel the livestock people have forfeited their right to demand a reduction in the wild horses," Annie told a United Press International reporter.

In late September, the jurisdictional dispute was worked out between the state and federal agencies. Ninety-seven adult horses and 15 colts were water trapped during the first week of the revived Stone Cabin Valley roundup. Because of overcrowding, the horses were moved to Battle Mountain while state brand inspectors completed blood tests and other studies. Seven horses died, mostly of broken necks after the gate closed at the water hole; the animals had panicked and tried to escape the trap. A federal lawsuit filed by the American Horse Protection Association attempted to stop the roundup once again, but remained under review by a federal judge in Las Vegas while the roundup continued.

WHOA!'s adoption volunteers were able to process applications for 200 of the 230 horses gathered and placed them with private individuals within two weeks through Annie's organizations. A volunteer network of horsemen from WHOA! as well as the National Mustang Association and local humane societies monitored the welfare of the adopted horses in around-the-clock shifts at the holding pens and did follow-up visits wherever the horses were stabled after their adoption. The animals remained under the official ownership of the BLM to ensure they would not be sold for slaughter. Both BLM district manager Gene Nodine and Wild Horse Annie were pleased with the results of this government-nonprofit partnership. According to Nodine, the three-hundred-dollar cost per animal collected was increased threefold by the state challenge and the AHPA lawsuit in Washington, D.C.

Nodine worried that under the federal law, any horses that were gathered but not placed with private individuals would have to be destroyed. The waiting list of potential adoptees gathered by Wild Horse Annie's organization relieved him of his fear. The national publicity about Annie's horse adoption program brought in 1,600 applications for the 400 horses.

The deaths among the horses trying to escape were tragic, but the casualties may have been higher if more aggressive procedures were used. It was a phone call that Annie received in mid-July the following year that brought a greater sense of accomplishment and relief.

By unanimous decision on July 17, 1976, the U.S. Supreme Court ruled that Congress was entirely within its constitutional rights when it enacted the 1971 Wild Free-Roaming Horse and Burro Act. Speaking for the Supreme Court, Justice Thurgood Marshall said the power of Congress over public lands, under the property clause of the Constitution, "necessarily includes the power to regulate and protect the wildlife living there."

The Supreme Court decision denied the validity of the New Mexico, Idaho, Nevada, and Wyoming attempts to claim the 1971 law as unconstitutional and invalid. It took more than a year, but Wild Horse Annie won an unexpected but crucial legal victory. The stature of the Wild Horse and Burro Act of 1971 was returned to full effect, and the 19 captured burros in New Mexico were released to private individuals under the federal adoption program.

Wild Horse Annie boldly continued with her long-standing belief that the public lands were not designated for the exclusive use of special-interest groups or industries. It was very apparent to her that returning the control to the states would have made it easier to renew the exploitation of the wild horses and burros because local decisions could be manipulated to the benefit of the exploiters. "Yet," Annie interjected, "it is because of overuse and abuse by many among these personal profit-motivated operations, that our public land resource has been brought to a state of near-depletion so seriously that in many areas, wild and domestic animals are threatened with starvation, and in some, the point of no-return has already been reached."

Annie had cause to celebrate. "Well—June seventeenth was a 'red, white and blue champagne kind of a day!' The news of the unanimous decision by the Supreme Court was telephoned to me at my home, just as I was leaving for work. I stopped at the florist's and picked up a big floral arrangement of red, white and blue, tied with a huge bow of the same colors, and an American flag tucked in beside them. Thence to the market where I bought champagne, and some proper glasses."

While the champagne chilled all day in the office refrigerator, Annie and her crew answered the telephones—congratulatory calls and coast-to-coast interviews with news media. That afternoon representatives from the BLM met with Annie to discuss how to resolve philosophical and management differences. When the formal aspects of the meeting were over, the BLM employees joined Annie in a glass of champagne. "We toasted America first," wrote Annie, "because only in America could this incredible saga have been written; then the Supreme Court whose unanimous decision put the frosting on the cake; then the wild ones; then each other—until the last cork had been popped."

When Annie returned home, Trudy Bronn requested they put a particular record on the stereo. Annie had ordered a copy of *America Sings,* and fortuitously the disk arrived that day. Mother and daughter put the album on the stereo phonograph. As she wrote to a friend

A bit of "eye moisture" came with "This Land is Your Land"; a bit more with "Battle Hymn of the Republic," and when "O Beautiful for Spacious Skies" came, the dam broke and I cried as I haven't cried for years! That was what was played at the funeral of my beloved friend, Congressman Walter Baring, who fought so hard for the wild ones and me first in 1959 and again in 1971. Guess it was the release of the tension that had been building up ever since February 1975 when New Mexico declared our law unconstitutional. Or maybe it was the bubbly. At any rate, it did me a world of good. And we are still on cloud nine![4]

As a result of the clear violation of PL 92-195 by the New Mexico Livestock Board, the Bureau of Land Management attempted to bill the New Mexico organization for expenses incurred as a result of their actions. Jim Scott asked the federal government for $9,060 to cover expenses for housing and taking care of the burros from February 1974 (when the animals were initially impounded at the auction) until March 1975. He also billed an additional $10,000 for caring for the burros from March 1975 until the Supreme Court awarded custody to the Bureau of Land Management. The Bureau of Land Management claimed since the livestock board was responsible for the roundup, the board was obliged to pay the $9,060.

With the issues of jurisdictional legislative dispute cleared in the U.S. Supreme Court, the Stone Cabin Valley roundup was also able to conclude without interference from the Nevada Department of Agriculture or anyone else. After taking the winter off, the roundup of the last of the 400 was restarted in September 1976. All but 21 of the horses were adopted, mostly stallions between the ages of ten and fifteen. If the horses were not adopted, they would be shot and buried the next month. "We've tried our damndest to place these animals," Gene Nodine expressed with regret, "but we've just not had any takers."

Annie did agree to the reduction of 50 percent of the wild horse herd; only 17 percent of the livestock was reduced. That was not within the intent of the agreement. In the affidavit signed on September 12, 1975, by Wild Horse Annie, she acknowledged the Stone Cabin Valley rangeland was in critically depleted condition and was subjected to decades of irreparable damage. "In order to preserve wildlife habitat," Annie continued, "to provide adequate forage for healthy wild-horse herds deemed to be within the carrying capacity of the range, to allow for recovery of the range, and to protect other resource values in the Stone Cabin area, an immediate reduction in ALL grazing pressures must be carried out there and in adjacent areas." She advised that the reductions should not be limited to wild horses, but apply equally to the present permitted domestic livestock use, "with immediate removal of all unpermitted domestic livestock."

SOME WILD HORSE SITUATIONS baffled federal investigators. The twelve hundred square miles of barren salt flats composing Dugway Proving Grounds in western Utah, adjacent to the Cedar Mountains, is one such example. Death was no stranger at Dugway, for its military mission at the time was to test and develop chemical and biological warfare weapons.

Sometimes, only when a tragedy occurs does the public become acutely aware of a place's existence and purpose. During the 1976 Fourth of July holiday, forty-nine horses mysteriously died on the Dugway Proving Grounds in Utah. The horses were found at the edge of Skull Valley, where forty-five hundred sheep died in 1968 during open-air nerve gas testing. The acting Dugway commander, Colonel James Templeton Jr., reacted to the possibility that the horse deaths were caused by nerve gas. "I can categorically rule that out," Templeton stated when he called Annie to describe the situation. "Hot weather and the limited water supply, which stressed the horses, were the predisposing factors that led to the deaths."[5]

A panel evaluation seminar was held in Utah on July 27, 1976, with an inordinate number of extremely high-ranking officials with doctorate degrees. The board included James L. Shupe, head of the Department of Veterinary Medicine at the University of Utah; Ross Smart of the Veterinary Diagnostic Laboratory at the University of Southern California; Richard Watkins, a practitioner, representing the Bureau of Land Management and Intermountain Laboratories; A. C. McChesney of the School of Veterinary Medicine at Colorado State University; George Klover, district veterinarian with Veterinary Services at the Department of Agriculture, in Denver; J. I. Moulthrop, a veterinary epidemiologist at the USDA; Robert Roulson, the chief of brand inspection and an assistant state veterinarian with the Utah Department of Agriculture; Tairi Fukushima, an epidemiologist with the Utah State Division of Health; David Waldron, a deputy commissioner of agriculture and director of the animal industry; and F. James Schoenfeld, a state veterinarian with the Utah Department of Agriculture.

Exhaustive laboratory analyses of the victims' blood and tissue ruled out any toxic substance, virus, bacteria, chemical agent, pesticide, or African equine encephalitis as contributing factors to the death of the horses.

Although the panel's findings were impressive, several mitigating circumstances remained.

Annie did not accept the "predisposing factors" diagnosis. "Over the many decades that wild horses have made Dugway their habitat, they have surely become adapted to the intense heat, and as for the water," wrote Annie, "BLM had just increased the supply at Orr Spring from 350 gallons to 2,800 gallons every twenty-four hours, completing the work on May 28 and the horses had been using it ever since. Something or someone kept those animals from water overlong. I would like to know what it was."[6]

During a "routine" army security flight by helicopter, the pilot and observer in the area of the watering hole at Orr Springs spotted twenty dead wild horses. Questions arose later when Wild Horse Annie obtained two different copies of the pilot's log. One log, written the day before the discovery, stated no wild horse carcasses could be spotted. Annie wondered why the pilot would be looking for dead wild horses the day before the forty-nine horses were first found dead. Although the majority of deaths occurred in close proximity to the springs, two more horses were found eighteen miles to the west, and four more were found dead five miles to the northwest.

Scientific, laboratory, and clinical data were presented to the panel by the various agencies and laboratories. The findings were discussed with the panel as they inquired into all aspects of the chronology of the incident and the findings. The panel met in an executive session behind closed doors following all presentations and issued the following conclusions: "Hot weather and the limited water supply, which stressed the horses, were the predisposing factors that led to the death of [fifty-four] wild horses during late June and early July at Dugway Proving Grounds. Since body temperature is regulated by sweating in horses, the environmental conditions and dehydration evidently results in body temperature imbalances."

The report stated that the premature drying of some water holes forced the horses to move to other watering areas, which were in the final stages of reconstruction by the Bureau of Land Management. It became necessary to quickly complete the reconstruction of their former watering areas. When those water holes were reopened, other bands of horses overdrank and died of hyperhydration or from an electrolyte imbalance (particularly potassium). Physiological changes within the animals' bodies affected their lungs, hearts, and brains and resulted in immediate death of the animals without a struggle. The panel concluded that a series of events, although individually insignificant, resulted in the deaths of the fifty-four horses.

Wild Horse Annie studied the photographs. "There were no limb or facial contortions. Twenty-five bodies were lying along one small gully, some on top of each other, some touching, some only a few feet apart. Bloodstained froth was at the nostrils and mouths of those already dead when the discovery was made. Such was not the case with those that died later." She continued, "Every effort was made to revive the horses still on their feet, huddled together in extreme stupor when rescuers arrived on the scene. In a matter of a few hours, they too, simply laid down and died without a struggle."[7]

Dr. Delbert A. Osguthorpe investigated both the 1968 sheep deaths and the 1976 wild horse incident. "We feel that these horses were stressed by not having access to water during this particular time. . . . I would swear on a stack of Bibles that no one is covering up anything on this incident."

According to BLM wild horse specialist Ron Hall, the survivors were lethargic, weak, and disoriented. "In all my years working with wild horses," Hall reported to Annie, "I've never seen anything like this."[8] When BLM investigators found the survivors, Hall explained the horses, in a stupor, could be slapped on the flanks without a reaction. They would just fall over, foaming at the mouth. Something had scared the horses to death, according to Hall.

The base officers and staff were courteous and helpful. Colonel Reddin, the doctor of veterinary medicine representing the army in the investigation, accompanied the BLM's Ron Hall and Wild Horse Annie on an inspection of the equine death site. Annie described her findings in her newsletter:

Our helicopter came in low over the freshly turned earth where more than half the wild horses that customarily watered at Orr Springs lie buried. Fifty-four of them . . . from wobbly little foals to veteran stallions and mares. Nearby, a small band stood listless in the merciless heat, barely lifting their heads at the sound of the craft overhead. They had become used to that kind of disturbance, for it had been going on ever since the discovery of the tragedy at Dugway Proving Ground that brought hordes of investigators to their bleak and forbidding habitat. They have adapted, too, to the intense heat that has conditioned them and generations before them. They instinctively conserve their energy, just as they instinctively search for and find the few seepages that provide them with the water they must have or perish. The survival instinct is strong, and they do find it!

Annie was finally reduced to tears, she said in a letter describing the scene. Dugway's environment was particularly harsh, with temperatures well above one hundred degrees. It was a lonely place, where at best survival hangs by a thread. "For fifty-four wild horses, that slender thread was not strong enough to withstand whatever happened at or near Orr Springs that left them dead and dying. I did not look back as we were airborne once again, to leave behind the desolation, the loneliness, the silence that is Dugway, and the new-made grave like a scar on the desert floor."

ANNIE HAD A DIPLOMATIC WAY of addressing issues, especially the emotional ones affecting the wild horses and burros. She clearly listened to the guidance of her father and that of Charles. In a 1965 letter to Helen Reilly, she explained that the wild horse campaign had to be focused on the protection and safety of the wild horses and burros on all the public lands. It was too easy to be sidetracked by every emotional wild horse issue that arose. "I had to keep in mind always that reaching the ultimate goal was more important than 'squaring off' at any group or individual," Annie explained to Helen, "for I knew that when legislation was won, it would automatically provide a solution to most of those issues."

As others saw the success of Wild Horse Annie's campaign, grassroots and established humane societies jumped into the fray with their own version of wild horse and burro protection. Instead of joining forces, Annie found she had competitors claiming to have her interest in mind. "I don't get too upset when the children are given the credit, for they have indeed accomplished miracles. After all, they are the ones who will be running the show some day, and this is good for them. What I do get a little upset about are the recent passengers on the gravy train who have a tendency to forget how it all began. But that is true to human nature, I understand, and goodness knows I had my share of accolades in the winner's circle."[9]

Using her favorite self-description when times were difficult, Annie cinched her girdle tightly and opened another case of hair spray as she leaped back into the fight. "I'm pretty rugged and I never go out on a limb by being unable to back-up my position. I learned that a long time ago—in another life almost. And—there are rewards—that from time to time—when a victory, be it ever so small, is won; or when there is a glimmer of hope that if not Utopia there will be a measure of security for the Wild Ones. I honestly believe that BLM would miss me if I were to retire from the ring now. And I don't mean the kind of missing that one experiences when a tooth quits aching." But she had no plans to retire, as the job was not yet finished. "When I do, though, I want to write a book. What a wealth of material there is—all star-spangled red, white and blue—sprinkled with tears here and there—fear, at times—triumph tempered with concessions—all tied together with bull-dog determination."[10] That dream of peacefully writing her memoirs was left in volumes of notes for others to use in scholastic papers and biographies.

WILD HORSE ANNIE'S FINAL CHAPTER

With a sense of surrender, Annie gradually began turning the daily worry and stress over to Helen Reilly and adoption coordinator Dawn Lappin. Annie would remain the public image of the International Society for the Protection of Mustangs and Burros as well as WHOA! But her primary responsibility now was to do "everything in my power to 'baby' my heart." Gone were the field trips, breathtaking glimpses of a band of wild horses cresting a distant hilltop, or maintaining an active travel schedule on behalf of her "wild ones." News of her medical condition was kept within her circle of friends. Publicly, she was not throwing down the velvet glove. "Damn!" she wrote to a friend. "But don't let 'them bureaucrats' back there think I'm going to let them win by default. I've sent out the word for the reserves, and am having a meeting with them." She was to have debated a spokesman for the cattlemen's association at the University of Nevada on May 7, "but my medical man says 'No way!'"[1]

The fight was long and hard. Sometimes the battles were private. Annie's physical appearance exposed her to the cruel nature that lies hidden in so many of us. Outwardly, it did not matter to her that her frail body was marred by the penalties of polio. Inwardly was a different matter. During the early years when Annie was gaining national attention in the newspapers, she was invited to appear as a sign-in guest for the Emmy Award–winning television show *To Tell the Truth* during its run as a game show (1956–68). The objective was for a panel of four celebrities to distinguish a person of some notoriety from two impostors. The casting director requested a photograph (for publicity purposes). Shortly after sending her best picture, her scheduled appearance on the television show was canceled without explanation. Annie confessed that the rejection hurt, but it also toughened her for other criticism.[2]

In a letter to Dean Bibles of the Bureau of Land Management, she reflected on a photograph that was taken of her in a conference room in Washington, D.C. She thought her critics would consider her to be "suspicious, dour, emotional, given to 'vapors' at the mention of anything bordering on biological impulses of animal life, and thoroughly unpleasant describes that picture of Annie."[3]

The year before her second federal law passed in Washington, the glare of the television lights and newspaper photographer flashbulbs reminded Annie that the gremlins from her days of polio had not completely abandoned her. In a personal letter to Mary Lea, a professional photographer, Annie let her emotions flow:

> You would never know how heartbreaking it is to want to be beautiful—because you who are [beautiful], accept it as a way of life. I was, to Charlie. But that was because he loved me much. Now I want to be beautiful to all the children to whom Wild Horse Annie has become a living legend. It isn't difficult while I am alive, because I give them what is inside me, and they think it beautiful. But I would like a photograph someday to leave behind—one that will ease the wrinkles of time— at an angle that will minimize the lack of alignment of my eyes—the cheekbones that are askew—and the chin pushed back from that damnable cast that dislocated my jaws. Can the magic of your camera do that some day?[4]

Other times, the losses were public and hurt even more. In the closing days of the Ninety-Fourth Congress (1975–77), a coalition of western lawmakers inserted an amendment into PL 92-195 under the Federal Land Use Policy Act of 1976. The BLM now had legislative approval to use helicopters on wild horses. It was the one thing that Annie had fought hard to prevent from happening, but she lost that battle. On October 21, 1976, President Gerald Ford signed the "Organic Act," as it was known.

Wild Horse Annie attended many federal legislative sessions that pertained to the wild horses and burros. Courtesy of the author.

Annie's campaign from the county courthouse in Nevada to the Capitol steps in Washington was beginning to unravel.

After Annie received word the Organic Act enabled the Bureau of Land Management to allow the use of helicopters to gather the horses, the painful memories of those roundups conducted by amateurs brought out a side of Annie few people saw. Coupled with the physical pain of her medical problems, Annie exhibited pent-up anger, particularly toward the government officials who turned their backs on years of negotiating a multiuse range-management conservation program, according to Helen Reilly. Annie was also angry about the rapid growth of "wild horse and burro protection" groups that provided little benefit to her own work but collected thousands of dollars for their organizations. "She just was angry with everything and everyone!" Helen Reilly privately explained.

Annie could hold on to her other accomplishments. Wild horses and burros still roamed the public lands. A few illegal roundups were still conducted, but the rush to eradicate the herds had diminished. Annie wanted to see wild, free-roaming horses and burros on the public land, not gathered and restricted to artificial sanctuaries.

Through her two nonprofit organizations, Wild Horse Annie introduced an awareness of the plight of the wild horses and burros to classrooms throughout the world and ultimately to the legislative offices in Washington. Her organizations developed and successfully marketed an adoption program between 1969 and 1974. It demonstrated great success as a public-nonprofit partnership at the Stone Cabin Valley roundup, as sixteen hundred applications to adopt four hundred wild horses successfully demonstrated. With only volunteer workers, Annie was able to help develop an effective adoption program in situations where legitimately excess wild horses and burros needed to be removed from the public land. The Bureau of Land Management incorporated her program less successfully into the federal program.

Annie recognized that nonprofit organizations, government agencies, and the private sector could develop a tripartite management system on behalf of the wild horses and burros and for the betterment of range conservation. The process had worked successfully on a small scale in Stone Cabin Valley, but could it work on a national level?

In correspondence with Helen Reilly, Annie explained that she had tried to avoid controversial issues in which she was not directly and intimately

involved. Often, disagreements stemmed from misunderstandings and could be resolved between battling entities and programs enhanced through coordinated efforts among competing organizations. "I realized," wrote Annie, "that it was of utmost importance that the Department of the Interior not be confronted with a divided army of mustang fighters, and I believe that was one of the greatest single factors in the success of the campaign."[5] Annie welcomed the opportunity for wild horse and burro organizations to become less ideological, for government agencies to become more flexible in their range-management objectives, and for both entities to be more open to compromise on solutions that would benefit the land stewardship and not just special-interest groups.

Similar sentiments were expressed a few years earlier when Nevada senator Cliff Young wrote a letter to the editor, offering some optimism about the passage of the Wild Free-Roaming Horse and Burro Act of 1971. He cautiously noted that "the BLM is encouraging public participation in its land-use planning process from which decisions governing future use of the public lands will be made, and they must be made on scientific principles where basic soil and vegetation are at stake. All of us interested in public-land management in Nevada, must participate in the land-use planning. The end result will be a healthy and productive rangeland with increased forage not only for livestock but for wildlife as well."

Wild Horse Annie was a separate entity from Velma Johnston. Her legacy of preserving the wild horses and burros was "their" gift to the children of America. She beamed over the telephone lines while talking about the five wild colts WHOA! had adopted that were being professionally trained. With her 1972 three-quarter-ton pickup truck and custom-built trailer, Annie planned to bring some of the wild horses to schoolchildren throughout the country. After all, it was the effort of schoolchildren that brought the issue of wild horses and Annie to the nation's capital on two different occasions.

Annie delegated Helen to attend a meeting on wild burros in June 1977. By now Wild Horse Annie's medical conditions (lung cancer and a deteriorating heart condition) had landed her in the hospital. Before leaving for the meeting, Helen stopped by Annie's room to get instructions and was shocked to find her mentor chain-smoking More menthol cigarettes. "The doctor said I was so far gone," Annie told Helen, "that what the heck, I might as well enjoy them." When Helen returned, she called Annie's hospital room to see if it was all right to drop by and report on the outcome of the meeting. "She told me that I must be tired and to just go home," Helen explained several years later. "She said she felt fine and she'd see me in the morning."

In the predawn light of June 27, 1977, her medical gremlins took the life of Velma B. "Wild Horse Annie" Johnston at the age of sixty-five. She was married to Charlie Johnston for twenty-seven years, fought on behalf of the wild horses for twenty-seven years, and passed away on the date that would be a tribute to the two favorite events in her life.

The *Los Angeles Times* wrote a standard obituary, but it was the follow-up feature that best described the legacy Annie left behind. Annie had always wanted to write a book about her campaign on behalf of the wild horses. She did not want to write it as her autobiography, but as a series of stories about how the wild horses and burros touched the lives of so many people. *Los Angeles Times* staff writer Lynn Simross took the month after Annie's death to meet with those who would keep her legacy alive. Simross's "Gentle Women Who Protect Wild Horses" followed ISPMB and WHOA! chairperson Helen Reilly and Dawn Lappin during the weeks following the death of their matriarch.

Like Annie, who answered her front door with a loaded .38 revolver discreetly held behind the door while her free hand was extended in friendship, Helen and Dawn were also threatened by vigilantes with guns and tire irons. Even the FBI informed them that they were once on convicted serial killer Charles Manson's hate list because Annie and her staff often worked in cooperation with the federal government. Dawn expressed her concern when she found the name of Squeaky Fromme, one of Manson's disciples, in the WHOA! membership file along with a letter requesting information about the horse group.

While the women talked about Annie, eighty-two-year-old Trudy Bronn joined in the conversation, occasionally pointing to Annie's desk. All the paperwork was cleared off for the first time. Only a small bronze statue that was presented to their absent leader by the National Cowboy Hall of Fame and Western Heritage Center in Oklahoma City was still there.

Wild Horse Annie's organization nurtured a membership of approximately ten thousand people in the United States, Japan, Spain, Australia, New Zealand, Norway, Pakistan, Germany, France, and England. A handful of volunteers helped the two salaried employees (Helen Reilly earned eighty-four hundred dollars and Dawn Lappin seventy-two hundred dollars annually in 1977). Louise Harrison discreetly funded the office's administrative costs.

Annie had maintained her twenty-seven-year campaign mostly from her modest northern Reno home. Her marketing was through the generosity of the national and international press, and her research team was composed of academics willing to share their work. She used a well-developed talent to negotiate and arbitrate disputes among her followers, livestock-industry representatives, and all levels of government administrators because she could not afford the legal teams that other organizations maintained.

Helen Reilly and Dawn Lappin dreamed of using the seven thousand dollars left in the organization's bank account as seed money to build a memorial to their friend in the form of a wild horse park, visitors' center, and museum, preferably in Colorado.[6] But without their charismatic chief executive director to lead the organization, the dream began to fade. WHOA! was closed, only to be resurrected by Lappin and maintained through a post office box address. The ISPMB was turned over to Karen Sussman shortly before the passing of Helen and John Reilly and is currently maintained from an office on the Cheyenne River Reservation in South Dakota.

As Lynn Simross concluded the article in the *Los Angeles Times*:

> The mustangs standing in the corral are a scruffy bunch, with ribs showing on their sides. Cattlemen often say they can't understand why anyone would want to save such ugly animals. But, as Annie used to tell them in her many speeches, "I have never referred to the wild horses as beautiful, noble creatures, because they are neither. Today's wild horse is not the glamorous mustang of long ago. He is, for the most part, underfed, scrubby and inbred."
>
> "Yet," she would continue, "the people of America have fought hard to save them (and the burros), these colorful remnants of two animal species that so uniquely represent the American spirit—freedom, pride, independence, endurance and the ability to survive against unbelievable odds. Should the future of these animals remain in doubt, the fight will go on."

After Annie died, BLM director Robert Burford called all the wild horse and burro groups together for the purpose of providing an opportunity to meet directly with the BLM staff to share their views on how the wild horse and burro program should be implemented by the federal government. Each wild horse and burro group arrived in Denver with its own personal agenda; it was clear there was no consensus among the groups.

After patiently listening without comment to each organization's "wish list," Burford called for a morning break. When the workshop reconvened,

BLM director Robert Burford addressed representatives of national wild horse and burro organizations after the death of Wild Horse Annie. Seated closest to Burford was Helen Reilly, Annie's successor at the International Society for the Protection of Mustangs and Burros. Courtesy of the author.

Burford explained that his department needed to address the deteriorating range condition. If the wild horse and burro groups could not come up with a plan for the animals, he would have to order substantial reductions in the herds within sixty days. The unexpected announcement stunned many of the representatives of the attending groups; for others, the mandate sailed over their heads. Instead of uniting behind a common cause, each group went its separate direction. If they had joined together, they would have been a formidable coalition to pick up where Wild Horse Annie had left off. It was a wonderful opportunity that was lost by a lack of unity and common purpose among the horse and burro groups.

As Bob Burford was leaving his political appointment as director of the BLM, I had an opportunity to meet privately with him at his office in the Federal Center outside of Denver. I refreshed his memory of that meeting in Denver. I asked him if he was aware that his surprise two-month deadline for the wild horse and burro groups would splinter the effectiveness of the groups. He looked up slightly, and a wry smile crossed his lips. "No, Alan," he said softly. "I had absolutely no idea that would happen." The tape recording of the conversation told one answer; the wry smile that only we knew about provided another interpretation of his intentions.

WILD HORSE ANNIE had two Hollywood role models—John Wayne (she often compared her husband to the western actor) and Ronald Reagan. She did not live long enough to see Reagan elected as president of the United States; if she had, she probably would have left John Wayne by himself on that pedestal of admiration.

During the Reagan administration, the wild, free-roaming horse and burro field budget was decreased, while administrative costs increased. A series of administrative errors by Bureau of Land Management director Robert Burford eradicated the waiting list of several thousand wild horse and burro applicants that had been generated through Wild Horse Annie's advocacy of adopting the animals into private ownership.

Burford proposed making the previously "free" federal adoption program economically self-sustaining by charging an application fee. The rate of $200 to adopt a wild horse was selected arbitrarily and exceeded the fair market value perceived by those individuals who were on the adoption waiting list. The demand for adoptable wild horses and burros dropped significantly. Burford attempted to correct his error and dropped the adoption fee to $125. By then, the poor marketing judgment reversed the public interest in the federal Adopt-a-Horse/Burro program.

Faced with the legislative need to administer the wild horse and burro program, then secretary of the interior James Watt began to lobby Congress on behalf of the Bureau of Land Management. Senator James McClure (R–Idaho) and others proposed legislation that would enable the BLM to sell any "excess" wild horse or burro that could not be distributed through the Adopt-a-Horse/Burro program within forty-five days of capture. The predicted purchaser of the excess wild equines would predominately be slaughterhouses and carcass-rendering plants. The proposal failed. Any remaining successful aspects of Annie's wild horse and burro program began to deteriorate.

Some elements of Annie's success do survive—a national advisory board, an adoption program, some use of range-management research, an end to airborne and mechanized roundups by weekend cowboys, and the establishment of many more designated wild horse and burro management areas. In 1980 the National Academy of Sciences proposed the first independent research project that would provide eighteen studies necessary for effective wild equine management. The management study was never implemented by the federal agencies because of budget cuts to the program.

Without a charismatic advocate like Wild Horse Annie but with humane organizations that could not form a coalition to continue Annie's vision, the Bureau of Land Management was able to return to its playbook without public challenge. The BLM began to repeat Kay Wilkes's faulty claim that wild horses were experiencing a "population explosion" and "excess" horses and burros had to be removed. Without the friendly adversarial relationship they had with Annie, the BLM was able to repeat the same misinformation frequently enough until legislators began to believe it was factual.

The livestock industry provided the constituent support the government and western legislators needed to weaken the two federal wild horse laws. Without accurate census counts and few objective research studies, the new range-management plans were capricious and arbitrary. And without their wild horse and burro mentor, advocates became vocal in their opposition to government plans for the wild horses, but failed to offer constructive alternatives. As William K. Reilly, president of the Washington-based Conservation Foundation, once wrote, "The nation and its environment have paid a high price for the diverse and contentious climate in which environmental protection is not proceeding. It is the interest of environmentalists, business leaders and administration . . . to restore a climate of credibility, constructive bipartisan debate, and regulatory vigor."

Ever since the Bureau of Land Management was created as part of the Taylor Grazing Act, administrative behavioral scientists have been critical of the management style of the agency. Management solutions are "satisfied" by implementing the first possible solution, even though it may not necessarily be the most effective. The public has always viewed the Bureau of Land Management as a closed-information system with little opportunity to allow the general public to participate in policy- and decision-making processes. The clients of the agency—the livestock operators and more recently the energy developers—became the agency's major influence, often augmenting the mission of the federal agency to meet private-sector objectives while using the heavily subsidized public lands. While the conservationists and environmentalists may have sporadic and momentary influences on specific land-use questions, it is the formal clientele hierarchy that maintains the most significant influence on the agency.

Public hearings were merely a formality for notifying interested parties of decisions that were already made behind closed doors by public land managers on behalf of commercial enterprises. Federal budget cutbacks reduced the research capabilities critical to public land management. Decision making was based on past research, often using outdated information or outmoded procedures. As a result, the only resource left to the nonprofit organizations was to file federal appeals or court injunctions, jamming a very costly federal system for the express purpose of participating in the bureaucratic planning process.

Universities began teaching creative management skills for nonprofit administrators, replacing letter-writing campaigns with the protests that cast a negative image on community organizations during the 1960s and 1970s. Instead of arbitrating conflicts, the adversarial sectors began to find themselves in courtrooms fighting on a new level of disagreement.

Regional legal foundations, like the one administered at the time by former secretary of the interior James Watt (Mountain States Legal Foundation), were incorporated "in the public interest" on behalf of private developers as nonprofit organizations to countersue the environmentalists. Public land conflicts stalemated without any resolution. A line of court cases wound its way through various levels of the judicial system, draining nonprofit coffers, increasing the cost of public administration programs, and delaying the development of public management programs.

Gifford Pinchot, President Theodore Roosevelt's natural resources director, proposed that public land should be developed and preserved by the majority—not for the profit of a few. Paul Culhane, author of several publications on public interest-group pressure and their relationship with public land-use issues, further developed Pinchot's concept. Culhane wrote, "This principle is embodied in the statutory responsibilities of the Forest Service and the Bureau of Land Management—public-land resources are to be managed for 'multiple-use,' in theory an optimum and high level of mix-of-uses, and for 'sustained yield,' the maintenance of those high levels of use 'in perpetuity.'"

The federal legislators who actually once listened to their constituents when thousands of schoolchildren and adults brought their concern for the welfare of the wild horses and burros to Washington, D.C., are now gone. Long lines of lobbyists who now have the ears of our elected officials have replaced them. To appease the public since the passage of the Wild Free-Roaming Horse and Burro Act of 1971, the Bureau of Land Management used to appoint a director of the wild horse and burro program. BLM administrators who were ready to be put out to pasture usually filled the position. No practical value ever came from that post, and the political appointment has remained unfilled through many administrations.

Wild Horse Annie and Pearl Twyne served on the original National Wild Horse and Burro Advisory Board that was established through the 1971 act to advise the secretaries of the interior and agriculture. Instead of developing an effective plan to protect, manage, and control the wild horses as Wild Horse Annie proposed, the BLM and Forest Service have perpetuated a plan to remove wild horses from the public land. As a result, more than thirty thousand wild horses were recently gathered from the public rangeland and housed for many years in elaborate holding corrals at public expense. Instead of strengthening the marketing capabilities of Annie's adoption program, the government continued to gather horses through poorly conceived wild horse and burro management programs.

The groundwork for a viable public land management program can be found in the moccasin prints of Velma Johnston, John and Helen Reilly, Pearl Twyne, and Dawn Lappin. Their research reflected the respect for land stewardship that was forged among previously polarized viewpoints about public land management. Much of their work has faded with the memory of Wild Horse Annie.

Thirty years prior to her death, Annie reflected on her mission in a letter to Howard Caudle:

> There is no question in my mind but that our cause is getting stronger all the time, but it is still not strong enough to arbitrarily buck the BLM all the way. These separate instances take our time and our money, and all we gain is a reprieve for the animals. Sure as shootin', the BLM has more time and money than we have, and if there are not those younger ones coming along to take our places with the zeal and dedication that we have we will have won the battle but lost the war, for the BLM has only to bide its time until we have run our course. The only ones to suffer will be the horses and burros in that event.[7]

Velma B. "Wild Horse Annie" Johnston was able to draw from her compassionate family upbringing and the lessons learned from dealing with a severe distortion of her physical body. For thousands of young people, Annie went out of her way to mentor youth during a socially turbulent period of American history. She shared her lifelong belief that the legacy of the West followed the hoofprints of the horse.

In a quiet moment at home, Annie reflected on a piece of prose she had kept available her entire career. Historian and author John Trotwood Moore (1858–1929) penned the words, and it served as her lifelong inspiration:

Out from the past, the dim, bloody, shifting past, came this noble animal, the horse, side by side with man, fighting with him the battles of progress, bearing with him the burdens of the centuries. Down the long, hard road, through flint or more, through swamp or sand, where ever there has been a footprint, there also will be seen a hoof print. They have been one and inseparable, the aim and the object, the means and the end.

And if the time shall ever come, as some boastingly declare, when the one shall breed away from the other, the puny relic of a once perfect manhood will not live long enough to trace the record of it on the tablet of time.

EPILOGUE

I heard about Annie's death the same way the rest of the country learned the news. Like most youth in their twenties, I was transitioning from career to career with a myriad of different residential locations —where could I go to be of help to Annie while independently developing a career? I was in the process of preparing for a move to Denver when I read Annie's obituary and engaged in a little mourner's remorse for not finding even more time helping Annie when she needed the support during her final year.

When Wild Horse Annie died in 1977, I lost a friend and mentor. She was instrumental in guiding me during our seven years of friendship that led to many more years working with Helen Reilly. Even in the Vietnam and post-war era of political cynicism, their example showed me that one could dislike some of the actions of elected officials and government employees, but never become disillusioned with one's own abilities to participate in that democracy. Annie often told me her greatest accomplishment was the encouragement of young people to actively participate in the government process for any cause that means so much to them.

Reflecting on the years I knew Annie, there was only one secret she ever asked me to preserve, and I'm proud to say that I have honored her request until this time. Although Annie and Charlie were avid horsemen during their days on the Double Lazy Heart Ranch, their move into town and away from constantly being around horses caused a change in Annie's immune system. At the height of Annie's international attention as the matriarch of the wild horses, she was actually allergic to horses. She thought her opponents would literally have a "hay day" if they had that information, and it remained our secret.

After reviewing many storage cases of personal documents written to and from Velma "Wild Horse Annie" Johnston, and in the seven years I personally knew her, I never heard her speak ill of anyone. In the 1980s, I contacted Joan Blue of the American Horse Protection Association with an offer to add her side of the Howe, Idaho, story for inclusion in Wild Horse Annie's library files. To save herself time, I invited Joan to send a tape cassette of her comments. The transcript of the tape could then be included as a permanent part of the Wild Horse Annie collection at the Denver Public Library. Mrs. Blue's response to the invitation was caustically to the point: "I haven't had such a good laugh in years! Imagine your suggesting that I squander any of my time talking into a machine about Wild Horse Annie. I couldn't care less about her alive or dead."

BETWEEN THE PASSAGE of the Wild Horse and Burro Act of 1971 and 1986, approximately $5 million was cumulatively spent on the wild equine program by the Bureau of Land Management. At the time of this writing, the BLM's 2011 budget for the program climbed to $75.7 million—an increase of $12 million over the previous year. A separate land-acquisition fund of $42.5 million to purchase land for one wild horse preserve was also included in the 2011 budget. The plan was to put the program on "a sustainable track," but no explanation of the plan was provided. According to the BLM's website, "The current path of the wild horse and burro program is not sustainable for the animals, the environment or the American taxpayer."

A 2010 web video produced by the Bureau of Land Management described U.S. Department of the Interior secretary (and rancher) Ken Salazar's wild horse and burro initiative. Amid shots of wild horses and "Marlboro country"–style music, subtitles explained the objectives. "They are 'Living Legends' of the American frontier, protected by federal law since 1971 and cared for by the Bureau of Land Management. They are no longer threatened by extinction, yet their own over-population endangers them. Herd populations and the cost of managing them have become unsustainable, threatening the health of the landscape and the health of the horses, and competing with native wildlife."

Mismanagement of the wild horse and burro program for more than four decades and mismanagement of livestock use on the public land for even longer are the problem. Wild Horse Annie confronted Kay Wilkes and the Bureau of Land Management about his false claims of overpopulation and other myths that were continued through subsequent administrations. Today, the exact same range-management issues are still using the wild horses and burros as scapegoats for land mismanagement. The Bureau of Land Management's "Myths and Facts" page on their website perpetuates the controversy.

The blame does not fall exclusively to the Bureau of Land Management. Wild Horse Annie struggled with other nonprofit organizations that saw a cash cow inherent in the wild horses and burros. Just as in the past, a picture of wild horses and a plea to "save the horses" are sufficient to generate contributions from well-intentioned but misguided contributors. Annie saw the risks of warehousing wild horses and commercially exploiting them. She opposed moving them off the public lands and onto nonnative grasslands; PL 92-195 was originally written to ensure the wild horses remained on their existing rangeland as part of a multiple-use concept of the public land. Once the government was no longer responsible for their protection, the sanctity of the federal laws was no longer valid.

Perform a Google search for "wild horse organization," and you will find more than a half-million potential hits. Many organizations will make claims they are continuing the work of Wild Horse Annie, a misrepresentation that would upset her. Some of the more dominant organizations have attempted to create coalitions to bring their united concerns to the Bureau of Land Management and U.S. Forest Service. Other organizations that were once active players in the fight for the wild horses are now just mail-drop addresses. But like BLM director Robert Burford astutely noticed after Wild Horse Annie died, the wild horse groups are easy to scatter when challenged. Only the largest of the groups are equipped with legal counsel and benefactors to underwrite counterchallenges against the government agencies.

Annie recognized that government land managers are ingrained in the culture of the ranching community. The nonprofit sector had a large number of followers and the ability to raise money, but lacked the necessary technical expertise. The private sector had access to expertise and money, but had yet to recognize the commercial value of "branding" with the wild horses and burros as a part of the legacy of the West instead of the emotional appeal that was advocated by the nonprofit groups. The Philip Morris Corporation and Ford Motor Company were among the few to recognize the value the legacy of the wild horses and burros had as potential corporate brands without exploiting the animals. Blending the three sectors theoretically looked good on paper, but Annie recognized that at least two of the sectors were laced with people with ulterior motives that could sabotage a collaborative effort at any junction.

For Annie, educating the government officials was almost as important as educating the young children about the wild horses and burros on the public land in terms of conservation. The Bureau of Land Management's culture was steeped in the commercial value of the public land. Annie talked about setting up an educational center where the various sectors could learn about the legacy of the wild horses and burros. Offers were made to provide land in Lovell, Wyoming, as well as in the Ken-Caryl Ranch area, southwest of metropolitan Denver. Architectural models were developed, but the long-range funding was not available.

Few innovative ideas reflected the legacy of Wild Horse Annie. In a rare demonstration of how the wild horse and burro program could be incorporated into contemporary needs, Ron Zaidlicz, an innovative and compassionate Colorado veterinarian, was able to demonstrate a creative use for "excess" wild horses. In 1978 he worked to incorporate the need to gentle the wild horses so a greater number of people could safely adopt them. Until his passing in 2008, "Dr. Z" worked with the Wild Horse and Inmate Program at the Colorado State Penitentiary in Cañon City. His concept for bringing civility to the wild ones was mutually beneficial to both man and beast. This innovative concept continued as the Cañon City program expanded its training of wild horses for use by patrol agents along the country's borders. Sixty mustangs were in service to Homeland Security in 2011, exemplifying the same hardy characteristics once admired by preaircraft cowboys of the 1800s.

We live in a culture where housing subdivisions spread across open space and forested lands. Instead of walking along deer trails and seeing foxes, mourning doves, pheasants, and other wildlife, we now live on paved streets named in honor of the animals that can no longer live there. Perhaps the U.S. Department of the Interior can create a museum where stuffed replicas of the wild bison, horses, and burros can be put on display so schoolchildren can visit and learn about the animals that were so important to the development of the West. In the gift shop, tourists could purchase copies of the books of Karl May and Zane Grey so that young readers can once again have their thoughts filled with wonderful stories about the romance of the West and the freedom and independence of the wild, free-roaming horses and burros that once roamed the western plains.

NOTES

Unless otherwise indicated, the sources cited below are located either in the Velma B. Johnston Collection (VJC), which is housed at the Denver Public Library, or in the author's private collection (AC).

1 | WILD HORSE BLOOD

1. Velma B. Johnston and Michael J. Pontrelli, "Public Pressure and a New Dimension of Quality: Horses and Burros," paper presented at the Thirty-Fourth North American Wildlife Conference, March 4, 1969, 241, AC.

2. Johnston, "Mustang Exploitation," testimony submitted to Representative Walter S. Baring, February 28, 1958, AC.

3. Johnston to Ray Gard, October 11, 1968, AC.

4. Johnston scrapbook, unidentified Reno newspaper, July 3, 1952, VJC.

5. Deanne Stillman, *Mustang: The Saga of the Wild Horse in the American West* (Boston: Houghton Mifflin, 2008), 246.

6. Johnston scrapbook, unidentified Reno newspaper, July 3, 1952, VJC.

7. Handwritten notes from Trudy Bronn to Alan J. Kania, undated, AC.

8. Johnston to "Phyllis," August 29, 1959, VJC.

9. Trudy Bronn, interview by the author, Reno, Nevada, April 26, 1980, VJC.

10. Johnston to Robert Froman, January 8, 1959, AC.

11. "Why Wild Horse Annie Fights for Mustangs," *Examiner,* AC.

12. Johnston to Howard H. Caudle, November 10, 1967, AC.

13. Bronn interview.

14. Marguerite Henry, "In Her Moccasins," press release, Rand McNally, AC.

15. Johnston to John J. Ahrend, April 27, 1973, AC.

16. Johnston to "Phyllis," August 29, 1959, VJC.

17. Bronn interview.

18. Herman Weiskopf, "Wild West Showdown," *Sports Illustrated,* May 5, 1975.

19. Bronn interview.

20. Johnston, longhand notes, undated, AC.

21. Johnston to Mary Lea, May 26, 1974, VJC.

22. Ibid., October 10, 1972.

23. The original Bucket of Blood was located in Virginia City, Nevada. There could have been several saloons that used that name, or Velma's records may have combined several events. Gabbs, Nevada, is located near Ione, Nevada.

24. Some references call the Bronns' ranch the Painted Rock Ranch, while others refer to it as the Lazy Heart Ranch.

25. Jack Barnes, "Wild Horse Annie: A Living Western Legend," *Reno Evening Gazette*, April 20, 1960.

26. Johnston to John McCormack, February 21, 1971, VJC.

27. Ibid.

28. Johnston to Mary Lea, December 5, 1970, VJC.

29. "Why Wild Horse Annie Fights for Mustangs."

30. Johnston to Mary Lea, October 10, 1972, VJC.

31. Ibid., December 5, 1970.

2 | ROUNDING UP NEWSPAPERS AND POLITICIANS

1. Johnston to Ernest F. Swift, January 27, 1958, AC.

2. Johnston to Baring, January 7, 1958, AC.

3. The horses were too far away, and Annie explained to me that the negatives were too "thin" to produce a usable photographic print.

4. Johnston to R. W. Faulkner, vice president of Woodmen Accident and Life Company, January 7, 1958, VJC.

5. "Battle Rages over Protection of Wild Horses," *Reno Evening Gazette*, June 10, 1952.

6. The reference was to Marlon Brando in the Stanley Kramer film *The Wild One* that was released the following year. Apparently, Velma saw the wild horses as an outlaw gang shunned by the local authorities.

7. Johnston to Robert Froman, January 8, 1959, VJC.

8. *Territorial Enterprise* editorial, circa June 1955, as reported in "Mustang Exploitation" (see chap. 1, n. 2).

9. Johnston to Gordon W. Guillion, February 23, 1955, VJC.

10. Johnston and Pontrelli, "Public Pressure," 251 (see chap. 1, n. 1).

11. Johnston to Yvonne Spiegelberg, September 17, 1959, VJC.

12. Ibid.

13. Johnston to Attorney George Rudiak, February 7, 1955, VJC.

14. *Mustang: Wild Spirit of the West* was written for children, but Velma maintained that the anecdotes in the story were factual.

15. Johnston to Walter Whitacre, chairman, Public Morals Committee, February 7, 1955, AC.

16. "Protection for Wild Horses," *Territorial Enterprise* editorial, February 11, 1955 (another source says the editorial was from the *Elko Daily Free Press*, February 13, 1955).

17. Johnston and Pontrelli, "Public Pressure," 243; Johnston to Mary Lea, February 27, 1972, AC.

18. Johnston to Tex Gladding, February 7, 1959, VJC.

19. Johnston to Whitacre, February 3, 1955, VJC.

20. Johnston to Gladding, February 3, 1955, VJC.

21. "Mustang Exploitation," *Nevada State Journal,* circa March 2, 1955.

22. Johnston to Margaret Sinkey, January 13, 1959, AC.

23. Johnston and Pontrelli, "Public Pressure," 240–52.

24. Johnston to Froman, January 8, 1959, AC.

25. Johnston to Helen Reilly, April 19, 1966, AC.

26. Johnston to Froman, January 8, 1959, AC; Johnston to Thurm Lowery, May 23, 1974, AC.

3 | THE FINAL DAYS OF LEGAL MUSTANGING

1. Johnston to Froman, January 8, 1959, VJC.

2. Johnston, typed report, April 21, 1959, VJC.

3. Earl Thomas, acting director, Bureau of Land Management, Washington, D.C., to Johnston, August 14, 1958, AC.

4. Johnston to an unknown recipient, draft, March 17, 1959, AC.

5. Johnston to Froman, January 8, 1959, VJC.

6. Ibid.

7. Johnston, telephone notes to an unknown caller, June 29, 1959, AC.

8. Johnston, typed report, March 17, 1959, AC.

9. Ibid.

10. Ibid., April 21, 1959.

11. Johnston to Walter S. Young, December 8, 1958, AC.

12. Barnes, "Wild Horse Annie" (see chap. 1, n. 25).

13. UPI, "Newsmen in Washington See Wild Horse Annie Without Shootin' Irons," July 15, 1959, AC.

14. *Kiplinger Washington Letter,* July 18, 1959, AC; *Christian Science Monitor,* July 21, 1959.

15. *Wright Slant on Washington,* July 20, 1959, AC.

16. Johnston, "Mustang Exploitation" (see chap. 1, n. 2).

17. Johnston to Gard, August 30, 1959, AC.

18. Johnston to unknown recipient, draft, August 11, 1957, AC.

19. Johnston to Corp. Iam E. Kaye and family (the Black Watch RHR), Cyprus, August 11, 1959, AC.

20. Johnston and Pontrelli, "Public Pressure," 240–52 (see chap. 1, n. 1).

21. Johnston to Lloyd F. Cecil, Paris, October 6, 1959, AC.

22. Johnston to Carlita Clark Boden, September 22, 1959, AC.

4 | GOING IT ALONE FOR CHARLIE AND THE HORSES

1. Johnston to Mrs. Harry Clark Boden, September 22, 1959, AC.

2. Johnston to Spiegelberg, September 17, 1959, VJC.

3. Johnston to John, Helen, and Susan Reilly, June 25, 1962, VJC.

4. Johnston to Mrs. H. N. Cherry, May 29, 1961, AC.

5. Johnston to John, Helen, and Susan Reilly, June 25, 1962, VJC.

6. Ibid., March 27, 1962.

7. Johnston to the Reilly family, November 21, 1962, VJC.

8. Ibid., August 22, 1963.

9. Ibid., June 10, 1963.

10. Johnston to "Louise," January 18, 1961, AC.

11. Johnston to the Reilly family, January 30, 1962, VJC.

12. Ibid., November 7, 1963.

13. Johnston to Duanne Sonnenburg, December 14, 1971, AC.

14. Johnston to "Mary Rose," May 6, 1964, AC.

15. Johnston to "Evelyne," December 7, 1966, VJC.

16. Johnston to "Kathleen," December 17, 1969, VJC.

17. Johnston to Sonnenburg, December 14, 1971, AC.

18. Johnston to the Reilly family, March 9, 1967, VJC.

19. Ibid., May 3, 1965.

20. Johnston to Billie Twyne, June 1, 1969, AC.

21. Johnston to "Marie-Rose," December 5, 1968, VJC.

22. Johnston to Sonnenburg, December 14, 1971, AC.

23. Helen Reilly, interview with the author, AC.

24. Ibid.

25. Johnston to John, Helen, and Susan Reilly, March 14 [no year], AC.

26. Ibid., March 15, 1963, VJC.

27. Ibid., November 21, 1962.

28. Ibid., May 1, 1967.

29. Johnston to "Hazel," December 10, 1967, VJC.

30. Johnston to Ed Phillips, November 22, 1966, AC.

31. Johnston to Helen, John, and Susan Reilly, December 13, 1966, AC.

32. Johnston, note, January 20, 1961, AC.

33. Johnston to Helen E. Jones, executive director, National Catholics for Animal Welfare, February 7, 1961, AC.

34. Johnston to Mary Lea, May 26, 1974, VJC.

35. Johnston to Helen B. Cherry, November 24, 1964, AC.

5 | PRYOR COMMITMENTS

1. Walter Sullivan, "U.S. Creates a Haven for Wild Horses in Nevada," *New York Times*, August 21, 1963.

2. Johnston to John Hopper, February 25, 1974, AC.

3. Johnston to Phillips, October 26, 1966, VJC.

4. Johnston to the Reillys, April 21, 1967, VJC.

5. Johnston and Pontrelli, "Public Pressure," 249 (see chap. 1, n. 1).

6. *Newsweek*, May 13, 1968, as described in ibid., 247.

7. William M. Blair, "U.S. Urged to Help Wild Horse Herd: Panel Asks Protection for 100 Montana Mustangs," *New York Times*, June 21, 1969.

8. Johnston to Pearl M. Twyne, June 16, 1959, AC.

9. Johnston to Ernest F. Swift, conservation adviser, National Wildlife Federation, Washington, D.C., April 10, 1968, VJC.

10. Although each organization expressed the same opposition to the government plan, each acted independently, instead of as a united front. This organizational independence among humane societies continues to reduce their effectiveness in negotiating meaningful management plans with the Bureau of Land Management and other federal agencies.

11. Johnston to "Kathleen," December 2, 1968, VJC.

6 | DIFFERENCES OF OPINION

1. Johnston to "Joyce," September 23, 1969, VJC.

2. National Mustang Association Organization and Objectives, undated, post-1968, AC.

3. Ibid.

4. Johnston to Mrs. Boyd Hunt, April 13, 1974, AC.

5. Johnston to the Reilly family, June 2, 1967, VJC.

6. Johnston to John, Helen, and Susan Reilly, February 10 [no year], AC.

7. Notes of phone call from Johnston to Bob Minarek, National Mustang Association, March 3, 1969, AC.

8. Notes of phone call from Dennis Hess to Johnston, March 7, 1969, AC.

9. Johnston, personal notes, March 9, 1969, AC.

10. Notes of phone call from Dr. Mike Pontrelli to Johnston, March 7, 1969, AC.

11. Notes of phone call from Johnston to Minarek, March 12, 1969, AC.

12. Notes of phone call from Johnston to unidentified person, March 12, 1969, AC.

13. Notes of phone call from McMahon to Johnston, March 13, 1969, AC.

14. Johnston, personal notes, March 19, 1969, AC.

15. Ibid.

16. Ibid.

17. Johnston to "Carroll Ann," February 10, 1972, AC.

18. Johnston, form letter, August 10, 1970, VJC.

19. Johnston to Mrs. Boyd Hunt, April 13, 1974, AC.

20. Johnston to Twyne, May 15, 1971, VJC.

21. Johnston, form letter, August 10, 1970, VJC.

22. Emphasis added.

23. Johnston to Hope Ryden, October 10, 1969, VJC.

24. Michael J. Pontrelli, "Protection for Wild Mustangs," *Defenders of Wildlife News* (Fourth Quarter 1969): 446 (written on behalf of Johnston).

7 | ANNIE RETURNS TO WASHINGTON, D.C.

1. "Evaluation of Wild Horse Organized Assistance, Inc. (WHOA!) from Standpoint of Present Potential," undated report, AC.

2. Johnston to William Loeb, editor of the *Manchester (N.H.) Union Leader* (and personal friend), AC.

8 | UNFINISHED WORK

1. Johnston to Grey T. Larison, March 16, 1974, AC.

2. Johnston to Mary Lea, April 9, 1974, AC.

3. Johnston to Heddy and John Ahrend, April 13, 1974, AC.

4. During the Howe, Idaho, case that will be described in depth later in this book, Annie was being monitored by a nondescript organization that opposed the government and anyone who tried to force federal legislation upon "private" landowners. This group was self-described as a "vigilante group" that used the colonial coiled-rattlesnake symbol and "Don't Tread on Me" as their motto.

5. Johnston to Mary Lea, May 26, 1974, VJC.

6. Johnston to Joan Bolsinger, May 15, 1974, AC.

7. Johnston to Mary Lea, May 26, 1974, VJC.

8. Johnston to Thurm Lowery, May 23, 1974, AC.

9. Johnston to Mary Lea, October 10, 1972, VJC.

10. Johnston to Margaret S. Rice, October 8, 1974, AC.

11. Johnston to Caudle, November 10, 1967, AC.

12. Johnston to Rice, October 8, 1974, AC.

13. Ibid.

14. As full disclosure, I received approximately three hundred dollars to cover my airfare on several investigations that I covered for Wild Horse Annie.

15. Johnston to Mary Lea, August 1, 1974, AC.

16. Johnston to "Patsy," July 28, 1974, AC.

17. Johnston to "Phyl," July 28, 1974, AC.

18. Ibid.

19. Johnston to "Patsy," July 28, 1974, AC.

20. Committee on Interior and Insular Affairs for the United States Senate, June 16, 1974, 1–2, AC.

21. Statement of Hon. Jack O. Horton, assistant secretary, U.S. Department of Interior, Hearings Before the Committee on Interior and Insular Affairs, U.S. Senate, 93rd Cong., 2nd sess., on the Administration of Public Law 92-195, the Wild Free-Roaming Horse and Burro Protection Act of 1971, June 26, 1974, 49, AC.

22. Ibid., 50, 53.

23. Ibid., 50.

24. Ibid., 68.

25. Ibid.

26. Ibid., 70.

27. Ibid., 70, 71.

28. Ibid., 88.

29. Ibid., 89.

30. Johnston to "Patsy," July 28, 1974, AC.

31. Statement of Velma B. Johnston, Hearings Before the Subcommittee on Public Lands of the Committee on Interior and Insular Affairs, House of Representatives, 92nd Cong., 1st sess., on H.R. 795, H.R. 5375, and Related Bills, April 19–20, 1971, 91, AC.

32. Johnston, Minority Report, member of the National Advisory Board on Wild Free-Roaming Horses and Burros, Reno, September 18–20, 1974, AC.

33. National Advisory Board on Wild Free-Roaming Horses and Burros, Reno, Nevada, minutes, September 18–20, 1974, AC.

34. Ibid.

35. Johnston to "Hazel," December 6, 1968, VJC.

9 | THE LITTLE BOOKCLIFFS WILD HORSE AREA

1. Sometimes spelled "Book Cliffs."

2. "Congressional Inquiry: Wild Horses on Public Lands," Memorandum 9230 to Colorado State Director from District Manager, Grand Junction, March 21, 1968, AC.

3. Bureau of Land Management form letter from District Manager Keith Miller (written as a response to inquiries from the general public), June 17, 1969, AC.

4. Memorandum: Colorado State Director from District Manager Keith Miller, April 22, 1971, AC.

5. Johnston to Caudle, June 3, 1970, AC.

6. *Grand Junction (Colo.) Daily Sentinel,* circa 1972, AC.

7. Dr. C. Wayne Cook to the author, January 31, 1972, AC.

8. EAR Little Bookcliffs Wild Horse Movement, August 14, 1975, AC.

9. General Management Agreement for the Round Mountain Allotment and Little Bookcliffs Wild Horse Area between John D. Hill and the Bureau of Land Management, March 28, 1974, AC.

10. Little Bookcliffs Wild Horse Management Plan, August 1979, AC.

10 | THE "HOWE, IDAHO, MASSACRE"

1. The welcome sign at the town limits in 1973 indicated the population was 32 people. The 2007 population jumped to 168 males and 160 females. Estimated household income was $32,150, more than $12,000 below the rest of the state.

2. Typed documentation of the events surrounding the Howe, Idaho, horse roundup, February 1973, AC.

3. Instruction memo No. ISO 72-38, to All District Managers from State Director [William Mathews], Idaho State Office, Bureau of Land Management, February 16, 1972 (memo expired December 31, 1972), AC.

4. Ibid.

5. Johnston to Kay Wilkes, chief, Division of Range Management, Bureau of Land Management, November 5, 1973, AC.

6. Robert Amy, interview by Ralph Dyment (U.S. Forest Service) and Bill Jensen (Bureau of Land Management), January 9, 1974, AC.

7. Federal investigative report, Investigating Team: Jens C. Jensen, Kenneth W. Jensen, Culver D. Ross, Ralph R. Dyment, and Fred W. Prussing; George Woodie, March 9, 1973, interview by Fred Prussing and Ralph Dyment (U.S. Forest Service) and Jens Jensen (BLM), AC.

8. *Federal Register,* vol. 38, no. 157, August 15, 1973, Part 4710, "Wild Free-Roaming Horse and Burro Management," Subpart 4710.0-5b, "Definitions," AC.

9. Federal investigative report, interview with Walter "Ed" Jones; Investigating Team: Jens C. Jensen, Kenneth W. Jensen, Culver D. Ross, Ralph R. Dyment, and Fred W. Prussing, March 10, 1973, AC.

10. Ibid.

11. Johnston to Mary Lea, June 25, 1973, AC.

12. Federal investigative report, narrative, March 1973, 2, AC.

13. Ibid.

14. Ibid.

15. Ibid., 3.

16. Ibid.

17. Federal investigative report, interview with Dave Lindberg, March 6, 1973, AC.

18. Federal investigative report, narrative, March 1973, 3, AC.

19. Ibid., interview with Dave Lindberg, BLM, March 8, 1973.

20. Ibid., March 6, 1973.

21. Ibid., narrative, March 1973, 3.

22. Robison, interview by Jensen (BLM), Ross (U.S. Forest Service), and Dyment (U.S. Forest Service), March 7, 1973, AC.

23. Ibid.

24. Federal investigative report, interview with Bill Yearsley, March 9, 1973, AC.

25. Ibid., narrative, March 1973, 4.

26. Ibid., interview with Lindberg, March 6, 1973, 5.

27. Ibid., interview with Mrs. and Mrs. Robert Amy, January 9, 1974.

28. Ibid., narrative, March 1973, 5.

29. Ibid., interview with Lindberg, March 6, 1973, 5.

30. Ibid., interview with Robison, March 7, 1973.

31. Ibid., interview with Amy by Dyment, January 9, 1974, 5.

32. Ibid., interview with Robison, March 7, 1963.

33. Ibid., interview with Jones, March 10, 1973.

34. Ibid., narrative, March 1973, 6.

35. Ibid.

36. Ibid.

37. Phone conversation between the author and Dwayne Struther, Central Nebraska Packing Company, March 6, 1973, AC.

38. Phone conversation between the author and Sheriff Lords, Butte County, March 6, 1973, AC.

39. Emphasis added.

40. Federal investigative report, interview with Robison, March 7, 1973, AC.

41. *Idaho Falls Post-Register,* October 15, 1973.

11 | ANNIE BRINGS THE WORLD TO HOWE, IDAHO

1. Johnston to George Turcott, October 1, 1973, AC.

2. Phone conversation notes between Johnston and Mathews, October 26, 1973, AC.

3. Press release, "Justice Department Declines Criminal Prosecution in Idaho Horse Roundup," U.S. Department of Interior, Herndon, October 11, 1973, AC.

4. Johnston, administrative report, subsequent to interview with assistant U.S. attorney in Boise, Idaho, on October 31, 1973, AC.

5. Phone conversation between Johnston and Joan Blue, October 31, 1973, AC.

6. Phone conversation between Johnston and George Lea, November 1, 1973, AC.

7. Phone conversation between Johnston and Bill Mathews, October 26, 1973, AC.

8. Anne Thatcher to Johnston, January 11, 1974, AC.

9. Johnston to George Turcott, January 23, 1974, AC.

10. Report to Chairman and Members of the National Advisory Board on Wild Free-Roaming Horses and Burros, November 7, 1973, AC.

11. Johnston to Gertrude Jupp, September 9, 1974, AC.

12. *Arco Advertiser,* November 15, 1973, 2.

13. Phone conversation between Steve Pellegrini and Johnston, November 12, 1973, AC.

14. Phone conversation between Johnston and Max Palmer, December 6, 1974, AC.

15. Ibid.

16. Ibid.

17. Ibid.

18. Phone conversation between Johnston and Frank Hartmann Jr., December 7, 1974, AC.

19. Ibid.

20. Mathews to Johnston, May 20, 1975, AC.

21. Hope Ryden, "Whatever Happened to the Howe Horses?," American Horse Protection Association, fall 1977 newsletter supplement, AC.

22. Johnston to Mary Lea, October 5, 1975, VJC.

23. Johnston to Bolsinger, May 15, 1974, AC.

12 | FEDERAL OR STATE LAW?

1. Johnston to Betty Kuphaldt, March 11, 1975, AC.

2. In addition to her responsibilities to the National Wild Horse and Burro Advisory Board, Annie was appointed to the BLM Multiple-Use Advisory Board for the Susanville District. Mike Pontrelli, a friend and consultant to Annie, likewise was appointed to the State of Nevada BLM Multiple-Use Advisory Board. Annie commented that there was a need to overhaul the advisory boards; the nineteen-member Nevada State Board was composed of six cattlemen, six sheepmen, and one each from the other seven categories of public land interests. Johnston to Mary Lea, October 5, 1975, AC.

3. Ibid., April 23, 1975, VJC.

4. Johnston to Betty and Roy Kuphaldt, June 24, 1976, AC.

5. Ibid., August 16, 1976.

6. Ibid.

7. "Requiem for Wild Horses" (unpublished document in Annie's files), 5, AC.

8. Associated Press, "Variety of Factors Led to Death of Wild Horses," *Grand Junction (Colo.) Daily Sentinel*, July 14, 1976.

9. Johnston to George Lea, July 28, 1971, VJC.

10. Johnston to Mary Lea, August 4, 1972, VJC.

13 | WILD HORSE ANNIE'S FINAL CHAPTER

1. Johnston to Mary Lea, April 23, 1975, VJC.

2. Johnston to John, Helen, and Susan Reilly, June 19, 1967, VJC.

3. Johnston to Dean Bibles, September 24, 1969, AC.

4. Johnston to Mary Lea, December 5, 1970, VJC.

5. Johnston to Helen Reilly, July 12, 1965, VJC.

6. Annie believed the livestock industry had too much influence in Nevada to enable a wild horse research institute and museum to survive anywhere in the state.

7. Johnston to Howard H. Caudle, November 10, 1967, AC.

INDEX